CLEAN MAIDS,
TRUE WIVES,
STEADFAST WIDOWS

D1508476

Recent Titles in
Contributions in Women's Studies

CLEAN MAIDS, TRUE WIVES, STEADFAST WIDOWS

Chaucer's Women and Medieval Codes of Conduct

MARGARET HALLISSY

Contributions in Women's Studies, Number 130

GREENWOOD PRESS
Westport, Connecticut • London

Library of Congress Cataloging-in-Publication Data

Hallissy, Margaret.
    Clean maids, true wives, steadfast widows : Chaucer's women and
medieval codes of conduct / Margaret Hallissy.
      p. cm. — (Contributions in women's studies, ISSN 0147–104X ;
no. 130)
    Includes bibliographical references and index.
    ISBN 0–313–27467–3 (alk. paper)
    1. Chaucer, Geoffrey, d. 1400—Characters—Women. 2. Women—
England—History—Middle Ages, 500–1500. 3. Women and literature—
England—History. 4. Social ethics in literature. 5. Women—
Conduct of life. I. Title. II. Series.
PR1928.W64H35 1993
821'.1—dc20   92–30016

British Library Cataloguing in Publication Data is available.

Library of Congress Catalog Card Number: 92–30016
ISBN: 0-313-27467-3
ISSN: 0147-104X

First published in 1993

Greenwood Press, 88 Post Road West, Westport, CT 06881
An imprint of Greenwood Publishing Group, Inc.

Printed in the United States of America

The paper used in this book complies with the
Permanent Paper Standard issued by the National
Information Standards Organization (Z39.48-1984).

10 9 8 7 6 5 4 3 2

Copyright Acknowledgments

The author and publisher are grateful to the following for granting permission to use selections from the publications of:

Larry Benson, editor, *The Riverside Chaucer*, Third Edition. Copyright © 1987 by Houghton Mifflin Company. Used with permission.

Ovid's Metamorphoses, translation by Rolfe Humphries. Copyright © 1955. Used by permission of Indiana University Press.

The Romance of the Rose by Guillaume de Lorris and Jean de Meun, translated by Harry W. Robbins. Translation copyright © 1962 by Florence L. Robbins. Used by permission of the publisher, Dutton, an imprint of New American Library, a division of Penguin Books USA Inc.

Gloria K. Fiero, Wendy Pfeffer, and Mathe Allain, *Three Medieval Views of Women*. Copyright © 1989. Yale University Press.

G. R. Owst, *Literature and Pulpit in Medieval England* (orig. 1933), rev. ed. 1961. Blackwell Publishers.

Saint Hildegard of Bingen, *Symphonia: A Critical Edition of the* Symphonia armonie celestium revelationum *[Symphony of the Harmony of Celestial Revelations]*, with Introduction, Translations and Commentary by Barbara Newman. Copyright © 1988 by Cornell University. Used by permission of the publisher, Cornell University Press.

Margaret Hallissy, "Widow-to-Be: May in Chaucer's 'The Merchant's Tale,' " in *Studies in Short Fiction* 26, no. 3 (Summer 1989).

"Broom Wizard," poem 52 from *Medieval English Verse*, translated by Brian Stone (Penguin Classics, 1964). Copyright © Brian Stone, 1964.

For Maria, Jennifer, and Megan

For there is under Heaven no king or count who would be ashamed of my daughter, who is so wondrous fair that her match cannot be found. Fair, indeed, she is; but yet greater far than her beauty is her intelligence. God never created any one so discreet and of such an open heart. When I have my daughter beside me, I don't care a marble about all the rest of the world. She is my delight and my pastime, she is my joy and comfort, my wealth and my treasure, and I love nothing so much as her own precious self.

—Chretien de Troyes, *Erec et Enide* (twelfth century)

Contents

Figures

Preface

For he was ever (God wait) all wommanis friend.   —Gavin Douglas[1]

Of all the descriptives that his nearer-contemporary, Gavin Douglas, could have seized upon to capture Chaucer, Douglas chose friend to women. Wary though I am of presuming to speak for my gender, I would postulate that if women define a friend as someone who is interested, who listens, and who therefore understands, then this long-dead medieval poet is indeed as Douglas describes him—all women's friend. To study the characterization of women in Chaucer's works is to realize that he was a close observer of the lives of women. He listened carefully and was able to extrapolate from what he heard women say to re-create what they probably said when no men were around. Chaucer also perceived a sharp distinction between what women did and what they were told to do. He knew the books that set forth rules governing women's lives. One key idea upon which these rules were based was the division of the lives of women into three stages, or estates: virginity, wifehood, and widowhood. This book's purpose is to recreate, for those interested in Chaucer and especially in his characterization of women, the resonances for the original audience of this powerful received idea.

Chaucer used a complex of interwoven associations well known to his medieval audience concerning proper behavior for women throughout their lives. On the basis of the estates concept, women characters in literature can be judged as conforming to or deviating from very specific behavioral norms. The goal of this book is to enhance understanding of Chaucer's thought processes by bringing into the foreground a set of common assumptions that affected the development of his women characters so that we may clarify when he adhered to and when he deviated from his culture's expectations of women.

Rules for women were promulgated both formally and informally, through sources both sacred and secular—scripture, theology, canon law, and homiletics on the religious side; civil law, inheritance customs, and didactic literature on the secular. All the sources had this in common: they were directed toward women and controlled by men. All the rules had a single purpose: the preservation of female chastity. In the interest of remaining clean, true, and steadfast, a woman was expected to suffer, even die. Saints' lives and Chaucer's own *Legend of Good Women* show that suffering in the defense of chastity was the culture's very definition of female virtue.

A woman began her life as a daughter in her father's house; ideally, she then underwent her one rite of passage, a safe transition to her husband's house. A disrupted transition forms the plot of the virgin's story; for example, a threat to her chastity culminates in the death of the virgin in Chaucer's "Physician's Tale." A successful transition culminated in marriage. The perfect wife, like Grisilde in the "Clerk's Tale," embodies all cultural expectations of women. The married woman's life was governed by a complex set of rules designed to preserve and demonstrate her fidelity to her husband and to ensure domestic harmony. Improper speech habits—gossip along with verbal aggression, or shrewishness—constituted one form, but not the only form, of rebellion against patriarchal authority. Other disruptive behaviors also characterized the rebellious wife or widow. Wandering in unenclosed space proclaimed a woman available for sexual purposes. Sartorial excess signified an excessive individualism in defiance of social convention. In addition, medieval people saw all these behaviors as directly related to the cardinal female sin: unchastity.

In widowhood, a medieval woman could achieve the greatest measure of self-determination available to women in her society. Some conventional associations with widowhood were negative. Widows were regarded as sexually insatiable, yet at the same time vulnerable, and these connotations influenced the characterization of Criseyde in *Troilus and Criseyde*. But widows were also regarded as feisty, independent women. Financially and legally, widows were often more powerful than at any other time in their lives. Contemporary ideas about widowhood influenced Chaucer's characterization of his Wife of Bath, who is not only the complete medieval widow but also a compendium of all negative qualities attributed to women.

Chaucer knew and evaluated the advice given to women in his day, and he discounted much of it as detrimental to the development of a full human person. Books were the source of most of the rules, and books were, in the Middle Ages, an instrument of patriarchal power. The debate between experience and authority crystallizes in the "Wife of Bath's Prologue and Tale" as a debate between books and life, between the written word and the spoken word, between the medium of masculine discourse and the medium of female discourse. The Wife of Bath, Chaucer's most decisive deviation from the received wisdom about women of his day, could only have been developed by an author who turned from books to life, from reading to listening, and who created in the pilgrim Geffrey a narrator who does the same.

The writing and reading of books removes one, for better or worse, from the concerns of ordinary life. One of the great benefits of academic life, and the reason why many people choose this life over more lucrative and prestigious alternatives, is the recognition that time must be available for intellectual activities. I therefore thank all those at Long Island University who have provided time for this book. To the Trustees of Long Island University, I express appreciation for conferring upon me their Trustee Award for Scholarly Achievement for my first book, *Venomous Woman: Fear of the Female in Literature* (Greenwood, 1987), and for granting a sabbatical leave during academic year 1990–1991 to complete this one. Such rewards for faculty achievement benefit the entire university community. Long Island University's Research Committee has repeatedly and generously provided grants of released time for research and writing. The department heads and scheduling officers of the English department, Drs. Samuel C. V. Stetner, Arthur Coleman, and Edmund Miller, have supported this project with helpful teaching schedules. Dr. Joan Digby and John Digby devoted time and attention to the visual material. My husband, Gerald J. Hallissy, F.A.I.A., and my elder daughters, Maria Hallissy and Jennifer Hallissy, deserve thanks for adjusting their own busy lives to my esoteric preoccupations, especially since ordinary life in our household is vastly complicated. Chaucer would have praised them for their "pacience in adversitee."

During the research and writing of this book, Megan Hallissy was born. When my third daughter is older, I hope that she will read Chaucer, and I hope that she will read my book. It took many hours away from her, but I do not apologize to her for that. She will learn that anything worth doing takes time. I do want her to know, when she is old enough to understand, that finishing this book was my way of telling her and her sisters that all the things that women can do are good to do, and should be done, even if sometimes they have to be done all at once.

CLEAN MAIDS,
TRUE WIVES,
STEADFAST WIDOWS

⋘ 1 ⋙

The Three Estates of
Women's Lives

This book is a special doctryne & techyng by which al yong gentyl wymen specially may lerne to bihaue them self vertuously as wel in their vyrgynyte as in their wedlok & wedowhede.
—William Caxton, preface to his translation of
The Book of the Knight of the Tower[1]

In the G Prologue to Chaucer's *Legend of Good Women,* the god of Love is castigating a shamefaced poet very much like Geoffrey himself. Aren't you the one, he says, who has rendered into English the book in which Criseyde forsook Troilus? And in so doing, have you not demonstrated the faithlessness of women? Why, the god continues, could you not find in all your old books—sixty of them, a huge library by medieval standards—stories of good women? God knows, and so do the clerks who have preserved these tales, that the ratio of good to bad women is 100 to one. A helpful librarian as well as a literary statistician, the god of Love knows his sources. What the poet must do is find tales from those books in which women are portrayed positively, as "clene maydenes," "trewe wyves," and "stedefaste widewes" (G Prol., 282–283).[2]

At the end of *Troilus and Criseyde,* the narrator apologizes to the women in his audience for the slander against their sex:

Bysechyng every lady bright of hewe,
And every gentil womman, what she be,
That al be that Criseyde was untrewe,
That for that gilt she be nat wroth with me.
Ye may hire gilt in other bokes se;
And gladlier I wol write, yif yow leste,
Penopeës trouthe and good Alceste.
(V., 1772–1778)

Blaming his sources, those "other bokes" in which Criseyde's tale is told, does not excuse the poet's sin in re-presenting Criseyde. So he must do penance, correcting the moral balance by creating a new book to offset the impact of the old. Penance is never pleasant, so the tales in the new volume will not be happy; rather they must arouse "pite" and "routhe" for the "wo" the women "endure for here trouthe" (G Prol., 286–287). Geoffrey must repent by writing his antidotal *Legend of Good Women*, consisting of tales of pure virgins, faithful wives, and steadfast widows.

The tripartite formula, used so economically here to encompass all women in secular life, might well come easily to Chaucer's pen, as it was a commonplace of his age. Writers contemporary with Chaucer, sacred and secular, saw the lives of women as divided into three stages, each with its own norms. The concept of the three estates was strengthened by repetition in oral sources and in other books. Readers of authoritative books, using them to make more books as Chaucer's narrator does, passed along the bookish concept of the division of women's lives into three estates. The tripartite formula is a commonplace in medieval literature, from didactic doggerel to Chaucer's masterworks. But it was no mere literary conceit; the concept itself and the behavioral rules derived from it were meant to guide women's real lives. Purity, fidelity, and loyalty: these ideal feminine qualities were developed and demonstrated by a host of specific behaviors prescribed in books for women written by male authorities. As William Caxton said in his preface, women were expected to learn to behave themselves, shaping their lives to words in books. The rules were well known; so when model behaviors, or their opposites, were presented in literature, such details served as a shorthand method of characterizing women. In creating his women, Chaucer depended upon his audience's knowledge of the most intricate details of correct role behavior.

This book's purpose is to bring into the foreground a detailed body of information instantly available to the medieval audience, to be called up by the writer's merest allusion. While all medieval writers operated within this tradition, Chaucer shaped it to his own purposes. In creating his women characters, Chaucer was able to work within a well-known and highly detailed complex of ideas about virgins, wives, and widows. Unlike his contemporaries who also used the tradition, Chaucer often did so in such a way as to question the validity of those received opinions. In creating his own books, Chaucer at first appeared to be like his bookish *Legend* narrator, a mere conduit of old notions; but in reality he shaped, modified, even flouted what everyone assumed to be true about women. Instead of merely passing along authoritative material, as the *Legend* narrator is instructed to do by the god of Love, Chaucer's narrators changed it.

To understand what Chaucer was doing with the rules set down for virgins, wives, and widows, the medieval concept of estate must be clarified. Medieval people loved *summae*, or compendia that organized all sorts of things into neat categories. These systems provided them with a sense of order, and with reassuring norms against which to measure individuals. One key organizing principle was the concept of *estat*, or social position. Every individual from king to serf occupied a specific and God-ordained niche within a hierarchy. Each part of the whole operated by its own rules so that the larger organism might run smoothly. The order encompassed in the term *estat* was considered so intrinsic to the good life that medieval people believed it persisted in the afterlife as well. In heaven, angels were grouped in hierarchies, and the blessed were ranked, too, in "a new, spiritual nobility of reward accessible to all."[3] On earth as in heaven, each individual had an allocated place within, and was subject to, the rules governing a larger system.

One major medieval schema was the *cursus aetatis*, the course of the ages. According to this concept, human life proceeds in chronological stages, each with its own characteristic virtues and vices. In *The Ages of Man: A Study in Medieval Writing and Thought*, J. A. Burrow explains this important medieval idea. Operating on the analogy of a solar day, many medieval thinkers saw human life as "a process of bodily growth and decline, rise and fall." Different authors composed "rival age-schemes," but all applied stringent behavioral norms depending on a man's position on life's arc.[4] A four-age system, such as that of Philippe de Navarre, included "*enfance, jovens, moien aage,* and *viellesce,*"[5] and compared each to a season of the year, a day of the week, or a time of the day. Dante's system of the ages involved four stages, each with its own "seasonable virtues and graces."[6] In *adolescenza*, to age twenty-five, a man must be submissive, agreeable, and deferential. In old age, a man must cast off worldly preoccupations in preparation for death. While "individuals are free to conform or not to conform to natural order," the value of order is assumed.[7]

Another important principle of order is social position. In *The Three Orders: Feudal Society Imagined*, Georges Duby sees three groups of medieval people: those who work, those who fight, and those who pray. Each segment of society performed its delegated duty on behalf of the whole, and each had its corresponding privileges. All must pray, but the *oratores* accepted special responsibility for the spiritual well-being of others. The group need for protection was provided by the *bellatores* or *pugnatores*, those men whose special duty gave them feudal power and the highest secular status. At the bottom of the social scale, the *laboratores* or *agricolares* supported the rest of society with their manual labor. Both salvation or damnation for the individual and order or anarchy for the society depended on each person's fulfilling the duties of his "order." The term *ordo*, Duby points out, meant to medieval people nothing less than "the just and proper organization of the universe."[8]

In addition to estates categorized by chronology and by function, another interpretation of estates is as social groups divided both functionally and hierarchically, as explained in Jill Mann's *Chaucer and Medieval Estates Satire*. Mann follows the *Middle English Dictionary*'s definition of "estate": "A class of persons, especially a social or political class or group." Group members were seen as sharing character traits, and the belief that this was so influenced literary characterization, so that, for example, Chaucer's Merchant or Franklin or Physician are not only individuals but representatives of their specific group. "Clerical or marital status" and the responsibility of work form further subcategories, each with its "particular duties and temptations."[9] Social class, work, and marital status, then, were further nuances of the estate concept, to be added to its additional meanings: the functional division of society into orders and the chronological scheme of the *cursus aetatis*.

But the messy social realities of the fourteenth century did not, according to Paul Strohm, obligingly conform to these neat patterns. In *Social Chaucer*, Strohm shows how rigid principles of hierarchical order were being adapted to accommodate " 'middle' or other intervening categories." Strohm cites, among other evidence, a 1375 sermon by Bishop Thomas Brinton in which the preacher added *mercatores*, merchants, to the usual trinity of nobility, clergy, and laborers. In another homily, Brinton employed the traditional metaphor of the "body politic," but with more elaborations, to encompass new parts of society. The nobility was society's head, the clergy its ears, the military its strong right hand, and workers its feet. To this traditional material, Brinton added a left hand, composed of "merchants and devoted craftsmen," and a new "middle position," a heart, composed of "citizens and burgesses."[10] Brinton's preaching thus acknowledged the changes that were to affect Chaucer's own social position. Situated at a "volatile and ambiguous point in the social structure of his day,"[11] a fault line that allowed major social shifts, Chaucer did not fit the more rigid hierarchical schemes; as a man in a "middle position," connected with the court but compensated by a salary,[12] Chaucer did fit Brinton's more flexible scheme.

Forward-thinking though he was, Brinton did not attempt to include women in his image of the body politic any more than did his more tradition-minded fellow social theorists. Estates concepts, whether simple and structured or multifaceted and nuanced, applied either exclusively or predominantly to men. In *The Ages of Man: Medieval Interpretations of the Life Cycle*, Elizabeth Sears's study of the concept in the visual arts, the image of woman is seen as illustrative of man's position on life's arc, not woman's own. For example, "ʒouthe" is a young man proclaiming his desire to "play and rage" with women; but the women themselves do not age.[13]

A chronological scheme like Burrow's obviously encompasses all humans, but medieval sources apply the behavioral applications of the concept only to the lives of men. Duby sees his three-order scheme as describing men's lives only; only men's labor is real work, only men can rise to the highest positions among the *oratores* and *bellatores,* while women have "no office, no function, no 'estate.' "[14] According to Mann, there are only "two estates of women—religious and secular."[15] To understand the estate concept as applied to medieval women, we can first divide women according to religious or secular status, then set aside the subject of women in religion as beyond the scope of this study, and finally subdivide the secular category further according to the tripartite formula. It is as virgin, wife, or widow that a secular women operated in medieval life and was portrayed in literature. Because the tripartite formula and the behavioral rules derived therefrom guided men's expectations of women, and women's of themselves, it also governed predictable audience response to literary characters.

Sources for the rules governing women's behavior are repetitive and overlapping, even monotonous, issuing the same dicta century after century, forming a continuum of thought not to be seriously challenged until our own time. So it is not necessary to postulate that a single literary work was influenced by any particular normative source. Rather, the point is that the tripartite formula contains within itself a whole host of implications that are part of what historian Barbara Tuchman calls the "mental furniture" of the age.[16] A single climate of opinion on the subject of women's behavior existed all through the medieval period, within which medieval writers great and small created their women characters. The tripartite formula influenced art and literature across the literary spectrum and provided a context in which to understand the characterization of women in all medieval literature. Chaucer, as we will see, transcended his contemporaries in his ability to make significant modifications of this familiar body of opinion.

The rules that Chaucer's audience knew so well shaped a woman's behavior according to what would best serve the man with whom she had her primary relationship. Of paramount importance, of course, was the preservation of sexual purity. All rules emanated from that cardinal principle, for only through the chastity of women was the integrity of the lineage guaranteed. Medieval people knew instinctively what psychologist Erik Erikson was to observe: "Man can be sure of his fatherhood only by restricting the female."[17] So a young girl must be "clene," maintain her virginity until marriage; a wife must remain "trewe" or faithful; and a widow must be "stedefast," persevering in her obligation to be a living monument to her husband's memory, which provides further evidence of her fidelity in his lifetime. A virtual chorus of voices for hundreds of years told women how to behave within their estate role.

Appropriate behavior for women was "defined by their relationship to men."[18] A daughter's or wife's estate depended on her father's or husband's. Her behavior must first conform to the class into which she was born, and it must then be adjusted to the class she assumed at marriage:

"A woman takes the estate of the man she 'serves,' of her 'master.' "[19] A married woman was thus in essence no different from a daughter in the matter of personal autonomy. But as a widow, a medieval woman could achieve the greatest measure of independence possible to a woman in her society. Depending on circumstances, however, she might also revert to the custody of her father or other near male relative, in effect being demoted to the lower status she left behind at marriage. Then perhaps she remarried. Her estate, then, was contingent upon relationships with men, and, unlike the "ages" of men, only partially dependent on chronological age.

Only as a consecrated virgin could a woman remove herself from these family relationships and focus solely on her relationship to God. The *legendae* of medieval saints are full of tales of nubile young women who defy their families' marital arrangements for them and instead vow themselves to perpetual virginity. Particularly in the early Middle Ages, convent life provided a way for young women to define themselves not as daughters, wives, or widows, but as individual souls before God. In the process of rejecting prescribed family roles, they gave themselves the opportunity to develop their own spiritual and intellectual potential. As nuns, they abandoned the lesser spiritual estate of wifehood in favor of the higher estate of the "bride of Christ," embracing a way of life that completely diverged from that of their secular sisters. Beginning with such pioneering works as Eileen Power's 1922 study, *Medieval English Nunneries*,[20] convent life in the Middle Ages, as well as the character of the nun in literature,[21] has been carefully studied by others. This volume will instead concentrate on those women who chose the other path, remaining within the world of marriage and family life.

Because, next to her duty to God, a woman's duties within the family were most important, proper behavior in her relationship roles constituted the chief element in women's education. Behavior appropriate to each estate was laid down firmly and authoritatively in what the *Legend* narrator called "olde bokes" (F Prol., 25), the authoritative texts of the day, official and unofficial didactic sources, both religious and secular: church doctrine, canon law, saints' lives, Mariology, and homilies, on the religious side; civil law, inheritance customs, and didactic literature, especially conduct books, on the secular. These written sources through which rules were transmitted had two important functions: they filtered down the less accessible points of law and doctrine through the literate to a wider, often illiterate, audience; and they provided specific, even petty, instructions on behavior, thus illuminating daily life. The rules formed a network of restrictions on women's behavior that was intended to be protective. For a writer to be able to depend on these detailed behavioral norms for use in delineating character, the norms had to be understandable, well known, and popular, so accessible that the merest allusion was widely recognized.

And they were: the concept of the three estates and the behavioral expectations for each were so all-pervasive as to constitute a set of shared assumptions, a commonality of opinion expressed in formal legislation and informal social controls.

Chaucer relied heavily on his audience's knowledge of the rules that governed women's behavior, but he went far beyond what his contemporaries could do. Often Chaucer used the common store of material, as did his contemporaries, but not in their formulaic fashion. Instead, Chaucer used the material with great psychological sophistication. Consciousness of the minutiae of the climate of thought within which he was working will enable us to gain greater appreciation not only for his artistry but also for his androgynous sensitivity to his female creations.

❧ 2 ❧

"As men in bokes rede":
The Giving of Rules to Women

Your desire shall be to your husband, and he shall rule over you.
—Genesis 3:16[1]

We should look upon the female state as being as it were a deformity,
though one which occurs in the ordinary course of nature.
—Aristotle[2]

Whatever her estate, woman needs rules. She needs them because she is
fallen, fallen through Eve, whose punishment was to be subordinate to her
husband, as are all her daughters to their husbands in their turn, to the
end of time. The purpose of the rules, as William Caxton says in his preface to his translation of *The Book of the Knight of the Tower*, a medieval
conduct book, is to guide a woman, that she may learn to behave herself
virtuously as virgin, wife, and widow. The medieval Christian would have
linked Aristotle's evaluation of female inferiority with the doctrine of original sin and assumed that the function of the laws was to compensate for
women's fundamental character defect inherited from Eve.

Men, too, were bound by rules. To understand in historical context the
prescribing of rules for the behavior of women, it is necessary to remember
that, while medieval people assumed that rules were necessary to all, the
rule-givers, the authorities, were men. The business of rule-giving is a
bookish business, a matter of literacy, in a time when literacy was a privilege of the "clerk," the educated man. Not all writers were male, nor all
readers; but writing as authoritative pronouncement was an exclusively male
prerogative. No one ever imagined any *auctour*, a writer with the authority
to teach, as female. The "olde bokes" that Chaucer's *Legend* narrator con-
sults—whether the Greek and Roman classics or the Judeo-Christian scriptures and the commentaries thereupon—were all written by men. The psy-

chological authority to present one's writings as rules for others to follow, to teach through writing, was the privilege of a very small number of clerically educated men.

The giving of rules to women must also be understood in the context of almost universal social subordination. Those at the top of a "hierarchy of authority and domination"[3] command; all below obey. To medieval people, hierarchy was the consummate principle of order, and divine in origin. As in heaven so on earth: "There must be a ruler and a ruled lest anarchy prevail."[4] Says political philosopher John of Salisbury: "The inferior must obey the superior, who in return must provide them with all that they need."[5] Says an anonymous preacher: everyone, high and low, is "morally bound to 'travaile in his degree.' "[6] The theoretical subordination of medieval women, then, must be seen in this larger context of a world view according to which everyone but kings and popes serves someone higher, and in which any kind of rebellion against one's position in the pyramid is unthinkable. Women are only one of many sets of inferiors, all of whom must remain in rank.

According to another mode of thought congenial to medieval minds, analogical reasoning, order in the microcosm of the family reflects order in the macrocosm. As pope is to church, as king is to state, so husband is to wife. Any rebellion in any of the interrelated hierarchies is a threat to all order. So, as Natalie Zemon Davis points out, "the relation of the wife— of the potentially disorderly woman—to her husband was especially useful for expressing the relationship of all subordinates to their superiors."[7] Thus it was that the *"topos* of the woman-on-top" became a standard symbol of disorder.[8] A "topsy-turvy" world of wifely domination[9] was so threatening to medieval people that "the conception that a husband is the 'lord' of his wife . . . brought the woman who plotted against the life of her husband under the law of treason, and subjected her to the death penalty in its severest form [burning alive]."[10]

Complementing this belief in fixed, self-evident, and all-pervasive hierarchy was the medieval passion for elaborate and detailed systems. No piece of information was so minute that it could not be subsumed into some vast intellectual schema. Scholastic philosophy is famous for its organization of details into systems. The fact that a brilliant thinker like Thomas Aquinas could aspire to a *summa theologica,* a single work encompassing all theology, is testimony to the medieval belief in the possibility and value of comprehensive systems. The tripartite formula, then, is just one manifestation of the larger propensity in medieval thought driving them toward schematizing reality. Once all womanhood, like all Gaul, is divided into three parts, it logically follows that rules could be prescribed based on the function of the part within the whole. In an age in which theological and philosophical "formalism" prevailed—that is, "the tendency of moralists . . . to express their demands by means of codes of duties, or lists of virtues and excellences"[11]—it is no surprise that lists of duties and detailed codes of behavior could be prescribed for women in secular life, just as they were for everyone else.[12]

Thus it was that rules of behavior for women were promulgated by authoritative voices, both sacred and secular.[13] Sacred sources included scripture as glossed by early Church theologians. Theological insights were filtered into the popular mind through sermons and saints' lives and then applied to everyday problems through the casuistical procedures of canon law. On the secular side, rules for behavior were embodied officially in civil laws on marriage and inheritance customs and communicated unofficially but no less effectively through behavior manuals and other forms of didactic literature. All these served the purpose of teaching men what kind of woman constituted the ideal and teaching women how they were expected to behave in order to approximate that ideal.

St. John Chrysostom's ideas are typical of the theological principles underlying medieval attitudes toward women. Chrysostom encouraged in women the qualities of submission appropriate to subordinate beings. Downplaying the version of the creation story in which Eve was created simultaneously with Adam, Chrysostom believed that "Adam's prior creation is understood to entail his headship and superiority,"[14] presumably even in the prelapsarian state. Eve's sin makes control over her even more important, since "God's original plan that man be the 'head' and woman the 'body' . . . was disrupted when Eve like rebellious women of later times tried to take charge."[15] While, as that vexed phrase *imago Dei* indicates, man and woman are both like God, man is assumed to be more like Him, and husbands are therefore entitled to authority within the small domestic kingdom.[16] For Chrysostom, the consequences of this in everyday life are obvious. Husbandly authority is unquestionable and any usurpation by women of "male functions" is "perverse."[17] To encourage women's acceptance of their role within the system, "Chrysostom brought forth Biblical examples of subservient women for his audience's admiration"[18] and prescribed for women lives of "service, silence, and submission."[19]

Other major theologians applied this basic line of reasoning to the estates concept. Augustine and Aquinas saw women's lives as being divided into the three stages for doctrinally correct reasons: "Because the existence of woman is ordained for that of man, her state of life is defined by her relationship with him: she is bound to a husband in marriage, or she is released from this bond by widowhood; the virgin alone is independent, her existence being directed wholly towards God."[20] The consecrated virgin would not be entirely free of subordination to men, as the all-male ecclesiastical hierarchy had authority over even the highest-ranking nuns. But unlike her sisters in secular life, her primary relationship was to God.

Any hard-line stance on female subordination is difficult to reconcile with the principle of the value of the souls of women before God. Theologians tended to stress one or another of these teachings at various points in their writings without successfully reconciling all.[21] Jerome, for example, took such contradictory positions on women that he is a controversial figure to this day. In his concern to stress the value of male virginity, Jerome denigrated God's female creation and deemphasized the value of Christian marriage. His remarks in this vein have been described as "misogynist," even "vicious"; but the same authors also regard his real-life relationships with women as being "extremely supportive," even demonstrating "personal devotion."[22] The paradoxical ability in Jerome to see women as "embodying the temptations of the flesh" but at the same time "intellectual and spiritual beings on the same plane as men" led another commentator to suggest that Jerome "may even be regarded as the father of Christian feminism."[23] Misogynist or feminist, Jerome embodies the tension about women that permeated the teachings of the early Church fathers, the difficulty they had in reconciling what they saw as physical inferiority with spiritual equality. Augustine regarded women as men's spiritual equals despite their inferior bodies, whereas Aquinas saw the spirits of men and women as irrevocably unequal because the inferiority of the female body drags her spirit down. Despite their differing emphases, however, both Augustine and Aquinas were at pains to set forth standards of appropriate behavior.[24] Most theologians proceeded from the assumption that women, being "disorderly," "fragile," "hysterical," and "unsteady," needed guidance and that therefore the function of authority was to keep them in check.[25] Given the theological heavyweights on the side of female subordination, it is only to be expected that canon law would reinforce these beliefs, assuming, as does Gratian, a mid-twelfth-century canonist, that "the natural order for mankind is that women should serve men and children their parents, for it is just that the lesser serve the greater."[26]

Despite the unpromising theoretical foundations in theology, canon law and Church policies during the Middle Ages had other influences clearly beneficial to women. Out of concern for the avoidance of lust in marriage, canon law restricted the marital act to prevent the use of a wife as a sex object. Defining sexual excess in marriage as sinful gave women, in principle at least, some relief from a lecherous husband. On the other hand, the concept of the marital debt gave a wife some relief, again in principle, from the neglect of an underzealous husband. Over the course of the Middle Ages, the Church attempted to gain authority over marriage, previously considered solely a civil matter. For one thing, canon law increasingly stressed the necessity for the partners' consent. Gradually through canon law the Church expanded its control over marriage by formalizing the marriage ceremony. Though they seem restrictive to us today, these rules had the practical effect of protecting women in an age which assumed that function to be the responsibility of men. And, more important for our purposes, these developments have important consequences for the understanding of the characterization of women in literature.

On the role of sex in married life, theologians and canonists were in agreement that it should be limited as to frequency and intensity. Since marriage was the refuge of those incapable of the higher estate of celibacy, it made sense to discourage harmful practices to further weaken these weak ones. The "mastery of spirit over flesh"[27] was considered good in itself, and practices to that end were encouraged. The assumption was, in Albert the Great's blunt words, that "coition totally emasculates the spirit."[28] Albert's phrasing here shows that his theology of sex was based on his male physiology. Loss of rational control over a bodily part can presumably be unsettling enough, at least for a would-be celibate, to make total rational control seem much more appealing. If such control is defined as manly, then the male experience of arousal and orgasm is unmanly. Women make men lose their manly control; ergo, women must be bad. Women make men lesser beings like themselves; they emasculate. Similarly, Augustine, said: "I know nothing which brings the manly mind down from the height more than a woman's caresses."[29] To Augustine, men represented mind and spirit and were therefore higher; women represented passion and flesh and were therefore lower. By associating with women, men risked being brought down to their level. As the Wife of Bath observes, men wrote the books; discussions of sexuality in medieval theology are colored by the experience of a mind trying to control an unruly male body.

Despite the fact that medieval marriage regulations were based on misogynistic assumptions, the development of increased ecclesiastical control over marriage led to two developments that in practice improved women's lot. The doctrine that the valid marriage was the chosen marriage[30] was advantageous to women, as daughters were even more likely to be subject to the unjust authority of matchmaking fathers than were sons. The increasing elaboration of the courtship ritual preceding the moment of choice was to give women increasing power, however temporary, at the dramatic point of transition between maidenhood and wifehood. Even more concrete improvement in the lives of women was to be gained from the gradual transformation of the marriage ceremony from a private civil act to a public ecclesiastical act. This discouraged clandestine marriages, which placed a woman in the inferior and tenuous status of concubine, and substituted public, official unions less easily repudiated.[31] The precedent that a wife could not be repudiated like a concubine was a better way, as Philippe Ariès bluntly but accurately put it, of "managing the stock of girls."[32] In addition to being able to enforce the existence of the marital bond and the legitimacy of offspring, a wife, like her husband, could take marital disagreements to an ecclesiastical court. More important still, the public ceremony in facie ecclesia gave the wife dower rights under civil law; in fact, the public transfer of property rights to a wife was a key element that differentiated marriage from concubinage.[33] To marry at the church door was to be endowed with property.[34] This ensured inheritance rights, a matter with great impact on the economic and social situation of widows.

Like canon law, sermons transmitted theology to the ordinary Christian, and so effectively, as G. R. Owst conclusively demonstrated in *Literature and Pulpit in Medieval England,* that the all-pervasive themes of sermon literature permeated medieval literature. However, by the fourteenth century, according to Edwin Charles Dargan, the heyday of preaching was past, and theology was "sadly distorted," "degenerate," and "decadent."[35] Dargan saw three major types of preaching as characteristic of the decadent thirteenth and fourteenth centuries: the scholastic, the mystic, and the popular. Preaching influenced by scholasticism stressed orderly and logical presentation, with fine distinctions and primarily intellectual appeal. Mystical preaching stressed, often in highly abstract terms, "union of the soul with God."[36] Neither syllogism nor flights of mystical rapture inspired literary creation as much as did popular preaching. Though a poor medium for transmitting sophisticated theology, popular preaching was characterized by the kind of detail that its audience remembered. What Dargan calls "overgrowths upon the gospel," such features as saints' lives and *exempla* (or illustrative stories), denunciation of sin, anecdotes, fables, "legends and tales,"[37] were useful to creators of story and character. Unlike scholastic or mystical preaching, popular preaching had to be highly specific about contemporary manners and mores. The duties of one's estate in life were a common sermon *topos,* and one that provided examples of official expectations of women. Estates sermons directed to virgins and widows conveyed a simple message: remain chaste. Because married life was more complicated, indeed a morally " 'dangerous' situation,"[38] many sermons focused on it. Restrictions on marital sex; avoidance of adultery; authority in marriage; validity of a marriage: all provided subjects for marriage sermons.[39]

But, while sermon literature often stressed the spiritual equality of man and woman in marriage and the spiritual advantages of holy matrimony,[40] sermons also served as a prime conduit of misogynistic lore. In sermons, women were too talkative or too critical—shrews or scolds. They were disobedient, contrary, quarrelsome, deceptive, overly attached to women friends.[41] They were spendthrifts, bent on wasting their husbands' money on "superfluous adornment"[42] and deceiving honest men through the vicious practice of face-painting. Worst of all, women were temptresses, leading men to sins of lust. According to Jean Delumeau, the Middle Ages, especially the fourteenth century, was an age particularly preoccupied with sin, indeed suffering from "scruple sickness."[43] No sin was more interesting than lust, and no one was immune. Women could be sources of temptation even to their own husbands; the married man, says a preacher, sins by being the "too ardent lover of his wife."[44] Scripture yields examples of great men brought low by women: Holofernes, says another preacher, was "distrowed by þe nyce aray and atyre of a womman."[45] David was "ouercome to synne" by "vnclene kyssynges, clippynges, and oþur vnhonest handelynges."[46] Preachers' handbooks encouraged promulgation of the idea that sex in marriage was sinful when it was not used for procreation but for "lustful pleasure alone."[47] Since virtue consisted in control of the lower over the higher, wives, like children and cattle, symbolized "deeds of the flesh and animal-like acts" that should be "reined in by the well-taught soul."[48]

Given the concentration on sexual purity, it is no surprise that medieval canonization practices stressed female chastity. Only by emulating Mary in lifelong virginity could a woman realistically aspire to certified sainthood. Widows, restored (though compromised) to an asexual estate, might achieve sanctity through a renewed commitment to asceticism and service. Although it must have been true that "the Christian life of the household . . . was developed through the ministration of women,"[49] wives and mothers were rarely considered as candidates for canonization.[50] For men as well as for women, the roster of saints "gives short shrift to those Christians who were married, as if that less-perfect state somehow disqualifies from public recognition of sanctity."[51]

Not that married women were expected to emulate only married women saints, however. All saints' lives served then—and do now—as role models of heroic Christian behavior. The saints' extremes of spiritual heroism were meant to excite admiration, their more ordinary endeavors imitation. *Legendae* of virgins, usually beautiful and high-born, who endured amazing tortures, were meant to encourage ordinary believers in the routine trials of their lives;[52] such stories were an "argument *a fortiori*" for daily virtue.[53] The question arises as to whether the virtues officially endorsed by the canonization of their practitioners differed for men and women, especially with regard to the value of suffering. On this point, scholars of medieval sainthood differ. As historian Richard Kieckhefer explains, the culture of the late Middle Ages saw the virtue of patience not as a "sign of weakness, and an invitation to further abuse," but as an "appropriate response to adversity"[54] in both sexes. Analyzing the hagiographic romances of the thirteenth century featuring virgin martyrs, Brigitte Cazelles sees a clear-cut opposition between the "representation of male sanctity, which essentially entails self-assertiveness," and that of "female perfection," which Cazelles sees as "grounded in bodily pain, silence, and passivity."[55] In a historical study of saints' lives employing methods of statistical analysis, Donald Weinstein and Rudolph M. Bell do see emerging a " 'masculine' type of saint—holder of temporal or ecclesiastical power, missionary to the heathen and fiery preacher of the word." But they are less certain than Cazelles is about the existence of a "feminine" type of saint, preferring the term "androgynous" to describe those saints of both sexes whose *legendae* stressed suffering.[56] Patient endurance of suffering, then, was a virtue expected of men and women that was embodied in the lives of male and female saints in different ways.

When the saintly sufferer was a married woman, a particular type of family drama was enacted. The husband's role was "to provide opportunity for patience," with his ability to do so limited only by his "imagination and . . . capacity for malfeasance."[57] The husband was cast as the sinner, against whose evil the wife's virtue stood out in higher relief. So powerful was her example that the story often culminated in his conversion. Such is the pattern in the well-known tale of the long-suffering Monica, recorded approvingly in the influential *Confessions* of her son Augustine. Of the few married women who were venerated as saints in the Middle Ages, Monica was held up for the particular emulation of "women who lived with difficult or abusive husbands and recalcitrant children"[58] because of her patient endurance of her husband Patricius's bad temper.

Because Monica managed her wrathful husband well, she avoided being beaten. Moreover, when beaten wives "would in familiar talk blame their husbands' lives, she would blame their tongues," advising them to regard the marriage agreement as "indentures, whereby they were made servants; and so, remembering their condition, [they] ought not to set themselves up against their lords."[59] Monica assumed, as does her son, that the women, not the men, are responsible for the beatings and can, by good wifely behavior, prevent recurrences. Neither Augustine nor Monica regarded Patricius as responsible for his own wrathfulness, a trait that made domestic violence a constant threat, to be controlled only by Monica's rare saintliness. The cult of Monica encouraged women to develop Grisilde-like qualities of passive endurance: "For a married saint, abuse at the hands of a spouse could be a prime occasion for patience."[60] Yet Monica triumphed in the end. Her passivity finally resulted in control of both Augustine and Patricius, both of whom reformed and were converted to Christianity. Monica's story sent a message to women that they could indeed get their way, but always indirectly, never by direct confrontation (which would be shrewish). While suffering, they would be able to dominate their men by aligning themselves with the power of God. Aside from Monica, the medieval wife had few saintly role models in her own estate.

Except, of course, for Christ's mother, Mary. No figure provided so perfect a model: "Mayden, moder, and wiff, and so was neuer non but she alon . . . þise iii divers states com neuer in on person till þe tyme of Oure Lady Mary."[61] Mary transcends all categories to embody the ideal of womanhood. But since the evangelists give her relatively little attention, non-Gospel inventions—those "overgrowths" of which Dargan speaks— allow Mary to serve as exemplar in as many areas as possible. One sermon describes her as taking care of Jesus not only in infancy and childhood but also when he was a "presynner," on which occasion she "helet hys sores wyth mylke of hur pappys."[62] The suspension of natural laws here would have been no surprise, given Mary's history. The "miracles of the Virgin" stories were intended to excite the admiration and emulation of women, who can see Mary as a compendium of all feminine virtues. She is "meoke & mylde,"[63] steadfast, detached from earthly goods, quiet, patient, humble.[64] At the Annunciation, as depicted in literature, she is mild of speech, complacent, obliging in accepting the will of God, as in the well-known lyric "I syng of a mayden";[65] in many lyrics she is portrayed as a loving mother to the infant Christ.[66] A major function of the Mary figure in literature is to deflect all criticisms of women derived from the behavior of Eve and to model appropriate feminine behavior.[67]

The ecclesiastical rules surrounding women were intended to enable her to work out her salvation within her estate. Avoiding Eve, imitating Mary, she would be guided by authorities who, all believed, had her best interest at heart. If the teachings of Church fathers, the rulings of canonists, the example of saintly lives needed additional reinforcement, it was at the ready in the form of the secular scriptures: civil law and conduct literature.

Influenced by contradictory ideas about women, medieval civil law is fraught with contradictions. On the one hand, inherited from Roman law and reaffirmed by Christian theology was the assumption of feminine *infirmitas* and *fragilitas*, which required protective legislation.[68] On the other hand, women, even married women, enjoyed greater legal rights than may at first appear, more than they were to have in later times.[69] The matter of women's rights under the civil law was complex due to local variations in such matters as rights to own land and property, to sue and be sued, to join guilds, to enter into private contracts, to control dower and dowry, and to make wills. This last is important, as the right to make a will implies recognition of independent ownership of significant heritable property.[70] In general, however, and subject to the intricacies of local law, "women's power waxed, waned, and waxed again over the course of the female life cycle."[71] Legal rights were most limited when a woman was under male protection—that is, in maidenhood and wifehood—and they expanded in widowhood.

A woman's position in the tripartite scheme interacted with her social class as determinants of her capacity for independent legal or economic action.[72] Women of the rising middle classes usually had more autonomy than women of the upper classes and nobility. In the homogeneously bourgeois community of fourteenth-century Brigstock, a woman's estate was the factor that determined her scope for autonomy. Judith M. Bennett observes "fundamentally similar access to public power" among the young of both sexes, compression of a wife's legal rights after marriage, and "a new equivalency in the public power of the sexes" in old age.[73] The most important legal matter affecting women was inheritance. As George Homans notes: "The customs of inheritance of a place are one of the best signs of the kind of family organization that prevails there."[74] If Homans is right about this, the fact that inheritance patterns favoring women became the norm indicates that women held a position of respect and responsibility within the family. Because money or property was customarily left to a wife, the widow was a formidable power both economically and socially, the bourgeois widow most of all.

Over the course of the fourteenth century, important economic developments were taking place,[75] one of which was that power was shifting from a land-based feudal aristocracy to a money-based capitalist meritocracy. This evolution eventually benefitted women, especially women of the bourgeoisie, in that it changed both the basis by which property was owned and the type of property owned. Under the feudal system, land was the basis not only of social rank but of ability to form a family at all: "no land, no marriage."[76] But land was held in return for military service, a function of men. Therefore a woman's rights to hold land independently were limited by her inability to perform the military service that came with the land.[77] It followed not unreasonably that a lord had the right and duty to control the marriage of an inheriting woman, lest she, by a poor choice, provide him with an unsuitable vassal, and her retainers, in turn, with an unsuitable overlord. The custom of *merchet,* whereby a lord claimed the right to consent to the marriage of an heiress, was not, then, an empty power play over women, but a way of ensuring that landholders were able to fulfill feudal obligations.[78] This is a logical reason why land might be legally held by a woman but controlled by a man during a marriage.

But the ownership of money, or even some money-generating businesses, did not require a man to provide manly service, so the urban townswoman could, and apparently did, have more financial control than her landholding sister. Civil laws authorizing women in trades to operate as *femmes soles,* financially independent of their husbands, acknowledged this change. The autobiography of the self-styled mystic Margery Kempe (c. 1373–1438?) recounts how Margery wrests from her reluctant spouse a promise to allow her to live in celibacy by offering to pay his debts. Margery has money, John has none; Margery uses her money to get what she wants—John's agreement to abrogate his conjugal rights. This power play does not strike Margery as unbefitting a saint, but merely as a pragmatic solution to a problem impeding her holy career.[79]

Margery's financial independence of John Kempe notwithstanding, marriage and widowhood offered most women greater financial opportunity than any other activity. Though women were gradually being caught up in the rising tide of technology and capitalism to become craftswomen, even entrepreneurs, marriage was still the ground base, the *sine qua non* of womanly success. Women could, like the Wife of Bath, marry well, inherit money, and earn more. Since a good marriage was so important, economically as well as emotionally, most young girls in secular estate needed the skills taught them by the conduct literature—skills involved in attracting a desirable husband, living contentedly with him, and continuing a respectable and comfortable life after his death. No education was more practical than that provided by the courtesy books.

For hundreds of years, the courtesy book shaped both men's and women's perceptions of appropriate behavior for women. As described by Diane Bornstein in *The Lady in the Tower: Medieval Courtesy Literature for Women,* the most comprehensive study to date on medieval courtesy literature, a courtesy book is a practical "guide for behavior in the real world."[80] Because in the Middle Ages "households of the nobility and ecclesiastical officials were the training schools for the aristocracy," "textbooks" were needed, and courtesy literature served that purpose. Written for both men and women by household superiors and circulated in manuscript,[81] the courtesy book encouraged in the young of both sexes a pleasing conformity to existing social customs. Since success for women meant making a suitable marriage, a further goal of courtesy literature was to teach such behavior as would make a young girl appealing to a potential husband. Until the time of Christine de Pisan (1364–c.1430), the conduct books were written by men for the women under their authority, circulating to other men for their use in guiding the women of their households. So, at any given time, through the courtesy books we "get men's ideas of what women should have been doing."[82] Conversely, we also see what women were in fact doing, or were feared to be about to do, as courtesy books described the aberrant behaviors that conjured up the "monstrous figure . . . of the disobedient female."[83] The task of courtesy literature was "to mirror proper social behaviors,"[84] and it was an especially necessary one in a time of increased social mobility such as the fourteenth century. But since the writers, the authorities on behavior, were male, and so was most of the audience, a metamessage was also conveyed: "In determining what kind of woman a woman should desire to be, these books also determine what kind of woman men should find desirable."[85] The books, then, educated men, formed their expectations, and caused them to judge harshly any woman who deviated from the norm.

Didactic poetry, a subspecies of this literature, briefly presented ideas similar to those more fully elaborated in the courtesy books. Like the courtesy literature, didactic poetry is highly repetitious. Typical themes across the genre include contrasting the temporary and fickle love of women with the eternal love of Christ;[86] the impossibility of totally condemning women because of the virtues of Mary;[87] the woes of marriage, especially to a shrew;[88] fashion abuses;[89] and general misogyny.[90]

Three representative examples of conduct literature circulating in the fourteenth century provide a general outline of its structure and content. These works are significant not by virtue of originality—all conduct books repeat the same advice—but because they show expectations across various social strata. It is not postulated here that Chaucer was influenced directly by any one work, but rather that works like these provided compendia of common ideas with which a well-informed man like Chaucer would be familiar, and with which he could expect his audience also to be familiar.

The didactic poem "The Good Wife Taught Her Daughter" (MS c. 1350), by an unknown author, is a monologue in which a mother passes along rules of behavior to her daughter. Both women are urban townspeople, affluent enough to have servants and to be concerned about getting along in society, but not so affluent as to replace the mother as not only the primary but probably the only educator of her daughter.[91] The poem begins conventionally, with an exhortation to the daughter to love God, to pray, to give alms, to behave properly in church. Then attention is turned to her major worldly need, finding and pleasing a husband. During courtship, she is to be encouraging, not standoffish ("scorne hym noght," advises her mother), but not so enthusiastic as to commit sin. When she is married, she has the duty of honoring her husband, soothing his temper, and being quiet and cheerful around him, "swete of speche," "of mylde mood," and "noght of many wordes." She is not to gallivant about "fro house to house," to tavern, town, or market; she is to stay at home. She is to be moderate in drink, since it is "grete schame" to be "ofte dronken"; in this, as in other things, "mesure," moderation, is appropriate. On the "werkeday," the good wife is to be busy (indeed the term "housewifly" seems in context to mean "busy"). On "haliday" she must worship God. Her clothing should reflect her husband's social status; she should "ne countirfete no ladijs, as þi lorde were a kyng," nor should she be envious of others' "riche atyir." She should not be stingy ("to harde"), but rather entertain her neighbors with "mete and drynke," in measure, after her husband's estate. She must make sure that her daughters are suitably married (presumably passing along to them the same advice that her mother is giving her).[92]

The Goodman of Paris (writing circa 1392–1394)[93] provides a handy guide for a wife young enough to be his daughter. The upper-middle-class household which this young woman is expected to run is sufficiently complex that the Goodman is concerned about educating his wife into her role. It is important to hear in his language what Eileen Power calls "the note of tenderness which is paternal rather than marital,"[94] demonstrating affection and a sense of responsibility for one young enough to be his daughter: "You being the age of fifteen years and in the week that you and I were wed, did pray me to be indulgent to your youth and to your small and ignorant service, until you had seen and learned more." The Goodman understands and accepts his wife's youth and inexperience along with the unnaturalness of the burden of domestic responsibility placed on one so young who might more suitably occupy herself with childlike amusements.

This is not condescension on his part but a realistic response to the fact that his wife is a child: "And know that I am pleased rather than displeased that you tend rose-trees, and care for violets, and make chaplets, and dance, and sing."[95] The Goodman sees himself as educator of this young person and writes for her reference after his death. Though his culture would have taught him that his widow should devote herself exclusively to his memory and not remarry, he hopes that she will "do him credit,"[96] demonstrating the competencies he has taught her, "either to serve another husband, if you have one, after me, or to teach greater wisdom to your daughters."[97] The Goodman's ability to empathize with the feelings of his wife marks him off as a particularly sensitive husband. While the Goodman believed, as did all men of his time, that "it was his wife's function to make comfortable his declining years," he also felt that it was his responsibility "to make the task easier for her."[98] In the person of the Goodman, we see the human face of husbandly authority in the Middle Ages.

The Book of the Knight of the Tower, written during 1371 and 1372, is, like the Goodman's work, an expression of concern for the education of young people, the Knight's three motherless daughters. His book is conceived as a substitute for maternal guidance through the hazards of youth, into their married lives and beyond, into widowhood. Despite the fact that he presents himself as a widower for twenty years, he describes his daughters as "yong and litel,"[99] no doubt sacrificing numerical accuracy (never a primary value to medieval people) to express how vulnerable they are without their mother to guide them. Caxton, who published his translation of the Knight's book in 1484, says that he translated it at the request of a "noble lady," the mother of many daughters.[100] Thus the work was seen in its time as an aid to the education of young women, and the Knight as a man who did what his culture told him was his duty: protecting and guiding women. As if his daughters were in a social position to be free of the practical concerns of life, the Knight devotes little attention to the work of a wife. His major topic, one common in conduct literature, is the absolute necessity of preserving chastity in all estates and demonstrating that it has been preserved. His specific behavioral prescriptions all emanate from this central concern. The finer points of behavior discussed by the Knight were seen in courtesy books as safeguarding virginity (and, later, marital chastity). Advice on such specific matters as enclosure, speech, and clothing form a large body of regulations, so large that separate chapters in this volume are devoted to their impact on literature.

The courtesy literature's advice to women depends on their position within the tripartite scheme and is clearly directed toward the preservation of the highest virtue. The virgin must be raised strictly and supervised carefully. She must learn feminine accomplishments like sewing and spinning, singing and embroidery; but learning to read and write is debatable. Some conduct writers think literacy suitable only for girls intended for the convent or for those who might have political responsibility. But girls of lower estate need no such skills for they can ask their husbands at home, as St. Paul advised. The young virgin must dress and ornament herself according to her father's rank, which will, in turn, influence the rank of the man chosen to be her husband, and she must avoid social climbing through inappropriate dress. Being in public is dangerous for her, so her behavior there must be circumspect in the extreme. Modesty of bearing must reflect modesty of character. The Knight cautions the young girl that, when she walks on the street at all (an activity ideally limited to chaperoned churchgoing), she must walk with eyes downcast, looking neither to right nor to left, and taking small steps; all this lest she appear flirtatious, or betray excessive curiosity concerning her surroundings.[101] Francesco da Barberino, writing between 1307 and 1315, expressed disapproval even of churchgoing, on the general principle that the hidden life leads to greater esteem, concealing whatever faults a young girl might have.[102] Barberino wants maidens to spend their time only with their mothers or other older women; to speak little and low; to avoid hearty laughter, which shows the teeth. Even their choice of flowers for their hair garlands—small, fresh ones only are suitable—must indicate their virginity.[103] A virgin's food and drink must be restricted, as hot spicy foods and wine rouse lustful feelings. A good woman must take care, says the Knight of the Tower, that even her dogs be abstemiously fed and denied "lychorous metes."[104]

The good wife must continue to avoid all temptations and to demonstrate loyalty and service to her husband. Advice on fashion is geared to reflecting her husband's estate, neither dressing up nor dressing down; a key phrase is "according to rank and fortune." In addition, be she peasant or queen, she must run her husband's household efficiently; advice on managing servants is a popular topic. She must also serve her husband in a public-relations capacity, being his representative to the larger world. With her husband, she is urged to be nonconfrontational, soothing his anger and reflecting his own thoughts back to him. She is to help him conserve his goods; it is "shameful" for a wife to be so wasteful that a husband is forced to take over this financial responsibility. When her husband is absent, all the modest behaviors must be practiced all the more; she may not even seem to enjoy herself, and she must behave like a quasi-widow. Some say she must tolerate her husband's infidelities; some say she must discourage them as they jeopardize his salvation.

The widow's role is to demonstrate grief and to pray for her husband's soul, a practical service for which medieval people were willing to pay enormous sums in the form of mass donations. She must become a living monument to her husband's memory, dedicating her life to good works and to prayer. Remarriage was discouraged on the basis of infidelity both to the husband and to the ideal of renewed celibacy. St. Jerome compares the remarriage of a widow to the scriptural image of a dog returning to its vomit; he sees it as only an excuse for lechery.[105] Children are mentioned more frequently in advice to widows than in advice to married women; husbands are clearly the first priority, and only with their deaths do children take center stage, with the widow enjoined to dedicate herself to their education. Like other women but with more intensity, she is urged to good works such as almsgiving, care of the sick, attentiveness to her parents, and visiting leprosaria and the humble cots of the poor. But she should avoid showing herself in public and attending entertainments of any sort, even those with a religious guise; she should live, according to Barberino, "in retreat."[106] A widow is responsible for the management of her husband's lands, prayer for his soul in purgatory, and the education of his children, even, according to Barberino, his bastards.

Throughout her life, whether as virgin, wife, or widow, a woman was hedged about by rules such as these, promulgated with great certainty by learned authorities. Theologians and homilists, lawgivers and courtesy writers: all the voices of authority were male. Their intent was honorable and consistent with the beliefs of the time on hierarchy and subordination. It was an age in which the right to teach was limited to a tiny elite, in which even that elite depended on a still smaller group of ancient *auctores,* and in which the rest of humankind, male and female, was expected to obey their betters. The givers of rules to women saw themselves as helping women approximate the ideals of the three estates. Only thus could women be happy in life and in the hereafter. Rules intended to help women follow the straight path might appear to the twentieth-century reader more as roadblocks than road signs. But no medieval women writers seriously challenge so all-pervasive a set of cultural assumptions. It would be surprising if there were any, considering the low level of education for women and the consequent paucity of women expressing themselves in writing. Instead of a woman chafing at the restraints, it is Chaucer who questions what obedience to rules might mean to women. Since of all the rules, the greatest involve the preservation of chastity, it is necessary to understand the lengths to which women were expected to go in defense of that cardinal virtue. To be clean, true, and steadfast required the choice of death over dishonor.

Suffering Women and the Chaste Ideal

In sooth all good is departed from maid or woman who faileth in virginity, continence and chastity; not riches, nor beauty, nor good sense, nor high lineage, nor any other merit can ever wipe out the ill fame of the opposite vice, above all if in a woman it be but once committed, in sooth if it be but suspected.

—Goodman of Paris[1]

Women . . . have a great advantage in one thing; they can easily preserve their honour if they wish to be held virtuous, by one thing only. But for a man many are needful, if he wish to be esteemed virtuous, for it behoves him to be courteous and generous, brave and wise. And for a woman, if she be a worthy woman of her body, all her other faults are covered and she can go with a high head wheresoever she will; and therefore it is no way needful to teach as many things to girls as to boys.

—Philip of Novarre[2]

In *The Book of the City of Ladies* (1405), Christine de Pisan retells old tales of virtuous women. Among them are a clutch of virgin martyrs who earned their salvation by incredible suffering. Martina is "slashed all over . . . drawn and staked down and broken . . . stretched out and set on fire with burning oil . . . ripped with iron hooks . . . thrown to the wild beasts . . . thrown into a large fire . . . her throat cut."[3] Lucy is "imprisoned in an asylum for crazy women,[4] Macra and Barbara have their breasts ripped off."[5] Fausta is "sawed in two . . . a thousand nails hammered into her head . . . placed in a cauldron of boiling water."[6] Christine's father "had her sprawled completely nude and beaten so much that twelve men wearied at the task." Then he "had a wheel brought in, ordered her tied to it and a fire built below it, and then he had rivers of boiling oil poured over her body." Finally he had her breasts ripped off and her tongue cut out.[7] The sadistic ingenuity of their tormenters did not, however, cause any of these women to accept violations of their chastity, even in marriage. Now these were consecrated virgins; but their extraordinary suffering was intended, as saints' lives were, to inspire admiration and thus bolster fortitude in the lesser trials of chastity to which all women were subject.

Lives of the saints conveyed important collective values, "concepts of ideal female behavior";[8] like other cultural messages, the *legendae* of virgin martyrs reinforced the idea that the preservation of chastity is a value so high as to warrant extreme suffering. The suffering woman is a good woman. Suffering is good for women, providing an opportunity to attain heights of virtue. So it is a radical move for a medieval author to question, as Chaucer did, the necessary correlation between chastity and suffering. *The Legend of Good Women* is often seen as one of Chaucer's minor works; it is too dull, too redundant, for twentieth-century tastes, and unfinished as well, as if its author lost interest. But it is significant in exploring the truism that chastity is a woman's only virtue and that women's suffering for chastity is a self-evident good. More importantly, Chaucer's work with the material in the *Legend* contributes to his more creative development of similar themes in the "Franklin's Tale." In this tale, Chaucer undercuts three interrelated beliefs of his day: that chastity is not only woman's primary but also her only significant virtue, that woman's suffering has special moral value, and that death is preferable to dishonor. In addition, in contrast to the disastrous pairings depicted in the *Legend,* the marriage of Dorigen and Arveragus, while far from perfect, is a complex human relationship, not just another redundant *exemplum* of masculine vice and feminine virtue.

In *The Legend of Good Women,* Chaucer does as his sources do, as most of his contemporaries would: he portrays woman as wholly defined by her sexual behavior or abstinence therefrom.[9] As virgins, wives, and widows— the formula occurs in the G Prologue—women are defined by "sexual relationships with men,"[10] and chastity is women's "only possible virtue, the only source of whatever value they have in society's eyes and their own."[11] Most twentieth-century critics feel that this reduction of all female behavior to a single element makes the *Legend* heroines lifeless abstractions. In the formulaic tale of chastity preserved, the heroine is defined by what she does not do; morality consists of *refraining from.* All other decisions or other actions are eliminated; this, by the standards of Chaucer's time, makes these women "good." As Ann McMillan points out in her valuable introduction to her translation of the *Legend,* Chaucer's plot patterns are based on *legendae,* saints' lives, particularly the martyrology. As in Christine's stories of the virgin martyrs, suffering is salvific; through the martyr's sufferings pagans are converted and Christians are inspired. If virtue consists in accepting suffering, and vice in the pragmatic avoidance of suffering, it is only a short step to the notion that the greatest virtue lies in soliciting opportunities for suffering, even the obstinate refusal to avoid needless suffering. The martyr cannot by definition take any steps to help herself; she chooses to be a victim. The martyr's story, like the *Legend* stories, is "formulaic,"[12] featuring ingenious tortures followed by miraculous recuperations that confound the torturers, leading eventually to the death that wins the martyr's crown. But because Chaucer's characters, mostly taken from pre-Christian sources, are not virgins but women involved with men, the pattern is altered. The torturers' function is assumed by the women's lovers, and so the women have chosen their torturers. Because "women are innocent victims, men vicious deceivers,"[13] the pathos of the good women's suffering is heightened by altering source stories to make the men more vicious, the women more innocent. Revision of sources to fit the "good woman" formula may require that a legendary character clean up her act.

Altering sources is a practice with many precedents in classical and medieval works. In Ovid's *Heroides,* classical stories are retold in the epistolary form. The viewpoint shift to the first person causes the tale to be told from the woman's viewpoint, which creates sympathy, however far-fetched, for Ovid's heroines. The rehabilitation of Medea is typical. In *The Metamorphoses,* Medea is a passionate woman; she is a witch-woman, allied with dark supernatural forces; she is a violent woman, capable of deeds of darkness from which other women recoil. But in *The Heroides,* Medea presents herself as the victim of Jason's perfidy so that the reader can easily forget her little failings; Ovid carefully cuts off the letter at a point before the child murders, leaving Medea a "good" woman, passive, suffering, and unavenged.[14] So when, like Ovid, Chaucer omits details that would make his women less good, his audience would recognize this technique. Chaucer often employs the rhetorical device of *brevitas,* a comment to the effect that time does not permit going into detail. As Lisa J. Kiser points out in *Telling Classical Tales: Chaucer and the Legend of Good Women,* Chaucer's use of *brevitas* "turns into something more like lying," because the practice "mask[s] those details in his sources which would complicate our moral judgments of these women and their deeds." By deleting the more controversial aspects of his source tales, Kiser says, Chaucer "succeeds in transforming these ladies of bad reputation into paragons of goodness."[15]

To effect this metamorphosis, Chaucer forces pagan heroines into the mold of Christian saints by eliminating all qualities considered unfeminine in his day. Thus his heroines become "less active, aggressive and passionate . . . less noble, more flawed and feminine."[16] Vengeful thoughts and retaliatory actions are deleted[17] to avoid violating medieval ideas of the value of women's suffering and the immorality of revenge. In the martyrologies, torturers often die in droves, but the saint must never wish for this. Proper martyr behavior is demonstrated by St. Christine, who, rotated by iron hooks in a cauldron of boiling oil, "sang melodiously to God."[18] At one point Christine does lose her serene disposition, spitting her cut-off tongue into the face of a torturer, "putting out one of his eyes,"[19] but such behavior is untypical. Not only must good women not take revenge, they must "never get angry."[20] In short, Chaucer's technique is to suppress all "independent actions" and "emotional forcefulness,"[21] qualities inappropriate for good women, who, like saints, endure torture cheerfully.

Because the medieval audience would assume that a good woman abstains from sex outside marriage, classical fornicators must be brought within the fold of some arrangement that might pass for Christian matrimony. In several legends Chaucer does this by alluding to a canon law issue of his day involving private marriage agreements. Over a period of several hundred years spanning Chaucer's lifetime, the Church attempted to regularize marriage procedures. One development was an increasingly precise definition of the words and actions requisite to contracting a legal and binding marriage. Medieval theologians followed the approach of Peter Lombard, a twelfth-century canonist, who defined marriage as being contracted in two ways: by words of present tense, whether followed by consummation or not; and by words of future tense followed by consummation.[22] In other words, once a verbal agreement was made to marry in the future, consequent consummation made the marriage legal and binding even without a formal, witnessed ceremony.

The second type of marriage contract posed enforcement problems. Too often, a verbal agreement "permitted an unscrupulous man to have sexual relations with a woman after an exchange of words of present consent and later free himself from the consequences of the relationship by perjuring himself and denying that the words were ever exchanged."[23] The ecclesiastical courts in Chaucer's day were cluttered with such cases, and futilely so, as these unwitnessed promises could not be enforced;[24] private promises were rescindable once seduction had occurred.[25] Such situations are depicted in several of Chaucer's legends: a man denies that he ever intended to marry the woman who thinks herself married to him by an implied contract. This canon law controversy is a mitigating circumstance explaining the behavior of Chaucer's good women. The women have accepted as binding the informal marriage agreement, the *per verbum de futuro* contract followed by consummation, and therefore see themselves as "trewe wives" suffering in defense of wifely chastity.

The story of Dido and Aeneas in the *Legend* is a prime example of Chaucer's alteration of sources to free his heroines from subjective guilt. In Ovid's *Heroides*, after the day in the cave with Aeneas, Dido laments her "ruin," her "purity undone," and attributes her present sorrow to her violation of chaste widowhood; she even offers to be Aeneas's concubine if he will not accept her as his wife.[26] In Virgil's *Aeneid*, the lovers' story is full of imagery of raging passions. The narrator does not see the couple as married, and regards them as guilty of sexual excess even by the norms of a culture uninfluenced by Christian asceticism. When Aeneas is ready to abandon the relationship, he simply denies that they were ever married.[27] Clearly the Dido of Ovid's and Virgil's account might appear a simple fornicator to medieval eyes. So, to maintain audience sympathy, Chaucer must get Dido married. In the *Legend,* then, Chaucer glosses over Dido's widowhood and portrays her as believing herself to be married on the strength of the private agreement. Subjectively she is innocent, just another deceived medieval woman, "victim of an unacknowledged clandestine marriage."[28] Dido's situation is, alas, all too common in the *Legend.* Medea, Ariadne, and Phyllis also believe themselves in legitimate marriages because of promises made in private.

Dido's swoon points to another alteration that Chaucer must make in his sources to keep his women good: transformation of anger into internalized and passive forms. Nothing is more unfeminine, no trait except unchastity more forbidden, than anger. Shrews get angry; martyrs do not. As Elaine Tuttle Hansen shows, Virgil's Dido "rages, insults and curses Aneas"; in Ovid, she is "pathetic, but still proud"; but in Chaucer, she "begs, kneels, cries . . . and faints."[29] Medieval behavior manuals uniformly discouraged expressions of anger and even angry feelings. Strong emotions in the good women are metamorphosed into passive forms: moans, wails, and especially swoons (Dido alone swoons more than twenty times). When a betrayed woman complains, the term means a *planctus,* a lament or self-pitying speech, not a forthright demand for male reform. The need in Chaucer's *Legend* for avoiding confrontational scenes in which anger might surface often means that the hero is depicted as skulking off in the dead of night, as do Aeneas and Theseus, while the abandoned women are asleep, safely quiet, virtuously passive. Avoidance of external expressions of anger also means that "the violence that women are unable to turn against men . . . they turn against themselves." [30] Thus several of the good women commit suicide. Control of anger contributes to women's suffering; a man might fear the wrath of a shrew, but he has nothing to fear from the "helplessness" and "almost catatonic passivity" of a good woman.[31]

Suppression of anger and vengeance is the editing principle in Chaucer's recasting of the Philomela legend from Ovid's *Metamorphoses.* The unacceptability of feminine anger is made clear in the memorable image of Philomela's tongue. In Ovid, the violated Philomela cries out the guilt of her brother-in-law Tereus; it is to deprive her of her outraged voice that he mutilates her. With her severed tongue "quivering, making a little murmur" on the ground,[32] Tereus rapes her several more times, adding a new level of perversity, but also suggesting the sexual basis of control of women's speech: to control a woman's speech is to control her in every possible way. In Ovid, Procne, discovering the crime against her sister and herself, incites her humiliated sister to revenge. "This is no time . . . / For tears, but for the sword," Procne says—no time for a feminine suffering but for a masculine retaliation.[33] Unhampered by the loss of *her* tongue, Procne cries out her desire to mutilate Tereus' eyes, tongue, and genitals. The actual revenge, horrible in its violence, is carried out without a hint of conventional womanly emotion: Procne kills Itys, her son and Tereus's, chops up his body, and feeds it to Tereus in a stew. Then Philomela, "with hair all bloody / Springs at him, and hurls the bloody head of Itys / Full in his father's face."[34] Surely this behavior is unladylike by medieval standards. So Chaucer finds himself much too pressed for time to tell this part of the tale, and stills the wrath of Procne when she sees the tapestry depicting her sister's fate: "No word she spak, for sorwe and ek for rage" (F., 2374). She feels anger, but may not speak it. Neither may Philomela, who has no speech. Medieval people would also note that Philomela's mutilation prevents her from "raising the hue and cry," a key element in pressing rape charges at law.[35] Both sisters are passive and pathetic in captivity, Philomela "dombe," "sittynge," and "wepynge"; Procne in "wo . . . compleynt and . . . mone" (F., 2378–2379). Chaucer cuts the story here, leaving them to their fruitless but ladylike lamentations.

In general, then, to maintain "the pattern of male treachery and female suffering,"[36] Chaucer deletes the source behaviors that place the heroines at variance with the norms of medieval culture for women. The good women are provided with as great a degree of chastity as can be made consistent with the well-known plot line, and with the supporting passive virtues that indicate, indeed contribute to, their suffering. Speech is either entirely eliminated, in the case of Philomela, or transformed from castigation to lamentation; anger is turned inward, to become depression and self-destruction, rather than outward, to revenge. The men are never taken to task for the bad behavior that causes suffering, nor do the women have the sense to avoid such men in the first place. Chaucer's heroines become the proper ladies of sermons and conduct books, the embodiments of chastity preserved by suffering. In thus adjusting the "olde appreved stories" (F Prol., 21) to medieval sensibilities, Chaucer provides his audience with an absolutely conventional piece of didacticism "designed to avoid awakening the characteristics . . . men feared and to instill accommodation and reconciliation to the carefully designed future role."[37]

Women's role is to suffer; thus, in the *Legend*, suffering is "the characteristic, defining act of the good women."[38] All medieval Christians were exhorted to accept trials sent by God as Job did, with patience. While the converse was never true, women were encouraged to embrace sufferings inflicted by men. Jill Mann reminds us that the *Legend* tales "contain three suicides and two rapes" specifically to stress "female suffering in its most extreme forms." Further, Mann stresses that betrayal is an important link between the *Legend* heroines and Criseyde.[39] The idea of suffering is another such link. Because the *Legend* is a work of atonement for the creation of Criseyde, the behavior of the *Legend* heroines shows that Criseyde should have remained true to Troilus, not just *despite* the fact that fidelity would have led to suffering, but *because* it would have. To save herself from suffering by taking the pragmatic step of securing the protection of Diomede is wrong. Criseyde's failure to embrace suffering makes her a bad woman. Good women, as the narrator tells us in the "Prologue," arouse "pite" for their "wo." "Wo" is good for them and makes them *exempla* of virtue. The more "wo" the better, then.

A woman who has already suffered may be further required to kill herself. The cultural assumptions of the pagan world from which Chaucer drew his source stories are that death is preferable to dishonor, that dishonor for women is coterminous with unchastity, and that suicide is preferable to the disgrace caused by loss of chastity. Chaucer does not attempt to solve the theological dilemma posed for his Christian audience by condoning suicide in the pagan sources; rather, he transmits the attitudes toward suicide of the ancient world. In *Tragic Ways of Killing a Woman*, Nicole Loraux argues that suicide in Greek tragedy is considered shameful, not heroic, therefore "a woman's death." A heroic death is a man's death, "by the sword or the spear of another, on the field of battle . . . a man must die at a man's hand."[40] An admission of abject helplessness in an intolerable situation, suicide in *The Legend of Good Women* is not only a last resort for the feeble-spirited but the logical culmination of a tendency in the good women to inflict suffering on themselves.

A further irony in the matter of self-imposed suffering is that it can be rendered absurd by the manifest inferiority of the men for whom the women suffer. As Ruth M. Ames points out, "the poem might better be entitled *The Legend of Bad Men*."[41] Chaucer's narrator describes his tales as involving "goode wymmen" and "false men" (F Prol., 484, 486). In other words, he is creating contrasting sets of character types. Except for Pyramus, with whom Chaucer "has exhausted the supply of good men in literature,"[42] all the other men in the *Legend* are "cads,"[43] bad men, not typical men; bad men behave with utter self-absorption, total insensitivity. Surely these men are not worth dying for. So it becomes clear that Chaucer's good women have a major character defect: they are attracted to men who are sure to make them suffer. When the bad character traits of the men are joined to the character flaws of the women who choose those men, the formula is established: good women love to suffer, and they find men bad enough to help them do it.

From the behavior of these characters, certain conclusions can be drawn about women who are good according to the norms of medieval society. Such women commit themselves unconditionally to men who do not keep promises. Good women center their lives on men; bad men discard women when opportunity beckons. Despite all contrary evidence, good women think they can change men's bad habits. Good women are attracted to men who appear weak and needy; in return for their help, good women expect undying love. Bad men, however, recognize no such bargain; when they no longer need help, they leave. Good women ignore men's potential for cruelty. Good women assume that men are willing and able to fulfill the culturally mandated role of protector. Operating on all these assumptions leads to disaster for good women, but bad men escape unscathed.

These contrasting patterns of male/female behavior work themselves out in the tales. A major problem area in these painful relationships is keeping "trouthe." In medieval literature, the verbal commitment between men is a common motif. Men pledge their honors with their words, and they would lose self-respect and the respect of others if they failed in "trouthe." But agreements between men and women in the *Legend* often involve misunderstanding as to what, if anything, is being pledged; the women believe themselves committed, be-trothed, while the men do not. "Ingratitude" in this work, as R. W. Frank observes, "implies a failure to supply a *quid pro quo*."[44] The good women and the bad men have different expectations of reciprocity. The women make a commitment in which nothing is explicitly promised them in return, yet they naively assume that generosity will be repaid in kind. Consequently, all the women believe themselves to be in the privileged position accorded to the legitimate wife in medieval law and custom; but the men see the relationship as concubinage, a lesser relationship, contingent and temporary, allowing the woman to be dismissed at will.

Good women also assume that men regard love as a central value. But all the men in the *Legend* see worldly success as more important. Thus Antony kills himself when he is defeated in battle; Aeneas leaves Dido and Jason leaves both Medea and Hypsipyle when destiny beckons. The conflict between love and achievement is reflected in the spatial motion of the tales. The women are stationary in space, ready to receive the men upon their arrival and to provide a haven, a place of comfort and security that the women believe to be permanent. The men perceive the women's place as temporary, a place of regeneration and a point of departure for their next adventure. Women's activities are directed toward the relationship and the domestic inner space, but men's are directed outward, toward the larger world of male action, where their true commitment lies.

Good women assume that by the force of their goodness they can transform known betrayers into model husbands. Cleopatra knows that Antony has grown bored with and abandoned his wife. As Elaine Tuttle Hansen points out, Phyllis's "instantaneous capitulation to Demophon seem[s] more foolish" considering his well-known "heritage of falsity from his father Theseus, whom we saw in action two legends back." These repetitive patterns of self-destructive behavior on the part of the women erode the reader's respect for them. Instead of being edified by their actions, the reader might ask "why, with so many literary examples of folly, women still fail to see the falsity of men."[45]

Good women love to help the weak. Men who have "the gift of eliciting sympathy"[46] are very appealing to such women. As Jill Mann notes: "Wherever the story makes it possible, Chaucer emphasizes that it is pity rather than sexual attraction which draws these women to love."[47] This stress on pity desexualizes the women, making them very good women indeed, fulfilling a nurturing, quasi-maternal function with respect to the helpless men. But once the men grow stronger, they leave.[48] This pattern is seen in the tales of Phyllis, Hypsipyle, Medea, and Ariadne, and especially in that of Dido. Aeneas comes to Dido's kingdom a clear loser, a refugee from fallen Troy. She is a widow ruling independently, an ideal woman and sovereign, loyal, competent, generous, desired by all. Aeneas arouses her pity because of his helplessness. He has an even more helpless small son, Ascanius, whose strong appeal to the childless Dido is expressed in the pleasant notion that the boy has been magically transformed into Cupid to make her fall in love with his father. When women like Dido are attracted to pitiable men, they rush to help them; in exchange for this help, they assume undying love will be given in return. Dido gives Aeneas refuge in her kingdom, stocks his ships, supplies his men with wine, treats him so royally that he thinks he is in paradise. She gives him a long list of gifts, he gives her far fewer. Even adjusting for the virtue of largesse, lavish gift-giving from host to guest, the imbalance in the list of gifts points to "that cascading emotional involvement of Dido, her heedless giving of herself," an attitude not shared by Aeneas, who on the contrary gives the "overall impression of a fellow who has fallen into a cushy spot and is enjoying it to the full."[49] Aeneas's behavior brings the once-dignified queen to her knees, then to her death.

In other *Legends,* similar unproductive feminine traits destroy other women too. Jason comes to Hypsipyle's island weak and needy; Hypsipyle offers help. They are married, he takes over her body and her property, begets two children on her. Then he leaves, returning to his quest. Even Medea, famous for her intellect, is taken in by Jason. "At nyght," in "hire chamber," Jason swears an "oth" never to "false" her (F., 1637–1640); in return, Medea agrees to use "the sleyghte of hire enchauntement" (F., 1650) to enable him to find the fleece. Fleece found, Jason will deny his private promise and abandon her. Arachne helps Theseus survive his encounter with the minotaur. In return, he promises marriage, but instead elopes with her sister. Yet she kneels and kisses his footprints in the sand. Demophoön is sailing from Troy to Athens; his men are sick and wounded; their ship, battered by tempests, is driven to land in Phyllis's kingdom. She helps them; he rests and recuperates, acting lordly and taking everything he wants. In return he promises marriage, but instead leaves her. These recurrent, even monotonous, behavior patterns lead us to ask, with

R. W. Frank, what intelligent women are doing in relationships like these, and how are we to feel about them? Frank says that "a man's betrayal of a woman's love cannot be made a matter to shake the heavens. The betrayed woman can win our sympathy and the betrayer can earn our contempt. But the lady's misfortune cannot quite seem high tragedy and the cad's actions cannot inspire horror."[50] While surely a woman's heartbreak is high tragedy to *her*, a matter to shake *her* heavens, nevertheless in the *Legend* the impression is inescapable: these women are volunteering for their own sad fates.

The similarities between the several stories move toward some generalizations about the contrasting natures of women and men. Chaucer sees women's instinctive need to help, their intuitive understanding of men's needs, their positive genius for self-sacrifice. But he sees these traits not as the behavior manual writer or homilist would do, as virtues, but rather as psychological handicaps putting them at a disadvantage in dealing with the more rapacious members of the opposite sex. The repetitive nature of the stories show it as "common and inevitable that men betray and women beg for more."[51] Good women, apparently, are trusting to the point of gullibility, poor judges of character, masochistically attracted toward pain, natural victims. They make assumptions about the nature of relationships, that there has been "a bargain struck."[52] But the men feel no responsibility to pay back such women's generosity and no sense of commitment in response to their sacrifice. They take sacrifices made on their behalf as their due, and move on.

To be abandoned by a man is not, after all, the worst fate that can befall a good woman. Rape, mutilation, imprisonment, and sexual slavery are worse. Chaucer's good women do not realize that bad men's proneness to violent gratification of their sensual appetites places women at risk, as the example of Philomela graphically illustrates. Tereus perverts the good: he takes his wife's charming devotion to her sister and his father-in-law's trust in him to betray the wife, to deflower the sister, to flout the sacred duty of protection pledged to their father. Even the narrator, anti-male as he is, realizes that few men are as bad as Tereus; nevertheless, on the off chance that they might meet such a one, he cautions his female readers to beware of all men.

Surely, Chaucer thinks, more can be expected of his own sex. Abandoning the *Legend* represents Chaucer's recognition that the received wisdom of his time on feminine virtue and male vice is totally inadequate to accommodate the complex psychology of fully developed literary characters. This realization, as Ann McMillan points out, helps in understanding the evolution of Chaucer's thought on marriage in more sophisticated works like the "Franklin's Tale."[53] By portraying such bad men in counterpoint with such good women, Chaucer lays the groundwork for his far greater achievement in creating the more complex and ambiguous marital relationship between Dorigen and Arveragus, in which the simple binary moral categories break down.

In the story of Dorigen and Arveragus in the "Franklin's Tale," Chaucer develops themes similar to those in the *Legend* but in strikingly innovative fashion. Here a virtue other than chastity is important for a woman; a woman avoids suffering without incurring severe condemnation; and a man acknowledges obligations in marriage, even if he fulfills them in less-than-ideal fashion. Considering the litany of exhortations on the preservation of women's chastity, Chaucer's advancement, through the character of Arveragus, of the idea that chastity is only one of the virtues appropriate to a woman is a sharp divergence from the norms of his time. In the tale, Chaucer develops an ethical theory that perceives men and women as equally capable of all virtues, with no virtue seen as sex-specific. Arveragus, albeit with some degree of self-concern, can nevertheless place his own interests to one side and engage in altruistic behavior; Dorigen, though dealing with the consequences of unwise behavior, can still hope to achieve the honor that accrues to one who keeps "trouthe." And both can make the unusual value judgment that, important as chastity is, it is not a woman's only nor even the most important virtue, nor is her suffering for its preservation inevitable, nor will a threat to her chastity, even a violation thereof, irrevocably destroy their marriage. What is more, Chaucer creates a portrait of a marriage in which moral compromise and acceptance of imperfection substitutes for the ethical absolutism depicted in the *Legend* tales.

Neither Dorigen nor Arveragus is an ideal exemplar of wife or husband, but of the two, Arveragus is the more unusual in attempting a new model of marriage. The relationship begins as a conventional courtship, described in conventional terms.[54] Arveragus is a "knyght that loved and dide his payne / To serve a lady in his beste wise" (V.F., 730–731). During courtship he follows the prescribed pattern: he "wroughte," did great deeds, for her "er she were wonne" (V.F., 733). Chaucer has a way of using short words for big concepts; here, great meaning can be seen as attached to "er," before. Courtly love is a relationship that by definition excludes marriage, because "marriage would destroy love . . . by reversing the order of things. The suppliant and servant would become the lord and master."[55] So, although Dorigen is Arveragus's "lady" to whom he does "meke obeysaunce" (V.F., 731, 739), this situation would ordinarily be reversed in marriage: "Courtly love requires the man's perfect obedience, marriage the woman's."[56]

But so dearly does Arveragus love Dorigen that he attempts to reconcile the competing systems by retaining in private the notion that Dorigen is his lady when he confers upon her the public dignity of taking her to wife. It is not she who, buoyed by her superior position in courtship, exacts the promise as a condition of the marriage, but he who "of his free wyl . . . swoor hire as a knyght" (V.F., 745) that theirs will be a marriage unknown in Chaucer's day and rare in ours:

> nevere in al his lyf he, day ne nyght,
> Ne sholde upon hym take no maistrie
> Agayn hir wyl, ne kithe hire jalousie
> But hire obeye, and folwe hir wyl in al,
> As any lovere to his lady shal,
> Save that the name of soveraynetee
> That wolde he have for shame of his degree.
>   (V.F., 746–752)

Arveragus swears to reject the "maistrie" associated with conventional marriage. He recognizes that his wife has her own will, as he does. Therefore he swears never to ask her to act against it. Chaucer accepted, indeed advocated, the notion of independent will in women, as we will see in the "Wife of Bath's Tale." Arveragus realizes that traditional male dominance/female subordination does not necessarily lead to joy for all concerned, that the condition of will-lessness prescribed in the conduct books is as unnatural for women as for men. Of his free will, Arveragus pledges not to limit his wife's. This does not guarantee that Dorigen will choose wisely, only that, wise or unwise, the choice is hers, and that he will do his best not to exert that authority which his culture would have assumed to be his right.

When Arveragus takes the oath that constitutes his marriage vow, he means to keep it. "He swoor hire as a knyght"—these words mean what they seem to mean, that is, that he swears on his honor as knight; but they can also mean that he swears as a knight would to another knight. As we have seen in *The Legend of Good Women*, "bad" men make no promises; they leave their options wide open. But Arveragus voluntarily makes a spoken commitment, which he regards as binding on his honor as a knight. Arveragus, then, believes his word to his wife to be as binding as his word given to another man. What Arveragus swears to do is a major modification of the customs of an ancient institution. This act is unusual enough in itself; so, while it is an imperfection, it is not surprising that Arveragus does not want to publicize what would surely be seen as an odd arrangement, even a violation of divinely ordained hierarchy. The additional fact that Arveragus does not perfectly achieve his goal of abnegating mastery does not subtract from the nobility of his promise. After all, what Arveragus is doing here is taking a new kind of marriage vow; and all marriage vows, be they innovative or conventional, are testimony to high ideals that often turn out to be difficult to maintain in daily practice.

Marriage as an institution has built-in expectations of which individuals like Dorigen and Arveragus are aware even as they try to change them. Male dominance was a major assumption in medieval marriage. It was impossible for any marriage to be completely free of it, and Dorigen's language when she accepts Arveragus's promise shows that she knows this: she thanks him, humbly, for offering her "so large a reyne" (V.F., 752–755). The image of an animal on a long leash is not a positive one in this context; a long rein is a rein still, and Arveragus can shorten it if he wishes. By thinking in terms of this image, Dorigen shows herself aware that she only has the degree of freedom that her husband wishes to give her; that no matter what he says about abandoning "maistrie," he is still her hierarchical superior, and she is under his authority. This brief comment prefigures the complex interaction between them at the moment of crisis in their marriage.

The couple, then, begins their life together with the highest possible ideal: their marriage will be different from all the others. The narrator describes such a union as a reciprocal relation of equals, that is, a friendship; and "freendes everych oother moot obeye, / If they wol longe holden compaignye" (V.F., 762–763). Marriage partners are "freendes." Friendship is characterized by "parity rather than the usual imbalances based upon sex." [57] The partners are equal, not master and serf, and if they want to "holden compaignye," stay together, they must obey each other. The vow of obedience traditionally taken only by the wife should be reciprocal. The univocal vow, the Franklin observes, particularly grates on women, who by nature desire to be free of domination:

> Love wol nat been constreyned by maistrye.
> Whan maistrie comth, the God of Love anon
> Beteth his wynges, and farewel, he is gon!
> Love is a thyng as any spirit free.
> Wommen, of kynde, desiren libertee.
> And nat to been constreyned as a thral;
> And so doon men, if I sooth seyen shal.
> (V.F., 764–770)

Arveragus begins his marriage, according to this ideal, regarding his wife as a friend, someone like himself, who wants liberty, as he does himself.

The plot revolves around the testing of Arveragus's commitment to this self-imposed standard. Testing a woman's virtue is a common plot element (as in the "Clerk's Tale"), but a plot revolving around testing a man's virtue in marriage is new. A separation generates emotional tension and triggers the plot events. In Arveragus's absence, Dorigen behaves as a woman is expected to do when her husband is away: "She moorneth, waketh, wayleth, fasteth, pleyneth" (V.F., 819). Her responsiveness to her friends' encouragement to "leve hire hevynesse" (V.F., 828), however, is a mis-

take. By the norms of the behavior manuals, Dorigen's situation is wid-
owlike, and therefore she is supposed to be inconsolable. She should not
be out in company, lest she be tempted to adultery. Dorigen's choice to
accept her friends' advice is a freely chosen error, a violation of the estate
of quasi-widowhood by tacitly acknowledging the possibility of consolation. What was expected to happen does happen. Violating seclusion, she
is seen by Aurelius, who falls in love with her in the classic courtly mode:
young bachelor in love with the lord's lady.[58]

Dorigen soon compromises herself. "In pley" (V.F., 988), almost flir-
tatiously, she makes the pact: if Aurelius "remoeve alle the rokkes," she
will "love [him] best of any man" (V.F., 993, 997). The degree of Dorigen's guilt here is a matter of debate among critics. It is true that Dorigen
makes this promise only to safeguard her husband, and that, moreover,
she regards the removal of the rocks as a physical impossibility. It is also
true, as Elaine Tuttle Hansen points out, that her words are a "joke," a
"roguish promise," not a serious commitment to be interpreted by the
male standard of the plight of troth but rather a light speech immediately
followed by a "violent retraction."[59] Nevertheless, bearing in mind the
strict standards for wifely chastity propounded to the medieval woman,
Dorigen has compromised herself merely by thinking about adultery, much
less discussing its possibility with an attractive young man. She may speak
"in pley," but adultery is no laughing matter. Since she utters the specific
words of the unbreakable oath, "Have heer my trouthe" (V.F., 998), it is
no surprise that Aurelius's understanding is that she has committed herself
(V.F., 1320, 1328). Thus the dilemma arises: which of two highly esteemed
virtues to violate, chastity or "trouthe"?

At the moment of crisis, when the choice of a course of action must be
made, both marriage partners abandon their egalitarian experiment and revert to familiar role models. Dorigen weeps, wails, and swoons, because
she perceives only the two standard alternatives offered her by her culture:
"deeth or elles dishonour" (V.F., 1358). Because both are unacceptable,
she is truly a "sorweful creature" (V.F., 1346). In her long "compleynt"
(V.F., 1354) she shows her inability to find an unconventional solution to
the problem; she reverts to stock feminine helplessness. Over and over she
repeats the formula, varying the words but not the thought: death or dishonor. Ideas neatly phrased seem truer; even the alliteration of the aphor-
ism contributes to the sense of inevitability: death or dishonor. Is there a
third alternative? Dorigen cannot see one. In another characteristic medieval thought process, Dorigen is persuaded by the weight given to accu-
mulations of *exempla*, the "stories" that "beren witnesse" to correct behavior, the tales of "many a noble wyf and many a mayde" who "yslayn
hirself, allas / Rather than with hir body doon trespas" (V.F., 1364–1366).
After Dorigen cites enough examples of this stock formula, she has convinced herself that she too must slay herself. But, unlike the *Legend* her-

oines, she seeks a way to escape this ultimate self-punishment. So she delays long enough ("a day or tweye" [V.F., 1457]) for Arveragus to come home, and tells him "al" (V.F., 1460–1465), thereby turning the problem over to him.

What is happening here is a complex human interaction involving vacillation between convention and innovation in marital role behavior. On the one hand, Dorigen is confiding in her husband because he has proclaimed himself her friend, and friends share problems. But she can also be seen as shifting moral responsibility for a difficult decision to him in conformity with the traditional hierarchical model of marriage. If he reverts to type, he will assume the authority he once rejected and solve the problem for her. If she wanted the decision totally in her hands, she could well have made it in the day or two that she delayed doing so. To share a decision with a partner in order to diffuse responsibility for it would be a psychological strategy not unknown to married couples. At the same time, she risks the consequences of righteous husbandly wrath if indeed Arveragus reverts to type. However mixed her motives, the effect of seeking Arveragus's help is that, instead of assuming that he will act the part of the stock betrayed husband, she gives him the opportunity to act like the friend he promised to be.

And Arveragus does. First, he hears her out, and with amazing calm: "with glad chiere, in friendly wyse" (V.F., 1467). When Dorigen finishes her tale, Arveragus responds in a way that shocks even his wife: "Is ther oght elles, Dorigen, but this?" (V.F., 1469). Is that all? The understatement of this must be set against the horror with which moralists of Chaucer's day saw the merest hint of threat to wifely chastity. Dorigen responds in this context when she says, "this is to muche" (V.F., 1471). Then, against prevailing belief, Arveragus maintains that not chastity but "trouthe" is "the hyeste thyng that man may kepe" (V.F., 1479), humanity's highest virtue, not only as important for women in general as it is for men in general, but so important that even his own wife must act accordingly.

Arveragus's intervention in his wife's decision at this point is interpreted in dramatically different ways depending on whether or not it is read as a violation of Dorigen's freedom. Jill Mann cites the argument that "at this point the special structure of the marriage relationship collapses into the traditional pattern of male dominance and female subservience" to disagree with it, seeing Arveragus as honoring the integrity of Dorigen's promise and insisting that she "live out the implications of her independent action." To Mann, Arveragus resists the conventional impulse to "assume control, to 'rescue the little woman' from the mess she has got herself into." Instead, his "refusal to forbid her to keep her promise deprives her of the alibi of male coercion" and leaves her freedom intact.[60] On the other hand, it is also true that Arveragus does assert the ultimate degree of husbandly authority when he commands her to conceal her infidelity under "peyne of deeth" (V.F., 1481). As Dorigen always knew, a husband can pull in the reins when he wants to. As Elaine Tuttle Hansen sees it, this order effectively denies Dorigen's self by silencing her: "There is an obvious irony in the fact that she is told in the same breath to keep her all-important word and to keep her mouth shut about doing so." More denigrating to Dorigen, in Hansen's view, is the fact that the tale's happy outcome is not the result of any action of hers but rather of the "chain reaction of male virtue." This reduces Dorigen to a bit player in her own story, just another traded woman, "kept in place even as she is passed around."[61]

Both of these conflicting arguments make valid points. Too much sympathy for Dorigen can blind readers to the fact that it is she who made the mistake, however well-meaning, with which Arveragus is now dealing, however imperfectly. Hansen points out that Chaucer is concerned throughout his work with the "difficulty that men face in securing masculine identity and dominance."[62] On these terms, Arveragus is dealing with a difficult role conflict. Arveragus has tried to exert less "maistrie" than usual in his marriage. But if this experiment in human relations results in his wife's having sex with another man, it is understandable that the idea of this unhappy outcome being noised abroad causes him extreme anxiety. Under stress, he reverts to the language of the traditional role he had repudiated. Like his wife, Arveragus has fallen into the error of impetuous speech. But the momentary lapse does not negate his achievement in redefining virtue: he has encouraged his wife to demonstrate a "male" virtue, trouthe, and has himself practiced a "female" virtue, "self-sacrifice and abnegation."[63] Such innovative behavior breaks decisively with the heavy weight of tradition that governs relationships between husbands and wives, and it is thus perhaps as far as one marriage can be expected to go in redefining the institution.

Dorigen and Arveragus are able to resume their relationship as before, no mean accomplishment given the magnitude of the crisis they have survived: "Nevere eft ne was ther angre hym bitwene. / He cherisseth hire as though she were a queene, / And she was to him trewe for everemoore" (V.F., 1554–1555). Despite their mutual failure to live up to their own highest ideals—Dorigen had vowed perfect chastity, Arveragus had disavowed mastery—they have done well. Because Arveragus is able to transcend his culture's gendered definition of human virtue, and also because Dorigen is able to accept his more merciful counsel, she avoids the suffering of the good women of the Legend and he avoids losing her.[64] No one dies, and if Dorigen is dishonored to some extent by her technical violation of the most stringent norms for chastity, the relationship absorbs the imperfection.

The moral compromise made to sustain a marriage and a life in the "Franklin's Tale" does not, however, represent the typical pattern of medieval thought on the virtue of chastity. The overt value system of the saints' lives and *The Legend of Good Women* more clearly represents prevailing opinion: chastity is all, and the suffering and death of women is virtuous. Because chastity was so major a value, rule-givers related every aspect of female behavior to it. Therefore in literature, a complex of apparently unrelated details of women's lives was perceived as preserving chastity or conducive to losing it. In all three estates, the chastity of women is preserved by their subordinate status in that women are not ordinarily perceived as free moral agents. Subordination, seen negatively, means control of women; seen positively, it means protection. A woman's first protector, or controller, is her father, whose duty it is to preserve her virginity until responsibility for her protection, or control, can be passed along to a husband of his choosing.

4

Perfect Virgin, Perfect Wife: Transition

A daughter at all comely, or any one else of the household that takes the fancy of a man of property, is merchandise displayed for sale to attract the customer.

—John of Salisbury[1]

In a good wife the following conditions are necessary: that she be busy and devout in God's service, meek and obedient to her husband, gentle in word and deed with her servants, generous and liberal to strangers, merciful and friendly to the poor, mild and peaceable with her neighbors, circumspect and prudent in things to be avoided, strong and patient in things to be suffered, busy and diligent in her work, modest in her clothing, serious in her conduct, careful in her speech, chaste in her looking, honorable in her action, sober in her walking, shamefast in public, pleasant with her husband, chaste in her private life. Such a wife is worthy of praise.

—Bartholomaeus Anglicus[2]

I want a wife who is kind, meek, modest, quiet, hard-working, humble, young, and pure of mouth and hands, wise and graceful, and at least fifteen, sixteen, up to twenty years old.

—Eustache Deschamps[3]

He who finds a good wife finds a good thing, and obtains favor from the Lord.

—Proverbs 18:22

In medieval literature, the marriageable young virgin and her valuable chastity belong to the father and are given by him to a husband. When a woman is given and taken in marriage, the father transmits his authority over and his responsibility for protecting his daughter in a world unsafe for women. The paternalism of the *pater* includes two key elements: authority and responsibility. *Authority over* is a concept repugnant to many moderns, but, as we have seen, a universal principle of order to the medievals. To understand *responsibility for* as medievals saw it, we must think of that age's universal longing to be members of a group united under a strong leader. To be "unconnected" was to be "unprotected," so, according to John Boswell, persons who found themselves in such a situation often " 'commended' themselves to the service of someone more powerful . . . in return for economic security or simple personal safety."[4] The right and duty of protecting women must clearly be seen against the background of a stringently hierarchical society, joined by interlinking "systems of dependence,"[5] in which the stronger has the duty to protect the weaker, in return for which the weaker owes the stronger loyalty and service. Women, being perceived as physically and morally weaker, had the right of protection, as did relatively weak men. The lord protected his male retainers as the father did his daughter, and both imitated God in His role of protector of all humanity. Granted, one possible definition of the daughter was that of John of Salisbury: she was a piece of marketable property transmitted from one owner to another at the volition of those others. Another major component of the complex father-daughter relationship was the father's duty to protect the virginity of his daughter so that he might present her intact to the man who would guard her chastity as his wife. Thus both men safeguarded in her the integrity of their mutual lineage.

Of crucial importance in this process is the smooth transition of a virgin from father to husband. The young girl in the space between father and husband is in that most threatening of situations, a borderline state. She is the "liminal or 'threshold' person in family space,"[6] her "betweenness" involving risk, as she is temporarily removed from a fixed position in "cultural space."[7] Until her only meaningful journey is safely completed, she is in danger. The virgin's story, then, is a story of passage from stasis through liminality to stasis, from father through "betweenness" to husband. If the passage is safe, she can be described, as is the Man in Black's Lady White in Chaucer's *Book of the Duchess,* but she has no real story. Disruption of any element of the transitional process, obstacles to its fulfillment in the new stasis of marriage, constitutes the plot—the only possible plot—of a virgin's story.

In scripture, the term "daughter" is often used synonymously with "woman," as in the phrase "daughters of Israel." Multitude of progeny signifies success, prosperity, and happiness, so that both sons and daughters are grouped with sheep, camels, oxen, and asses as sign of God's restored blessings on Job (42:15). There is much ado in the Old Testament about the giving and taking of daughters in marriage, to whom and under what circumstances they might be given (see, e.g., Neh. 10:30). The father's absolute power over his daughter is apparent in the passage in Exodus discussing selling a daughter as a slave (21:7); but most Old Testament references to daughters are far more positive in tone. Except for the episode in which Christ cures the daughter of Jairus (Mark 5:22–23), there is little interest in the New Testament in daughters as such, probably because of the decreased emphasis on giving and taking in marriage in a religion that places a higher value on perpetual chastity. Instead, the image of the daughter is used by Paul to represent the new spiritual relationship of the Christian to God (2 Cor. 6:18).

More important than the term "daughter" in scripture is the more specific and more emotionally charged term "virgin," she who, like Rebekah in Genesis, "no man had known" (24:16). Only such a one is fit to marry a priest in Leviticus, who "shall take a wife in her virginity. A widow, or one divorced, or a woman who has been defiled, or a harlot, these he shall not marry; but he shall take to wife a virgin of his own people, that he may not profane his children among his people" (21:13–14). To accuse a new wife of not being a virgin is a serious matter, requiring her parents to produce "the tokens of her virginity" and present them to the "elders of the city" as evidence that they had done their job. If the husband is wrong, he is whipped. But if the woman is found guilty, "the men of her city shall stone her to death with stones, because she has wrought folly in Israel by playing the harlot in her father's house" (Deut. 22:13–21). Rape of a betrothed virgin is a grave offense, punishable by death for both parties if not sufficiently resisted (22:24), death for the man if the rape took place "in the open country" where "there was no one to rescue her" (22:27). Rape of an unbetrothed virgin must be atoned for by marriage and a cash payment to the father (22:28–29; cf. Ex. 22:16). Loss of virginity is, of course, shameful; Tamar, raped by Amnon, rent the costume of virginity, the "long robe with sleeves," placed ashes on her head, and "went away, crying aloud as she went." For such a one as she, the future is bleak: dishonored, Tamar "dwelt, a desolate woman in her brother Absalom's house" (2 Sam. 13:19–20), unacceptable in the house of father or husband.

In scripture, virginity or its lack is often an image of God's relationship to man. Israel's infidelity is like that of two young women who "played the harlot" (Ezek. 23:1). In contrast, the term "virgin" is a superlative, a synonym for special, precious, exalted, a thing of peculiar value, Israel as God's betrothed, "virgin Israel" (Jer. 31:4, 21; Amos 5:2). The joy of God's union with His people is like that of a man marrying a virgin: "As the bridegroom rejoices over the bride, so shall your God rejoice over you" (Is. 62:5).

In the Hebrew scriptures, the virginal state is temporary, a prelude to marriage, and the death of a virgin lamentable because her destiny was unfulfilled (Judges 11:34–40). The New Testament and the early Christian tradition exalts permanent virginity as representing complete devotion to God. Christ's miraculous birth of a virgin manifests His divinity. Considering the weight Christian theology has placed on the concept of virginity, it is surprising that Christ is silent on the subject; St. Paul is the main source for the theology of virginity. Paul uses the idea of the virgin bride much as the Old Testament does, as metaphor for special and exclusive commitment: "I betrothed you to Christ to present you as a pure bride to her one husband" (2 Cor. 11:2). Unlike the Hebrew scriptures, in which virginity is mentioned only as a female characteristic and only as premarital, Paul values virginity in both sexes as a permanent state superior to marriage (1 Cor. 7). This strand of the tradition diverges into the study of convent life in the Middle Ages and away from the study of the three estates of the lives of women. For marriageable women, there is only one lesson: preserve virginity until marriage.

The theological significance of premarital chastity was complemented by an important social function: preservation of the integrity of the lineage for purposes of inheritance. In feudal society, the "main principle" of inheritance was, as George Homans succinctly defines it, that "an established holding of land ought to descend intact in the blood of the men who had held it of old."[8] Therefore that bloodline must be pure. The virgin bride becomes a chaste wife who provides offspring to her legitimate husband only. Like the priests of Levi, medieval men were urged to take a virgin as wife. Because "family honor depended . . . on the behavior of womenfolk," and because women were believed to be morally frail, fathers and husbands were needed to protect women from error and themselves from shame: "A father had to marry off his daughters so as to guard himself against the dishonor they might otherwise bring on him."[9] This pressing need for female chastity is a good reason for girls to be married young in the higher social classes, those most concerned with family reputation and blood inheritance. Once a daughter is married off, "it was a husband's duty to shield his wife from temptation," lest she subvert legitimate inheritance by raising up "children of a blood different from that of the master of the house [who] might one day bear the name of his ancestors and succeed to their inheritance."[10] Blood purity, then, is most essential where inheritance is at stake. In the nonnoble and unlanded, the perceived need for premarital chastity diminishes.

Marriage involves the movement of the young virgin from her father's house to her husband's house. "House" means the family, the lineage, and the protecting structure. Georges Duby, the preeminent historian of medieval marriage, defines marriage as the union of two houses "to ensure the survival of one" and its "central rite" as the "procession that conveyed a woman, the bride, to a house, a chamber, a bed, in the expectation that she would soon become a mother."[11] The exchange of women between houses is an important political act;[12] the daughters of a house represent opportunities for potential alliances with other houses.[13] While John of Salisbury's cynical comment shows that traded women could be regarded as mere commodities, the function of women in linking families by bearing offspring of the blood of each[14] was nevertheless crucial to the smooth transmission of power between generations.

The physical movement of traded women is between houses, the two physical structures representing the two linked families. As will be discussed in detail later, a good woman's space is within an enclosure. Unlike the male hero in literature, who "always has to leave home," the good woman is "essentially located at home." Her "transition or passage from childhood to adulthood"[15] is her motion in space from father's house to husband's house, in accordance with the arrangement made by the two men. This ritual is crucial. In the early Christian centuries, "the two concrete elements necessary to make the marriage valid were the *consensus,* or mutual consent of both parties, and the *domum-ductio,* or leading of the wife to her husband's house."[16] To have a story at all, the virgin must be caught at the moment of motion: out of her father's house, toward the loss of her virginity.

The father's role in maintaining the virginity of the daughter until he arranges for its surrender is beautifully explained by Lynda E. Boose in "The Father's House and the Daughter in It." Boose stresses the role of motion in space as representing the transition process. The daughter's inaccessibility in her father's house is a sign of her purity: "the perceived worth of the family appreciates in direct proportion to the daughter's absence from outside space."[17] The father's house represents his sphere of protection, the husband's house his, and "daughters belong to either their father's house or their husband's, there is no neutral space."[18] Never must a daughter be allowed to wander in unenclosed space, because "an unenclosed daughter culturally signifies a 'loose' commodity available for competitive male possession. . . . Outside terrain [is] a space of jeopardy for one's daughters."[19] Unenclosed means unprotected, therefore sexually available.

So, according to Boose's theory, a woman between houses is in danger. It follows that the crucial *passage between* should be accomplished in as brief a time as possible. The traditional marriage ceremony, in which the bride is ritually escorted by her father to be turned over to her husband, embodies these beliefs. One way of looking at this is as an exhibition of the male power of gift-giving, in which the woman becomes a symbol of a bond between men.[20] But the rite can also be seen as a formal delegation of the special responsibility for the well-being of a prized possession. The woman and her precious virginity "belong to" her father[21] and are his to give. To have a protector is a woman's right, and it is the father's duty to arrange for one. Once safely over the threshold of her husband's house, a wife, she is no longer liminal but "absorbed into the closed structure of marriage and home,"[22] her rite of passage completed. Boose's explanation of the need for a smooth transition from liminality to stasis also suggests the significance of deviations from the ritual pattern. If a virgin's smooth transition is disrupted, disaster threatens. This complex of ideas stands behind both the action and the characterization of the women in Chaucer's "Legend of Thisbe" and his "Physician's Tale." Both women die because of a disrupted transition between houses.

In Chaucer's *Legend of Good Women*, though Pyramus is the one "good" man in the group, his incompetence as protector leads to tragedy. Pyramus and Thisbe are the children of two families whose lands adjoin. The proximity of the houses suggests equality of rank and stresses the absolute appropriateness of the match, which would join two adjacent landholdings and render the linked families all the more powerful in the next generation. But the wall erected between the two family properties stands as image of the irrational enmity between the two fathers, which prevents the obvious match. Thisbe's father is particularly at fault, since he should actively be seeking, not preventing, her marriage to just such a man as Pyramus.

Nevertheless, Pyramus is wrong to disrupt the orderly transition of a marriage arranged between men. What Pyramus does is in medieval law termed a *raptus*, or kidnapping, and it is an illicit way of getting a bride. *Raptus*, like its cognate, rape, is forbidden. Although a *raptus*, unlike a rape, could be arranged with the woman's consent, as is this one, and although a valid marriage requires only the consent of the couple, a *raptus* nevertheless violates the value attached to the father's right to form an alliance with another man through his daughter. Deviation from accepted practice has another important consequence: the gap in protection during the time when Thisbe is between husband and father places Thisbe, literally and figuratively, in the dangerous space between two houses. When Pyramus encourages Thisbe to flee the safety of her father's house, he assumes responsibity for her protection. Once he and Thisbe had "plyghten trouthe fully in here fey" (F., 778), that is, exchanged words of present consent, they are married, even though the relationship has not been consummated. By his vows, Pyramus places himself in the accepted role of husband/protector, but, having done so, he botches the job. Foolishly, he allows her to leave her father's house alone—against all custom. A woman of Thisbe's status would never be alone, much less at night in a forest. Wilderness is always threatening in medieval literature, even to men; the unenclosed forest, then, represents a breach in the web of protection that should surround such a one as Thisbe. Dangers for the unprotected woman are embodied in the "wilde lyonesse" (F., 805) from which she narrowly escapes. She should not be in such a situation at all. By allowing this to happen, Pyramus is showing himself ineffectual in his protector role. Inexplicably, he is late. Then, he thinks Thisbe is dead. Young romantic that he is, he laments and apostrophizes her blood-soaked wimple, but he neglects to mount a thorough search. He knows her death is his fault:

"Allas, to bidde a woman gon by nyghte / In place there as peril falle myghte!" (F., 838–839).

The purpose of marriage laws and customs is to avert just such a hiatus as Thisbe experiences in the network of protection surrounding the marriageable virgin. Maidens, the narrator comments at the beginning of the tale, are kept "ful streyte, lest they diden some folye" (F., 723). It does indeed turn out to be folly for Thisbe to meet "pryvyly" with Pyramus (F., 733). When she "stal awey ful pryvyly" (F., 796), forsaking all her "frendes" (F., 798), she loses the network of protective affiliations surrounding a high-status woman. Privacy is no asset here. Instead of a public betrothal, in which she assures herself of the protection of a husband without forsaking the protection of a father, she accepts a clandestine relationship. True, Pyramus is a good man, and "hardy, in this cas" (F., 803), brave to do this, but in the event undependable. Obeying her irrational father would have been safer. Too late, as she prepares to kill herself, she realizes this: "And lat no gentil woman hyre assure / To putten hire in swich an aventure" (F., 908–909).

The narrator praises her for her bravery, but women like Thisbe were not supposed to be brave; they are to be kept safe. Her wandering alone and unprotected by night, in the dreadful space between, is a distortion of the proper pattern—public conveyance of the bride to a new house, a safe house. The fate of Pyramus and Thisbe is catastrophic, not only for themselves but also for both their houses, as the lineage fails with their deaths.

In Chaucer's "Physician's Tale," Virginia's violent death illustrates the extreme reaction triggered by the threat of a daughter's loss of virginity. Jean de Meun's continuation of *The Romance of the Rose,* through which Livy's tale of Virginius reached the medieval audience, sees the story as an *exemplum* of legal corruption; the conflict is mainly between the father and the unjust judge, and the fate of Virginia gets short shrift. Chaucer tightens the focus by eliminating Virginia's fiancé,[23] thus reducing the number of important relationships to those between Virginia and her father and between Virginius and his daughter's would-be corruptor. The plot revolves around Virginius's response to the tensions generated by the judge's disruption of the proper ritual transmission of the virgin. The moral dilemma in which Virginius finds himself involves conflicting medieval cultural assumptions about women's chastity. By choosing the wrong assumption upon which to act, Virginius destroys his daughter.

In terms of the standards for behavior for the unmarried girl as set forth in the didactic sources, Virginia is perfect. In language alluding to the all-pervasive distrust of cosmetics in the didactic literature,[24] Chaucer describes Virginia as nature's child. No artist could "peynte" or "countrefete" such a creation (VI.C., 12–13). By stressing the concepts of painting and counterfeiting, Chaucer alludes to the conduct books' prohibitions on use of artificial aids to beauty, a complex of ideas to be discussed in detail later. The allusion here shows that Virginia, natural and unadorned, is a being wholly in accord with both esthetic and moral norms for beauty and behavior. Like the heroine of lyric and romance, Virginia is very young, only fourteen years old. Her skin is white, her cheeks red, her hair golden, her limbs graceful. And she is as virtuous as she is beautiful. It is not for lack of virginal perfection that Virginia comes to grief.

In an article entitled "The Maidenly Virtues of Chaucer's Virginia," Karl Young traces the influence on the description of Virginia's virtue of Vincent of Beauvais's early thirteenth-century tract *De Eruditione Filiorum Nobilium*. This tract is typical of behavior literature in its specifications for maidenly virtue: chastity (of course), prudence, generosity, humility, shamefastness, constancy, industriousness, and temperance. Chaucer alludes to all of these, but he devotes most of his attention to Virginia's speech habits, a key element in characterizing women in Chaucer, as we will see. Virginia refrains from using affected terminology to appear wise, but rather employs language "ful wommanly and pleyn," which is also "after hir degree," suitable to her rank (VI.C., 50–52). Her manner is correct, her content is "sownynge in vertu and in gentillesse" (VI.C., 54). Even at social events, feasts, revels, and dances (situations thought to encourage violations of speech propriety), she persists in habits of virtue. This is good in a virgin, because "al to soone may she lerne loore / Of booldnesse, whan she woxen is a wyf" (VI.C., 70–71). She even pretends to be "syk" to escape "occasions of daliaunce" (VI.C., 62, 66); the role of illness in demonstrating sanctity in the lives of women saints has been pointed out by Donald Weinstein and Rudolph M. Bell.[25] Perfectly correct in her behavior in every detail, Virginia is an authoritative source of maidenly lore, a veritable courtesy book of a girl: "For in hir lyvyng maydens myghten rede, / As in a book, every good word or dede / That longeth to a mayden vertuous" (VI.C., 107–109). She is, then, in Beryl Rowland's felicitous words, "the yet unravished angel in the house, the good book which other maidens must read."[26]

To further the plot, Chaucer must account for this paragon's being seen at all by the lecherous judge. He does so by sending Virginia to church: "This mayde upon a day wente in the toun / Toward a temple, with hire mooder deere, / As is of yonge maydens the manere" (VI.C., 118–120). Among conduct book writers, some few strict constructionists forbade even churchgoing because of the risk of being seen by a lecher, who might, as Appius does, "his eyen caste / Upon this mayde" (VI.C., 123–124). Jerome, in his "Letter to Eustochium," warns the young virgin thus: "Go not out from home. . . . Diana went out and was ravished. . . . I would not have you go about the corners of the city."[27] More common, however, was the notion that churchgoing could be tolerated for the higher good, if the young girl were properly chaperoned. Chaucer adds to his source the fact that Virginia went to church "with hire mooder deere,"[28] and that, moreover, her churchgoing was "the manere," the custom, among virgins of that community (VI.C., 119–120). Virginia's mother, having performed her brief but crucial role, vanishes from the action. The virgin's chastity is a matter between men.

Appius's lust places Virginius in a difficult position. Appius has not asked Virginius to give his daughter, "the most precious of gifts,"[29] in marriage but intends to take her as a concubine, an act that would dishonor both the woman and her family. Instead of considering how he might use his own power to counteract that of Appius, Virginius turns his attention toward the person more easily controlled: his daughter. If she loses her chastity, the daughter disgraces her father. It is true, as Emerson Brown says, that Virginius suffers from an "incapacity to see Virginia except as an extension of himself."[30] Chaucer stresses this by the identity of names. But if Virginius identifies his daughter's honor with his own, he comes by this perception honestly; few medieval fathers would have thought otherwise. But it is also true that, as Anne Middleton points out, "in the *Physician's Tale*, and in the *Canterbury Tales* generally, Chaucer encourages us to examine, define, and redefine ethical abstractions that are treated as givens in his originals or regarded as unexamined moral categories by the Canterbury narrators."[31] In addition to identifying his own honor with his daughter's, Virginius operates on the basis of another cultural "given": that in a situation in which female chastity is threatened, "Ther been two weyes, outher deeth or shame, / That thou most suffer" (VI.C., 214–15).[32] Caught on the horns of this dilemma, Virginius sees no third alternative to losing his daughter or losing his honor. A substantial body of medieval thought would have supported Virginius's action as a proper expression of his paternal concern for his daughter's eternal salvation, even though Virginius in his distress does not think through the problem with any degree of theological sophistication. Nevertheless, because of the obvious injustice done to an innocent person, Chaucer questions the "unexamined moral category" of the given alternatives: death or dishonor.

In medieval moral theology, theologians debated the subjective moral guilt of the rape victim. While the general principle was that "unwilling victims of rape remain, morally, virgins,"[33] early Church fathers also considered the morality of suicide to preserve virginity in the face of threatened rape. Ambrose and Jerome regarded suicide as permissible, even praiseworthy, while Augustine, in a rare moment of sympathy for women, believed that no guilt redounded to the woman from the sin of the rapist[34] and that therefore suicide was unnecessary. Though Augustine's view was to prevail in the mainstream of Christian theology, with such heavyweights coming down on the other side of the issue, there is an element of moral ambiguity. Guidelines existed, but not such as to be appropriately considered by an innocent like Virginia. The very young were assumed to be capable of moral choice, of course (the Wife of Bath first married at twelve), but a virginal girl would compromise her integrity merely by thinking about such a matter as the theology of rape. Because of her age and the moral complexity of the situation (the corruption involved in merely examining her options), a father might reason that the choice between death and dishonor should not properly be Virginia's. To further complicate the issue, the situation debated by the Church fathers is an isolated rape, serious enough to be sure. But what the evil judge intends is a form of sexual slavery; he intends to make Virginia his "thral" (VI.C., 189). Again because of her impressionable youth, Virginia could well be educated into consent. The habit of submission, encouraged in a young girl as a positive character trait, would tend to corrupt her and lead to the consent requisite for serious sin.

Since neither suicide nor surrender are clearly morally correct alternatives, Virginius could be seen as sparing his daughter the risk of sin by killing her himself. It is never sinful to be a victim, which is by definition a state of being acted upon rather than acting, and thus not contingent upon the will. No sin, then, can be involved for Virginia if her father kills her, neither the sin of suicide nor the possible sin of eventual consent to a series of repeated rapes. When Virginius says that he kills his daughter "for love, and nat for hate" (VI.C., 225), the members of the medieval audience sophisticated in the intricacies of medieval casuistry could have seen the act of his "pitous hand" (VI.C., 226) as deflecting all moral responsibility onto himself.

It is true that, as J. D. W. Crowther points out, Virginius "lacks faith in God's grace" when he does not allow his daughter to "confront the man who lusted after her" and try to convert him as did many virgin saints. Crowther is right, too, that Virginius "sees his daughter as his alone to dispose of as he believes fit,"[35] as was typical for a medieval father. Virginius sees himself as the father of a marriageable young virgin, not as the father of a potential saint. It is his duty to give her in marriage just so as not to allow her virtue to be sorely tried, lest she fail. The stakes are high: the father's reputation, the daughter's salvation. Since the illicit actions of Appius have disrupted the orderly process, a father might legitimately take the responsibility for settling her fate by sending her home to her God. By this line of reasoning, killing his daughter is the final service of a protector more concerned for her eternal salvation than for his own.

Thus reasoning on the basis of the death/dishonor dichotomy leads to the morally shocking conclusion that the duty of a good father is to kill his beloved child, a girl "fostred up with . . . pleasaunce" (VI.C., 219), one who is, moreover, an only child, her father's only hope for the continuation of his lineage. But matters have come to this not so much because the father has reasoned through the theology involved as because he has assumed that there are only two alternatives, and that the sufferer must be

Virginia. It is she who must manifest the feminine virtue of patient endurance. Why is it that a third alternative is never considered: that Appius suffer death at the hands of Virginius? Virginius is no peasant Janicula, helpless to protect his daughter. Rather he is a powerful man, a knight "fulfild of honour and of worthynesse, / And strong of freendes, and of greet richesse" (VI.C., 3–4). Such a man as this should be able to uphold the honor of his daughter while preserving her life, or die in the attempt himself; that is his proper paternal role. Virginius could have directed his violent impulses against Appius, not Virginia. Appius, though capable of abusing his power as a judge, is nevertheless not strong enough to protect himself when his crime is discovered: the people promptly cast him into prison, whereupon he slays himself. Virginius shows sufficient influence at that point to exact a lesser punishment for Appius's henchman Claudius (VI.C., 263–273). These details show that no drastic imbalance of power exists between the two men at the outset. Why, then, must Virginia—and not her would-be rapist—suffer at her father's hands?

The key to the conundrum embedded in the tale lies in R. Howard Bloch's discussion of virginity in *Medieval Misogyny and the Invention of Western Romantic Love*. Discussing the concept of virginity in the Old French lay, Bloch explains how fragile a conceptual structure virginity was:

It is sufficient for the question to enter consciousness as a thought, even an insinuation, in order for virginity to be impugned. The virgin is above suspicion; the virgin is one who is not thought not to be one in the mind of another. . . . This is another way of saying that there is no way of thinking the question of virginity that does not imply its loss. Or, to make a less radical claim, there is no way of speaking about virginity that does not sully it.[36]

In Bloch's terms, once the idea of the dishonorable loss of Virginia's virginity has been formulated in the mind of Appius and from thence passed along to the mind of her father, that virginity is already impugned. "Virginia is deflowered from the moment she steps into the street"; she is "dead, at least as a virgin, the minute she falls under Appius' gaze."[37] Bloch traces this idea to Tertullian, who says that "every public exposure of an honourable virgin is [to her] a suffering of rape."[38] But Virginia was seen by Appius while she was on her way to church, properly chaperoned; apparently no action, however innocent, is safe for her. Worse, one sin (public exposure) can be avoided only by means of another (neglect of religious duties). Following this convoluted reasoning, then, Virginia, though an intact virgin, must suffer still more in punishment for having already suffered rape merely because Appius "his eyen caste" upon her and plans rape.[39] Despite being a perfect practitioner of all the maidenly virtues, beloved, protected, and chaperoned, Virginia is sullied simply being thought of as vulnerable to being sullied.

The Physician narrator cautions those in charge of marriageable young noblewomen—their governesses, fathers, and mothers—to exercise extreme caution in their upbringing; but the tale meant to illustrate the need for protection of virgins undercuts his advice by showing that no precautions, however stringent, can really protect against loss of what Bloch calls "chastity as Idea."[40] If virginity as a concept is not identical with virginity as a physical fact, if it is even more frail as an idea than as a condition of the frail female body, then virginity is impossible to preserve. If even Virginia is somehow unchaste, who is chaste? The illogicality, the moral confusion of the tale is a consequence of the extreme anxiety aroused by the liminal state of premarital virginity, a state in which things can go terribly wrong. But Virginia has done no wrong. The men in the tale have: Appius by lusting rather than seeking lawful marriage; Virginius by failing in his paternal responsibility to protect his daughter from lust until such time as he conveys her in lawful marriage.

If, on the other hand, the transition process is successful, the perfect maid will become the perfect wife. Such a woman has no real plot, no story; she exists in literature as an image of perfection. In Chaucer's *Book of the Duchess*, the Man in Black confides in the Dreamer the story of his meeting and falling in love with his lady. The traits of body and spirit that attracted the Man in Black are those that Chaucer's age found desirable in a woman. Lady White stands out from the "fayrest companye / Of ladyes" (807–808) ever seen. She is in every way superlative. She exemplifies her age's definition of beauty: gold hair, well-proportioned body, pleasant natural complexion ("whit, rody, fressh, and lyvely hewed" [905]). The Man in Black's perception of his future wife's body is sufficiently detailed to be realistic rather than romantic:

> Ryght faire shuldres and body long
> She had, and armes, every lyth
> Fattyssh, flesshy, not gret therwith;
> Ryght white handes, and nayles rede;
> Rounde brestes; and of good brede
> Hyr hippes were; a streight flat bak.
> I knew on her noon other lak
> That al hir lymmes nere pure sewynge
> In as fer as I had knowynge.
> (952–960)

Her temperament was as pleasant as was her body. She is "glade" and "sadde" in measure and at appropriate times (860), natural and unaffected, affectionate without flirtatiousness. Her speech is soft and friendly in manner, reasonable and truthful in matter. She never flatters or backbites or chides; she is free of typical female faults. Her "trouthe" is like a man's (935–936). She is the very repository of virtue. "Chef ensample" of all nature's work (911), "chef myrour" of womanly virtue (974), as true as Penelope and Lucrece, she equals the good women of the old books.

Such a virgin promises fair to be a perfect wife, and so she is. Such perfection is irreplaceable. But Penelope and Lucrece have few other rivals. Like most ideals, that of the good wife often falls short of attainment, but not for any lack of instruction directed toward medieval wives. Suspended in the liminal state, the virgin can only be characterized by what she does not do; but a wife is characterized, positively or negatively, by activity. Many writers were, as Derek Brewer says of Chaucer, "more interested, imaginatively speaking, in being married than in getting married,"[41] and understandably so, as the married woman as character in medieval literature is active. Because her activity affects men, the married woman's behavior receives detailed attention in didactic sources and in the literature influenced by them. Normative behavior for the good wife forms a common stock of assumptions linking the medieval writer and his audience. Whether he creates a character who embodies the ideal of the perfect wife, as does Chaucer in the "Clerk's Tale," or when, more often, he depicts deviant behavior, the medieval artist draws on received ideas about the behavior of the married woman.

In the Old Testament, discussion of wives and marriage is often practical. Regulations on the giving and taking of women in marriage and procedures for dissolution of marriage in the case of a wife's adultery are set forth. The activities of wives are described in considerable detail. In addition, the marriage covenant stands as an image of an ideal relationship between God and man, adultery as the breaking of that covenant, as in the book of Hosea. On both practical and theoretical levels, marriage is generally held in high regard in the Old Testament. Having a good wife is an advantage to a man. The *locus classicus* of descriptions of the good wife is Proverbs 31.[42] She is useful, competent, busy, her efforts crucial to the domestic economy. She is a worker, a manager. She makes the household's purchase decisions, whether the item bought is "wool and flax," the materials of women's trade, or a major real estate investment, a field for a vineyard. Multitalented, she can spin the wool and plant the vineyard too. She is energetic; she rises early, goes to bed late, "does not eat the bread of idleness." Because she bargains effectively, her household is well supplied with clothing and food. By her accomplishments, her husband's reputation is enhanced before his peers. Her family vastly and explicitly appreciates her efforts: "Her children rise up and call her blessed; / Her husband also, and he praises her: / 'Many women have done excellently, but you surpass them all' " (Prov. 31:28–29). The good wife in the Old Testament, then, is a highly valued person. So important is marriage that a newly married man is excused from public duty for a long honeymoon: "He shall be free at home one year, to be happy with his wife whom he has taken" (Deut. 24:5).

Jesus does not diverge from His Hebraic forebears on the dignity of marriage: "A man shall leave his father and mother and be joined to his wife. . . . The two shall become one" (Mk. 10:7). Jesus regarded marriage as a permanent commitment, to women's advantage, as opposed to concubinage, a situation that allowed termination of the relationship at a man's will. Yet, while a high Christian value, marriage is not the highest. Following Christ may require a man to leave wife and children (e.g., in Luke 14:26), as spiritual allegiances take priority over familial.[43] What shall happen to the wife and children thus abandoned, Christ does not say; nor does He offer the same degree of freedom from family ties to His female followers. So Christ's main thoughts on marriage both continue the Hebraic tradition of respect for the married state and postulate a still higher state, celibacy.

Paul has much more to say on marriage than does Jesus and is more explicit as to correct behavior for both sexes in the married state. Paul's behavioral directives must be understood in two contexts: the analogy between the married couple and Christ and His Church, and the hierarchical view of the marital relationship traceable to Genesis 3:16. Because hierarchical thought assumes ruler and ruled, Paul says, as did God to Eve, that wives should be "subject to [their] husbands, as to the Lord" (Eph. 5:21 ff.), that they should "love their husbands and children [and] . . . be sensible, chaste, domestic, kind, and submissive to their husbands" (Titus 2:4). Following his culture's message, Paul reinforces women's subordinate status by regulating women's dress but not men's (1 Peter 3:3–6; 1 Tim. 2:9–10). He prohibits women from teaching and preaching. He encourages passive female suffering by assuming that evil husbands who "do not obey the word" will nevertheless be "won without a word by the behavior of their wives when they see [their] reverent and chaste behavior" (1 Peter 3:1–2). But it is unfair to find only misogyny in Paul. Because of his belief in marriage as metaphor of God's relationship to man, he orders husbands to love their wives as they love their own bodies, and yet more, "as Christ loves the Church" (Eph. 5:28, 25). That is, he demands of husbands commitment to the highest possible ideal of devotion. Paul's thought, then, is not as unbalanced as it seems if only his words to wives are taken into account. A husband who loved with the intensity that Paul requires would surely be worthy of the respect of his wife, even her obedience, since such a man would be Christlike.

Marriage customs of the Middle Ages embody this scriptural tradition as well as the prevailing belief in the absolute necessity of hierarchical order. In the nuptial blessing, conferred on the woman but not on the man, it is prayed that the woman meet many behavioral norms, that she be "faithful," "chaste," "amiable," "bashful," "grave," "reverential," "modest," "well-instructed in heavenly doctrine," "fruitful in child-bearing," "innocent," and "of good report."[44] Some influential medieval sources balance the demanding role of the good wife with comparably high ideals for the husband. In *De Proprietatibus Rerum*, Bartholomaeus Anglicus reminds a husband of his responsibility not merely to "rule" but to protect his wife. A husband's protection betokens not only his love and commitment, but his acceptance of the proper relationship of strong to weak. Because marriage confers upon a woman a respected position, a man must court an intended wife properly and publicly.

The public courtship culminates in a public marriage conferring upon a wife legal rights over her husband's property; this distinguishes the relationship from casual concubinage, in which the man incurs few or no responsibilities, can put away a woman and her children at will, and does not raise her to the status of wife. Bartholomaeus sees the husband's protection as a sign of the dignity of wifehood: "He is no less careful for her than he is for himself: in his love he corrects her, he appoints a guard for her safety, he watches over her conduct, her speaking and looking, and he carefully considers her comings and goings."[45] The underlying assumption is, of course, that wives need supervision; but at the same time, that which is valued is protected, and so such care is a measure of respect.

In return for protection, a wife's duty is to aspire to perfection within her role. Behind all the criticism of married women in medieval didactic sources lies the ideal of wifehood, and it is the tension between ideal and reality that gives the misogynistic material its resonance. The counterpoint between the Merchant's own cynical attitude toward a wife who is "the worste that may be" (IV.E., 1218) and the ideals expressed in the passage often referred to as the "encomium on marriage"[46] at the beginning of the "Merchant Tale" plays on this tension between ideal and reality. Ideally, a wife is God's gift, man's helpmate, his "paradys terrestre, and his disport" (IV.E., 1332). Marriage is an "ordre," an organizing principle of society, a Christian sacrament, and a good economic arrangement as well: "If he be povre, she helpeth hym to swynke; / She kepeth his good, and wasteth never a deel" (IV.E., 1342–1343). A good wife is obedient and conciliatory in speech: "She seith nat ones 'nay,' whan he seith 'ye.' / 'Do this,' seith he; 'Al redy, sire,' seith she" (IV.E., 1345–1346). Like the wife in Proverbs, a good wife is wise, giving "good conseil" (IV.E., 1369), so a husband can in confidence "do alwey so as wommen wol thee rede" (IV.E., 1361). Reciprocity of respect characterizes the ideal marriage: "Suffre thy wyves tonge, as Catoun bit; / She shal comande, and thou shalt suffren it, / And yet she wole obeye of curteisye" (IV.E., 1377–1379). The speaker's peroration echoes the highest Pauline ideal: "Love wel thy wyf, as Crist loved his chirche. / If thou lovest thyself, thou lovest thy wyf" (IV.E., 1384–1385). But in marriage as in much of life, reality often comes up short. Justinus says that a wife, instead of being "wys, or sobre," might be "dronkelewe"; instead of humble, proud; instead of meek and milk of speech, a "shrewe, / A chidestere"; instead of a frugal householder, a "wastour of thy good" (IV.E., 1532–1535). Justinus justly points out that many men—himself, for example—have failed to find the ideal wife. The failure of reality to approximate the ideal is perceived as the fault of women.

All women's faults were perceived by the medieval audience simultaneously as violations of the prime duties of their estate role and as threats to chastity. The interrelationship between common character flaws and sexual profligacy appears precarious to moderns, but was quite clear to the medievals. A woman who sins in any way was *ipso facto* in danger of committing sins against chastity. In 1616, one Thomas Tuke wrote a treatise formidably entitled *A Discourse against Painting and Tincturing of Women. Wherein the abominable sinnes of Murther and Poysoning, Pride and Ambition, Adultery and Witchcraft, are set foorth & discovered.*[47] Tuke's wild leap from using cosmetics to committing adultery and murder illustrates an attitude long in place regarding women: any sin leads to *the* sin, and thence to *all* sin. No feminine foibles are harmless; to be good at all, a woman has to be perfect. Perfection is, however, unlikely. Women are likely to prove troublesome, and that in three major areas: excesses of speech, instability of place, and immoderation of dress. The ideal submissiveness of the perfect daughter often lapses when, her transition accomplished, she becomes a wife. Chaucer's Physician knew that, had Virginia survived, her docile speech habits would end: she would "lerne loore / Of booldnesse, whan she woxen is a wyf" (VI.C., 70–71). Better to die a meek maid than live a bold wife.

❦ 5 ❧

"Silent tongue and still": Women's Speech and Domestic Harmony

"Tell me, broom wizard, tell me,
Teach me what to do,
To make my husband love me:
Tell me, broom wizard, do!"

"Silent tongue and still
Shall bring you all your will."

—Thirteenth-century sermon[1]

Wives, be subject to your husbands as to the Lord. For the husband is the head of the wife as Christ is the head of the church. . . . As the church is subject to Christ, so let wives be subject to their husbands in everything.

—Ephesians 5:21–24

Dear sister, this story was translated by master Francis Petrarch, crowned poet at Rome . . . to show that since God and the church and reason will that they be obedient and since their husbands will that they have much to suffer, and since to escape worse things it behoves them of need to submit them in all things to the will of their husbands and to suffer patiently all that those husbands will . . . by how much the greater reason behoveth it for men and women to suffer patiently the tribulations which God, who is immortal, eternal and everlasting, sendeth unto them.

—Goodman of Paris[2]

If you want your wife to obey you, love her as Christ loved the church; then she will obey you, as the church obeys Christ.

—St. John Chrysostom[3]

In the fourteenth century, two medieval towns attempted to legislate female silence. In one, it was "ordain[ed] by common consent that all the women of the township control their tongues." In another, it was "enjoined upon all the women in the township that they should restrain their tongues and not scold nor curse any man."[4] The success of this legislation is not recorded; but its existence is one of many pieces of evidence that medieval men considered women's speech habits deplorable. Women were thought to need speech correction in timing, mode and content: when to talk, how to talk, what to say. The medieval audience's perception of a character is therefore shaped by her adherence to (or more likely divergence from) the various *dicta* on women's speech. How she speaks, when she speaks, what she says—even her silence—all serve to characterize women in literature. Moreover, a woman's speech habits were seen as a prime factor in fostering domestic harmony or disharmony. As might be expected, the model of correct feminine speech is Chaucer's Grisilde in the "Clerk's Tale."

In scripture, women's speech habits are a litmus test of virtue, especially since sin itself entered the world through a talking woman. As R. Howard Bloch points out, in the Yahwist account in Genesis, the creation of Eve is "linked to a founding linguistic act": the naming of Eve by Adam. But Eve disrupts this proper hierarchy and "through speech sowed discord between man and God." Hence the connection between women and "verbal allurements," the "deception of which language is capable," the "annoyance of speech implicit to everyday life."[5] Negative associations between women and speech like those in the Genesis account of the Fall are a commonplace throughout scripture. In Proverbs, certain speech styles are decisive indicators of unchastity: "The lips of a loose woman drip honey, and her speech is smoother than oil" (5:8–9); the harlot is "loud" (7:11) and "noisy" (9:13); she "persuades" with "seductive speech" and "compels" with "smooth talk" (7:21). Excessive speech is likewise linked to equally untrammeled sexuality. If a wife uses her speech abilities not for seductive purposes but to defy her husband, she is an almost equal horror: "It is better to live on a corner of the housetop than in a house shared with a contentious woman. . . . It is better to live in a desert land than with a contentious and fretful woman" (Prov. 21:9, 19). This scriptural image of the contentious woman evolves into the shrew or scold, a stock character in medieval literature, especially the drama.

From St. Paul comes the dictum that women should keep silent in the churches, by which he meant that they were not allowed to function as preachers or even ask questions there; they should "be subordinate," and, "if there is anything they desire to know, let them ask their husbands at home." Paul sees silence as a sign of proper subjection, since Eve's sin precludes her daughters' teaching or otherwise having authority over men (1 Cor. 14:34–35; 1 Tim. 2:11–14). The good Christian woman is defined in early Christian sources as "meek, quiet, gentle, sincere, free from anger, not talkative, not clamorous, not hasty of speech, not given to evil-speaking, not captious, not double-tongued, not a busybody. . . . When she is asked anything by anyone let her not easily answer, excepting questions concerning the faith . . . remitting those that desire to be instructed in the doctrines of godliness to the governors."[6] In other words, her speech habits show proper acceptance of authority. Because the serious use of speech in teaching and preaching is off limits to women, they are then circularly defined as trivial in their speech, and so unworthy of wielding the authority forbidden to them.

In addition to teaching and preaching, another important medieval speech act is also out of bounds to women: oath-taking. The oath is an important ritual confirming a bond between men.[7] Vows of fealty are, of course, impossible between men and women, as such promises are based on the feudal duty of military service from which women are excluded. Because important words are men's words, the words of women are seldom considered worth recording verbatim in historical documents. As Georges Duby says of medieval historical records, "only males count," and not many of them. "The only women who take the stage even briefly are those related—and very closely—to the hero: mother, sisters, wife, daughters," and "they do not speak there; nothing of what they might have said, in any case, seemed worthy of being reported; all the dialogues are among men."[8]

The only spoken words between men and women that really count are the marriage vows, which subject the wife to the will of the husband thereafter. Having spoken these words, a woman, in theory at least, need speak no more. When a woman should speak is, then, a key issue, worthy of the attention of august theologians, but one with a simple answer: as little as possible. Criticism of women as talkative and quarrelsome is a commonplace of sermon anecdotes.[9] As a didactic poem of the late thirteenth or early fourteenth century puts it, woman's speech makes her "a barrel full of chatter / Uncorkable, her gossip makes a clatter."[10] Had Eve kept silent, sin and death would not have entered the world.

Offsetting Eve's bad example in the matter of speech is, of course, Christ's mother, Mary, who, being perfect, is supremely quiet. As a medieval homilist says: "Oure lady seyn Mary . . . was of so litel speche that nowhere in the gospel we fynden of hir speche but iiii tymes, and tho were wordes of gret discrecion and grete myghte."[11] This bit of apocrypha, attributed to St. Bernard, is often repeated in medieval sources, and Mary's taciturnity, sign of her "grett mekenes and lowlynes,"[12] is presented as a model for her daughters to emulate. Following Mary, a young "mayden" should be "of lytyll wordys," instead of being "a claterer, a ianguler, a flyter, a curser, a swerer, and a skold of hur mowþhe"; she must not violate the "old Englysch sawe: 'A mayde schuld be seen, but not herd.' "[13] The trivializing terms describing women's speech indicate the popular belief that it is impossible that she be saying anything of importance; her speech is the sinful symptom of an idle brain. It is noteworthy, too, that Mary's speech habits are seen as a consequence of her "vow of chastyte."[14] Many words mean loose morals. But control of speech will always be difficult for women, because Eve was made from a rib, and "bones are always rattling."[15]

Even having limited her speech to the barest minimum, a woman's task is not done. How she speaks is important too. Manuals advise on vocal quality: well-modulated, neither harsh nor shrill.[16] The Knight of the Tower advises his daughters to "speke . . . fayre and swetly."[17] A woman's voice should communicate seriousness and sobriety, not giddiness; she should refrain from loud or immoderate laughter, particularly if it shows the teeth (this repeated caution is probably as much a reflection of the dismal state of medieval dentistry as of feminine virtue). In other words, a woman must speak in such a way as to generate only pleasant sounds and thus avoid giving offense.

One exception to the rule of placating speech as sign of the virtuous woman is the bold speech of female virgin martyrs. Their typical story is a "drama that pits a defenseless heroine against a powerful male protagonist."[18] In such a situation the usual acceptable feminine speech pattern would amount to a pusillanimous conciliation of a persecutor of Christians. In a French hagiographical romance of the thirteenth century, St. Catherine of Alexandria is described as a woman of "mind . . . so enlightened" and "intelligence so keen" that "no cleric . . . would dare speak in front of her."[19] When she is brought before the evil emperor, she "stands up boldly" and "addresses the tyrant," engaging him in debate at great length and in a "clear and loud voice."[20] Her argumentative stance is justified only because she does not use these abilities to assert her own authority but rather to defend the faith against unjust authority. Chaucer's virgin martyr, St. Cecile in the "Second Nun's Tale," is castigated for "answeryng so rude" to accusations of the pagan judge who orders her to recant or die (VIII.G., 432). Undaunted, she taunts him, mocking his power as a "bladdre ful of wynd" and laughing at his threats (VIII.G., 439, 462). After the usual series of tortures, when she lies "half deed, with hir nekke ycorven," she continues to "preche" to the onlookers (VIII.G., 533, 539). The bold speech of saints like Catherine and Cecile, even probably the intelligence shown forth in their words, is a suspension of the natural order that bespeaks divine assistance. These saints' speech patterns are virtuous because they proclaim God's word, not their own, and because they are willing to die in consequence of the anger they arouse for having spoken.

Saintly women preaching with their last breath contrast with those other women famed in misogynistic lore who use deceptive speech to manipulate men. As Jean de Meun puts it in The Romance of the Rose, women are so clever that they can cause a man to doubt the evidence of his own senses:

Nay, though his very eyes had seen her sin,
She might convince him that his sight was bad.
She knows how to employ a double tongue,
Twisting this way and that to find excuse;
For there is no creature can more hardily
Than woman commit perjury and lie.[21]

Chaucer uses this motif to comic effect in the "Merchant's Tale," when May convinces Januarie that he has not indeed seen her in sexual congress with Damyan in the tree. So clever is May—or so gullible Januarie—that he believes her.

Let us assume that, contrary to what misogynistic writers believed was the habit of her sex, a given female character is speaking truth. Having duly modulated her vocal tones, what should she say? The content of her discourse should be governed by three further rules: respond to the moods of others; use an indirect rather than a direct approach; and express no anger. Each directive is designed to make the woman acceptable, nonconfrontational, and inoffensive. On responding to the moods of others, Garin lo Brun, a conduct book writer (1155–1215), uses a telling image: he describes the ideal woman as *"un diapason,"* a tuning fork.[22] This means that she has no vibrations in and of herself, but rather vibrates to the tune of others. An early fourteenth-century conduct book writer, Matfre Ermengau, says that with the joyous she must be joyous, with the serious, serious.[23] This notion, which is repeated in other works, implies that women should mirror the thoughts and feelings of others back to them. If any woman should perchance have thoughts and feelings of her own, she must learn to communicate them in subtle fashion, if at all.

One particular challenge in this respect is posed by the contradictory belief that women are morally superior to men, in charge of domestic morality, and therefore, in Diane Bornstein's words, "a wife should compensate for her husband's faults."[24] If their husbands are not men of virtue, it was believed to be the wife's responsibility to restore the balance of virtue within the spiritual economy of the family. A bad man needs a good wife, and, ironically, such a wife has a perfect opportunity further to increase her goodness by enduring his evil. But this involves suppression of any anger she may feel at her husband. This common belief explains why, for example, Grisilde becomes even more patient as the severity of her trials increases.

The wife who does not endure in silence but responds in anger is characterized as a shrew or scold. Her scolding is never seen as a justifiable reaction to real grievances; rather, she is a disturber of domestic peace. As the Goodman of Paris says, "there be three things which drive the goodman from home: to wit a leaking roof, a smoky chimney, and a scolding woman."[25] The Knight of the Tower agrees, advising his daughters to "be-gynne no strif" with a husband, "ne answere hym so that he take therby displaysyre," since it is "shame and vylonye to stryve ageynst [one's] hus-bond be it wrong or right."[26] So a wife must never respond to a husband's behavior with anger, whatever the provocation. Rather, "the good woman ought to pease the yre of her husbond whanne she seeth hym wrothe."[27] As the mother advises in "The Good Wife Taught Her Daughter," a wife should answer her husband "mekely," not shrewishly; thus she will "slake his mod and be his derlynge."[28]

Answer him meekly, slake his mood, allay his anger: what a wife says must be governed by these principles. She must speak little, and that little quietly and harmoniously; she must utter only pleasant and placating truths attuned to the needs of others. Her role in the household must be that of a peacemaker, applying unto herself Christ's teachings in the Sermon on the Mount as if Christ meant his words for women alone. If her husband does not obey Christ in this injunction, she is all the more responsible for correcting him by the force of her example. Thus she will achieve "the rewards of feminine submission,"[29] if not in this life, then in the next. Every wife must emulate the patience of Grisilde, whose story makes its appearance whenever wifely obedience is discussed.

Grisilde's story served in Chaucer's day as a convenient *exemplum* of wifely virtue. But in our own day, as Anne Middleton says, the "Clerk's Tale" "insists on its 'otherness' from all our habits of reading, our customs of approval, and our wishes for comfort."[30] Many critics have sought to interpret this "tale of passion, where passion means suffering,"[31] in some fashion more congenial to modern thinking on, among other things, ac-ceptable behavior between husbands and wives. Bridging the "chasm" that divides medieval and modern in regard to this tale, as Middleton further explains, requires a "dual course of instruction: to wean us away from that something which is ours, and to supply it with something 'medieval,' something we did not know or are unable to apply, to take its place."[32] Abstracting from, but not in any way minimizing, the many other com-plexities of the tale, this discussion will attempt to bridge the gap between medieval and modern by focusing on one aspect of it: Grisilde's speech behavior as manifestation of medieval norms of wifely virtue.

Grisilde's speech habits are part of a complex of her ideal qualities. Like Christ, Grisilde lives among "povre folk" (IV.E., 200). Like Mary at the Annunciation, she awaits her lord's will.[33] Like most female saints, she is pious and passive.[34] Because she has been "povreliche yfostred up" (IV.E., 213), raised in poverty, she has the humility considered desirable in a wife. She is, of course, chaste ("no likerous lust" runs through her heart [IV.E., 214]), sober (she drinks more water than wine), hardworking (she is un-willing to be idle "til she slepte" [IV.E., 224]), and loyal to her father (she sustains his life "with everich obeisaunce and diligence" [IV.E., 230]). She employs herself as befits a Christian woman: tending sheep and spinning their wool. She shows her aptitude for suffering (an aptitude she will have further opportunity to cultivate in her marriage) by sleeping on a hard bed. All of these traits indicate that she will be able to manage the virtue-vice seesaw recommended by the behavior manuals. As Walter grows more evil, she will grow better. Grisilde's progress in wifely virtue is reflected in the spouses' vocal interactions.

Walter and Grisilde's relationship is based on the dominance of lord over subject, as is apparent in the description of their first meeting:

> And she set doun hir water pot anon,
> Biside the thresshfold, in an oxes stalle,
> And doun upon hir knes she gan to falle,
> And with sad contenance kneleth stille,
> Til she had herd what was the lordes wille.
>
> (IV.E., 290–294)

She kneels "stille," that is, quietly, without talking, leaving matters to be arranged between her superiors, lord and father. Janicula's subservience to Walter is appropriate in a retainer but bodes ill for the happiness of the marriage. Grisilde's victimization by Walter is facilitated by the absence of a strong father whose anger would be aroused by mistreatment of a daughter and the consequent insult to her family of origin. Walter could not treat Grisilde as he does if she were the daughter of a peer.[35] The custom of forming kinship ties with equals or superiors through marriage formed a system of protection for women. For fear of male relatives, if for no other reason, a woman must be reasonably well treated. When Janicula surrenders his will to Walter—"my willynge / Is as ye wole" (IV.E., 319–320)—he is essentially leaving his equally will-less daughter at the mercy of Walter, who has will enough for all three of them. When Grisilde exercises her will to make the one choice available to her, to be Walter's wife and rule herself after *his* will, abandoning her own (IV.E., 326–327), all future choices are erased.

The paired speeches representing the verbal interchange between Walter and Grisilde demonstrate her commitment to this concept of marriage which, it must be remembered, is to medieval thought not an aberration but an ideal. Walter has the first speech and consistently initiates dialogue. He is master, so the tongue-tied Grisilde, awed at having "so greet a gest" (IV.E. 338), awaits his words. What Walter seeks is a wife who adheres to the highest ideals of behavior as propounded in the courtesy books (IV.E., 351–357). He demands, as the authorities told him he had a right to do, conformity to his will in speech and speech-related behavior. She must not say "no" when he says "yes" (thus is a good wife described at IV.E., 1345), nor must she show disapproval by facial expression, "by word ne frownyng contenance" (IV.E., 356). All forms of self-expression are governed by the same rules that limit speech. She must also conform in thought so that she can do his bidding "with good herte" and never "grucche it" (IV.E., 351, 354). Since this is no more than was generally expected of medieval wives,[36] Grisilde is not surprised, but agrees immediately.

> She seyde, "Lord, undigne and unworthy
> Am I to thilke honour that ye me beede,
> But as ye wole youreself, right so wol I.
> And heere I swere that nevere willyngly,
> In werk ne thoght, I nyl yow disobeye,
> For to be deed, though me were looth to deye."
>   (IV.E., 359–364)

As you will yourself, right so will I. Chaucer plays with this term, "will," echoing the language of the marriage ceremony. All women, not just Grisilde, were expected to commit themselves to this condition of personal will-lessness. It is no accident, though, that Grisilde echoes her father's words to Walter (IV.E., 319–320); in medieval life, subordination was not unique to women.

Once raised in station, moving from her father's house to her husband's, Grisilde shows ability not only in domestic matters ("wyfly hoomlinesse" [IV.E., 429]), but in diplomatic relations as well. Considering her poor upbringing, Grisilde shows preternatural ability at all the speech skills required of a marquis' wife. In diplomacy, she is very successful, "discreet and fair of eloquence" (IV.E., 410), extending into the public arena the duty recommended by the Knight of the Tower to his daughters, that is, to appease a husband's wrath. For this she is loved by the populace and effective as Walter's representative, playing the mediatrix role in imitation of the Blessed Virgin Mary.

> The commune profit koude she redresse.
> Ther nas discord, rancour, ne hevynesse
> In al that land that she ne koude apese,
> And wisely brynge hem alle in reste and ese.
>
> Though that hire housbonde absent were anon,
> If gentil men or othere of hire contree
> Were wrothe, she wolde bryngen hem aton;
> So wise and rype wordes hadde she,
> And juggementz of so greet equitee,
> That she from hevene sent was, as men wende,
> Peple to save and every wrong t'amende.
>   (IV.E., 428–441)

Grisilde, then, possesses the speech skills required in her public role. In her private role, the verbal interchanges between husband and wife follow a predictable pattern. Walter's speeches are always much longer than Grisilde's replies, assertive, accusatory, and dominating; Grisilde's are short and submissive, calming, placating, and restorative of harmony. In a study of speech patterns of men and women, sociolinguist Deborah Tannen sees certain vocal traits as characteristic of persons who perceive the world as organized in a "hierarchical social order," which, Tannen says, many men do. For such men, power is the ability to "give orders and get others to follow them," and particular modes of speech are adopted as a way to "achieve and maintain the upper hand."[37] If Tannen is right, Walter's speech behavior is characteristically male and Grisilde's characteristically female. Grisilde never initiates speech, but replies when addressed:

> Whan she had herd al this, she noght ameved
> Neither in word, or chiere, or contenaunce,
> For, as it semed, she was nat agreved.
> She seyde, "Lord, al lyth in youre plesaunce.
> My child and I, with hertely obeisaunce,
> Been youres al, and ye mowe save or spille
> Youre owene thyng; werketh after youre wille.
> (IV.E., 498–504)

This is the perfect reply. No emotion, no negative reaction, no willfulness is expressed. Walter, free to use his wife as his "owene thyng," as he sees fit, has achieved the mastery that he wanted in marriage.

As Walter's behavior deteriorates, Grisilde demonstrates the increase in virtue described by the behavior manuals as appropriate to the woman abused by her husband. Like Augustine's mother, Monica, when she was mistreated by his father, Patricius, Grisilde controls her speech, so her relationship with Walter remains unchanged: "As glad, as humble, as bisy in servyse, / And eek in love, as she was wont to be, / Was she to hym in every maner wyse" (IV.E., 603–605). Nevertheless, like Augustine's father, Walter is culpable as a free moral agent. Insatiable in his desire to "assaye" his wife, Walter violates the classical and Christian principle of moderation. According to Chaucer's clerk, "wedded men" often "ne knowe no mesure, / Whan that they fynde a pacient creature" (IV.E., 622–623). Chaucer sees an ethical complication. Too much virtue in a wife makes some men immoderately vicious.

Even the perfect woman, then, is caught on the horns of a dilemma. As the Knight of the Tower wordily advises his daughters, a wife's job involves compensating for her husband's defects. Thus "it is good and necessary to an euyl man to haue a good wyf and of hooly lyf and the more that the good wyf knoweth her husbond more felon and cruel and grete synnar the more she ought to make gretter abstynences and good dedes for the loue of god."[38] But, on the other hand, such a paragon has the duty of moral counsel. An early thirteenth-century penitential, Thomas of Chobham's *Manual for Confessors,* summarizes the issue thus: "It should always be enjoined upon women to be preachers to their husbands, because no priest is able to soften the heart of a man the way his wife can. For this reason, the sin of a man is often imputed to his wife if, through her negligence, he is not corrected."[39] In two important articles on the subject, Sharon A. Farmer traces the theology developing in the centuries preceding Chaucer on a wife's duty of counsel. Farmer argues that despite a decline in the economic and social status of women, and despite clerical prohibitions against women taking an official role as preacher, theologians increasingly saw women as properly exerting moral influence in both sacred and secular spheres by means of persuasive speech. A concrete result is that "pious wives" could motivate rich husbands to donate to religious orders.[40] More abstractly, the virtuous speech of wives, their domestic preaching, could render their husbands more receptive to the authoritative word of the clerical homilist.[41]

Chaucer works within this tradition concerning women's speech in the "Tale of Melibee." Victim of an injustice, an attack upon his wife and daughter, Melibee overreacts, weeping "lyk a mad man" (VII.B^2., 2165), and vowing vengeance. He is supported in this stance by an all-male group of friends and counselors. Prudence, his wife, opposes the "crueel ire" of her husband (VII.B^2., 2200), a deadly sin, with her counterbalancing virtue of patience. But before she can soften the heart of her husband, she must argue against the "predictable objections of the medieval male to accepting counsel from his wife: that women are wicked creatures, that to accept Prudence's counsel would give the appearance that she had the 'maistrie' over him, that women cannot keep secrets."[42] This is a difficult process, which requires of Prudence long and detailed monologues studded with citations of sacred and secular authorities. Prudence finally achieves her goal, not by winning an argument *against* her husband (she is no Alisoun), but by winning an argument *for* him. When Melibee's "herte gan enclyne to the wyl of his wif" (VII.B^2., 3060), it is for the salvation of his soul. The will of his wife is not her own, but is the will of God for Melibee.

In this theological context which, as the "Tale of Melibee" shows, Chaucer knew well, Grisilde might err in having too much patience, being too silent in the face of injustice, an excess of virtue that could cause her to fail in the duty of the virtuous married woman to counsel her husband. It would be a rare woman indeed who could avoid entrapment in this double bind, and Grisilde does not. Grisilde is too deferential, so Walter is deprived of her counsel. This jeopardizes his immortal soul. If there is "but o wyl, for as Walter leste / The same lust was hire plesance also" (IV.E., 716–717), a problem arises if that "o wyl" is flawed. To leave her own will and liberty in her father's house is a mixed virtue in a wife, because it leaves her husband in spiritual danger. So deferential is Grisilde that one critic accuses her of "idolatry" in that she "completely surrenders her moral freedom and disobeys God's law to follow the whims of a fellow creature."[43]

Grisilde, then, is as excessive in her way as Walter is in his. When Walter, blaming the populace's dissatisfaction with the "blood of Janicle" (IV.E., 632), informs her that he has a papal dispensation from their marriage so that he can marry another more acceptable to his people, she allows him to place his immortal soul in jeopardy in an invalid marriage. Walter dismisses Grisilde as abruptly as if she were a concubine and no lawful wife. As James Brundage points out, this was not an unusual practice: "Noble families adamantly maintained that they must be free to shift alliances, including those sealed by marriage, in order to promote family interests."[44] While such dispensations were routinely granted to the great, the marriage is subjectively still morally binding. More significant, she accepts the disgraceful position of the rejected wife. With no recourse to any legal or ecclesiastical procedures, Grisilde has no choice but to obey Walter's order to "voyde anon" the "place" of wife, and make way for another (IV.E., 806).

But before she does so, Grisilde delivers herself of a longer and slightly more assertive speech. In it, she simultaneously attempts to placate Walter, thus moderating his extreme cruelty, and to reinforce the assumptions on which their life together was based. The basic and insuperable difficulty between them, the disparity of social status, only emphasizes the total abnegation required of the ideal wife. In marriage, man is magnificent, woman poor. She is unworthy to be his chambermaid, much less his wife. Her house is not her own, despite the fact that she is "lady" of it, because he "maade" her, elevated her to that estate, and therefore can unmake her, cast her down (IV.E., 820); his will *is* Fortune's wheel. Everything she has is at his discretion. Grisilde's speeches are beginning, just slightly, to take on the tone of complaint.

Nevertheless, when Walter requires Grisilde's services as wedding planner, she approaches him "with humble herte and glad visage, / Nat with no swollen thoght in hire corage" (IV.E., 949–950), falling on her knees to greet him "reverently and wisely" (IV.E., 952), resuming the subject role that comes so naturally to her. Even when she believes herself set aside as wife in favor of a younger and better-born replacement, when she has lost the raiment and jewels of a marquise, yet she retains her diplomatic speech habits and her willingness to use them in Walter's service. She knows how to facilitate social gatherings:

> With so glad chiere his gestes she receyveth,
> And so konnyngly, everich in his degree,
> That no defaute no man aperceyveth,
> But ay they wondren what she myghte bee

That in so povre array was for to see,
And koude swich honour and reverence,
And worthily they preisen hire prudence.
                    (IV.E., 1016–1022)

Either Grisilde's "povre array" has fooled those who knew her as a marquise or Walter has an entirely new set of "gestes"; Grisilde has apparently
faded into complete anonymity.

At this point in the story, the audience's disgust with Walter (and probably to some degree with Grisilde as well) is exacerbated by his asking
Grisilde's opinion of the "beautee" of his new wife (IV.E., 1031). Now,
Grisilde takes her one stab at expressing a personal opinion. Her disagree-
ment with Walter is, however, morally excusable even by the high standards of the behavior manuals in that she speaks for the well-being of
someone other than herself, the new bride. She asks Walter not to treat
this young, tenderly raised girl as she herself has been treated, because the
younger woman could "nat adversitee endure" as could Grisilde herself, a
"povre fostred creature" (IV.E., 1042–1043). An act of perfection, fulfilling the last task of wifely responsibility, this speech shows some acceptance of her mandated responsibility for Walter's morals. Such extreme
selflessness causes Walter to accept her as his "wyf," she having at last
proved herself worthy of the title by his lights.

An irony of the tale is that Walter's definition of a wife is not different
in kind, only in degree, from the image routinely presented to medieval
men. Obedient, even subservient; capable of self-sacrifice; moral exemplar,
guide, and advisor; competent in domestic and political peacemaking;
adaptable to changing circumstances; and incapable of expressing or even
experiencing negative emotions, especially anger or resentment at past mistreatment: these are routine requirements for wives in the didactic literature. Walter differs from other men in that he actually has such a wife and,
having her, is still not satisfied, is indeed "insatiable."[45]

But a further irony is that having a perfect wife makes Walter a worse
man, not a better. The conduct sources that repeat the story usually distance themselves from Walter's behavior.[46] Similarly, Chaucer's Clerk dis-
agrees with the model of marriage propounded in it. According to the
Clerk, Grisilde is not really a wife at all but an allegorical figure of the
soul triumphant over adversity, an *a fortiori* argument for the soul's subjection to God's will:

For sith a womman was so pacient
Unto a mortal man, wel moore us oghte
Receyven al in gree that God us sent;
For greet skile is he preeve that he wroghte.
                    (IV.E., 1149–1152)

But unlike Walter, God, who made man, knows man's limits and will not "preeve" him beyond these. In the behavior manuals, the presumption concerning the difficult husband is that he is difficult by nature, not that he has freely chosen to be difficult, to cultivate bad traits in order to increase his wife's virtue. Walter, as Chaucer rightly perceived, is culpably sinful and presumptuous in his decision to test the virtue of another human soul. Since humans, unlike God, can err, "mankind should respond to God the way Grisilde responded to Walter, but wives should not respond to husbands the way Grisilde responded to Walter."[47] Wives could safely be subject to their husbands as to the Lord, as Paul commands, if, as Chrysostom glosses, those husbands truly loved their wives as Christ loves the Church. Chrysostom continues to advise husbands thus: "The partner of your life, the mother of your children, the foundation of your very joy should never by enchained by fears and threats. . . . For what sort of union is it where the wife trembles before her husband?"[48] Since the unconditional love Paul and Chrysostom desire from man to wife might not be forthcoming, wives must be wary.

The "Envoy" argues that women *should not* emulate Grisilde. Addressing himself to the "noble wyves" in his audience (IV.E., 1183), Chaucer explains how women's words are an instrument of power.[49] To achieve power in marriage, he advises women to do the exact opposite of what Grisilde does and what the behavior manuals advise, that is, to disregard false definitions of virtue and speak their minds. "Lat noon humylitee youre tonge naille" (IV.E., 1184): the cruelty of the image of the nailed tongue shows how Chaucer feels about male control of women's speech. Instead, he advises women to imitate Echo, who always responds. There is a little problem with the Echo image here in that an echo by definition always agrees; but the rest of the "Envoy" makes clear that Chaucer does not mean this at all. He urges wives not to be disempowered, not to take the advice of those who would control the voice, that powerful instrument with which a woman can seize power, "taak on . . . the governaille" (IV.E., 1192). With that weapon wives may become "archewyves" (IV.E., 1195), powerful women, ready for battle, strong, submitting to no one. Even if the feminine body is not suitable for battle, if women "clappeth as a mille" (IV.E., 1200), keep their tongues moving, they will be strong.

The metaphor Chaucer uses to describe this strength is one of penetration:

> Ne dreed hem nat; doth hem no reverence,
> For though thyn housbonde armed be in maille,
> The arwes of thy crabbed eloquence
> Shal perce his brest and eek his aventaille.
> In jalousie I rede eek thou hym bynde,
> And thou shalt make hym couche as doth a quaille.
>
> (IV.E., 1201–1206)

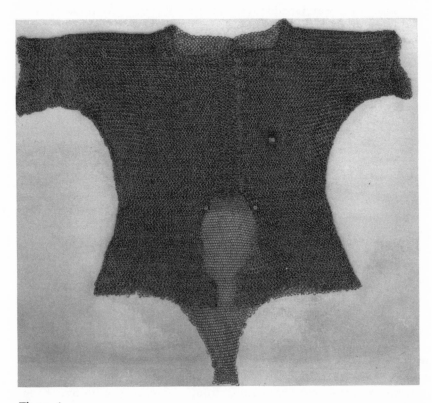

Figure 1
Chain-link armor (fifteenth century).

The image of a wife's sharp tongue piercing male armor is a telling one, inverting the image of rape. In literature, the voices of women are often described as shrill and sharp to the male ear. The armor image refers to chain-link armor, made of small interlocking metal circles (see Figure 1). Chaucer uses the metaphor of chain-link armor to show how something so small and fine as the feminine voice can serve as a weapon against a well-defended man. Though more penetrable than the heavy hinged armor customarily imagined as the universal garb of the medieval knight, chain-link armor was lighter and allowed more freedom of movement.[50] The male puts on his psychological armor to close off the voice. As the knight wearing a mail shirt such as this can be wounded with a very fine arrow, so a man's defenses can be breached by the woman's sharp shrill voice; the arrows of her crabbed eloquence can pierce it. With this weapon, which, though tiny, is penetrating indeed, she can get through to him and so achieve dominance over him.

The "Envoy" of the "Clerk's Tale" ties the character of Grisilde to that of the Wife of Bath as representatives of two dichotomous models of female behavior. On the subject of women's speech, Chaucer deviates sharply from received opinion. His imagery shows that he senses that women see men as being hard to reach. Men wear armor in defense against women, so the force implied in the arrow image is required. To "perce his brest," only distinctively feminine, sharp, shrill speech will do. In the "Envoy," Chaucer encourages in women what Patricia Meyer Spacks calls "the authority of talk."[51] What women must do, if they want to be "archewyves," amazons of wifeliness, is to make their opinions heard. They will, however, need to overcome the defenses thrown up against them in the form of two common stereotypes that would seek to trivialize their words. The stock figure of the gossip degrades women's same-sex loyalties; the figure of the shrew mocks their righteous anger. In creating his archwife, Chaucer draws upon the elements of misogynistic lore that use humor to deny the importance of women's words. He realized that a superficial domestic harmony bought at the price of female subjugation was not only unjust in principle but unworkable in practice. Men have a responsibility for correcting this; so do women. She who has allowed her tongue to be nailed has bought peace too dear. Were all husbands virtuous, wifely silence would indeed be golden. But as Jill Mann points out, "female shrewishness is the inevitable corrective to masculine selfishness. . . . The selfish husband creates the rebellious scold who is his daily punishment."[52] When a husband fails to love his wife as Christ loved the church, speech is a woman's best weapon.

✦ 6 ✦

The Gossip and the Shrew

As I'm a woman, I cannot keep still,
But will tell all, for women naught conceal.
　　　　　—Nature, in *The Romance of the Rose*[1]

　It is better to live on a corner of the housetop than in a house shared
with a contentious woman. . . . It is better to live in a desert land
than with a contentious and fretful woman.
　　　　　　　　　　　　　　　—Proverbs 21:9, 19

In soro and car he led hys lyfe
That haue a schrow ontyll his wyfe.　　　—An English carol[2]

Grisilde's story presents a woman whose self-expression is controlled to
the point that an independent self can hardly be said to exist at all. Such a
creature is a rarity. More common, according to medieval commentators,
are her contentious sisters, the gossips and shrews, whose speech habits
render them a threat to domestic harmony. A gossip is a woman whose
speech, though directed primarily toward other women, is considered anti-
male, because her relationships with women strengthen her in her relationship with her husband, thus undermining male authority. The shrew is a
woman who expresses anger directed against her husband. While the gossip
relationship is officially covert, the shrew openly challenges male authority. The two female types are separate by definition, but related: a gossip
is likely also to be a shrew, because her gossips encourage her to defy
husbandly authority. In both cases, the speech act is an act of domestic
rebellion.

　In Walter's house as in her father's house, Grisilde is unusual in her
isolation from other women. Apparently motherless, she lives alone with
Janicula. Married, she interacts only with Walter. In our twentieth-century

culture, the isolation of a woman, alone in her single-family house, had been the norm until the very recent past, and so the contemporary reader may miss the import of Grisilde's aloneness. A medieval woman of any significant social status would be surrounded by other women, family members, and attendants, as is Criseyde:

> Adowne the steyre anonright tho she wente
> Into the gardyn with hire neces thre,
> And up and down ther made many a wente—
> Flexippe, she, Tharbe, and Antigone—
> To pleyen that it joye was to see;
> And other of hire wommen, a gret route,
> Hire folowede in the gardyn al aboute.
>   (II., 813–819)

Criseyde has the companionship of her three nieces and a great number of her other women; elsewhere in the poem she is similarly attended. The number of attendants is at once an indicator of the dignity of the person attended, as well as testimony to medieval people's perception of solitude as undesirable, even unnatural.[3] Grisilde, then, stands out in her abnormal isolation, her deprivation of the retinue customary for a woman of her rank, a marquise, of their consoling presence, but more, of the conversation of a company of women—conversation that would have supported her in her estate as wife.

In the Middle Ages, two or more women friends having a confidential relationship were termed "gossips," or "gossybs," and the character of the gossip is a standard literary type. The *Oxford English Dictionary (OED)* defines gossip as a term describing the relationship between a godparent and godchild, between a godparent and the parent of the godchild, and, by extension, any woman who was "a familiar acquaintance, friend, chum." Such a woman would be invited to a lying-in, and from this group the newborn child's godmother would be chosen.[4] A gathering of women friends at a birthing or a christening would be characterized by casual conversation; hence the term's eventual connotation, which it retains today, of confidential yet trivial talk, mostly personal in content, and the speaker thereof as "a person, mostly a woman, of light and trifling character . . . who delights in idle talk." A homilist compares talking women in trivializing terms to jays and magpies, "iii claterers."[5] A gathering of gossips, a merry occasion, might be fueled by drink: a "gossip-cup" is a cup of good ale, and a "gossip-pint-pot" a hard drinker.

On a more serious note, the *OED* also defines "gossipred" or "gossipry" as terms denoting "spiritual affinity." The godparental relationship in medieval canon law was believed to create so close a spiritual tie that, contracted between members of the opposite sex, it precluded marriage. The relationship between the godmother and the birth mother was similarly close; they are "god-related."[6] The term gossip, then, before its trivialization, acknowledged that speech is the essence of the bond between women confidantes. Deborah Tannen, analyzing men's and women's different speech habits, points to talk as the *sine qua non* of friendships for women, in a way not true of men. Tannen says that for women, "the essence of friendship is talk,"[7] while men are satisfied with much less in the way of conversation with their friends. To women, men's taciturnity with their friends counts as peculiar behavior indeed. Conversely, the men who wrote the books in the Middle Ages regarded the speech habits of gossips as obnoxious, even sinful.

Not only do women talk too much, according to theologians and homilists, but the content of their speech is displeasing, too. In this the learned divines echo St. Paul's criticism of the young widows of Ephesus. These women seem to be having a fine time in the absence of husbandly jurisdiction, not only speaking at will but practicing the related vice of visiting for the purpose of speaking: "they learn to be idlers, gadding about from house to house, and not only idlers but gossips and busybodies, saying what they should not" (1 Tim. 5:13). Despite prohibitions in scripture and homiletics, women persisted in gossip and frequented the locations where gossip gatherings occurred. Gossip takes place, according to the didactic sources, wherever women meet without the supervision of men: church, the alehouse, and the home. Courtesy literature repeatedly enjoins women to keep silent in church, instead of taking advantage of the gathering to "rowne togedyr," exchange whispered observations with their friends.[8] The good wife tells her daughter to "be nought of many wordes" in general, but especially in church, where "iangelyng with fremed [or] sibbe" is especially inappropriate.[9] A special devil, Tutivullus, is assigned to write down the names of chatterboxes in church, *"ad missam garulantes."*[10] Though it provides the occasion of speech sins, churchgoing can hardly be prohibited entirely. But manual writers and homilists incessantly caution women against trips to taverns and against what St. Paul termed "gadding about from house to house." Unrepentant sinners that they were, medieval women continued to enjoy each other's company rather than isolating themselves in their separate domestic enclosures as moralists advised.

Gossip gatherings, wherever located, are regarded in medieval sources as hostile to men because during such gatherings married women habitually divulge intimate marital matters to their gossips.[11] This is an important theme in the didactic literature on gossip. The Goodman of Paris repeatedly cautions his young wife to "hide [her] husband's secrets."[12] He illustrates the point with an *exemplum* from Macrobius's *Dream of Scipio* of a mother who wheedles information out of her small son concerning the Roman senate's plan to allow male bigamy. This mother then "sped . . . to her gossips" and divulged all, leading to a female rebellion and the consequent failure of the senatorial scheme.[13] Obviously women's talk can upset the social order. In a long passage in that most influential medieval text, *The Romance of the Rose*, Genius cautions men never to tell their wives anything or perform any "secret act" before them, as they will "tell it to the world." If he reveals to her his participation in a crime, he may as well reconcile himself to being hanged. To wheedle secrets out of him, she will engage in seductive behavior, plead the sanctity of the marriage bond, and even allege that all her friends' husbands tell their secrets to their wives (an unmistakable clue to the information exchanged over a gossip-cup). If the deluded man confides in her, "she has now the upper hand" in the relationship, and he can never again defy her on any subject.[14] These *exempla* clearly illustrate men's fear that the gossip relationship is hostile to them, rendering private acts open to the glare of publicity and giving wives increased power over husbands.

The characterization of the gossip in literature draws on all these ideas, which were well known to the medieval audience. The gossip relationship stands as symbol of rebellion against male authority, endangering a woman's loyalty to her husband by substituting a stronger bond. The secretive nature of the relationship makes the husband fear betrayal. The whole situation is disorderly and unnatural. To mock the gossip relationship is to defuse its potential as a serious threat to the marriage; so the gossip is usually portrayed humorously, as in the "Noah" mystery play of the Chester cycle. As usual, however, Chaucer, with his understanding of woman's concerns, takes the relationship between the Wife of Bath and her gossip seriously, as one source of the Wife's independence of spirit.

In the mystery cycles, embellishments of the scriptural stories often show the reader what was on the mind of the dramatist and his audience. In the Noah plays, for instance, the domestic problems of Noah and his rebellious wife are a microcosmic image of the disorder in the universe caused by disregard for hierarchy. Noah's wife has no name; she is called Uxor (Latin, "wife"), probably to indicate her typicality: she is Everywife. In the Chester cycle "Noah," insubordinate Uxor refuses to board the ark. She lacks the unquestioning obedience necessary to all God's children, but especially His female ones. Uxor demonstrates stereotypically unpleasant speech-related traits: verbal expressions of insubordination ("I will not doe after thy red" [advice, l. 101]) and bad temper (she is "crabbed," "nevere . . . meke" [ll. 105–106], "froward" [l. 194], and "wraw," wrathful [l. 209]).[15] In other words, she is a stock scold. But her rebellious behavior in refusing to board the ark is motivated specifically by the fact that her gossips are not invited.

According to Uxor, who arrogates unto herself God's selection of the virtuous, the gossips must be saved from perdition. Though worldwide destruction threatens, these jolly drinking buddies declare their intention of imbibing "a pottell of malmesy good and strong" (l. 233) before they

drown. Even though her whole family, husband, sons, and (good, obedient) daughters-in-law are aboard, Uxor refuses, "But I have my gossopes
all" (l. 242). These women are clearly more important to her than family
or even life itself. Noah's behavior is based on the hierarchical and analogical thought processes characteristic of medieval theology. God speaks; man
listens and obeys. As in the macrocosm, so in the microcosm: husband
Noah passes God's command on to their mutual inferior, Uxor. But Uxor
does not accept the chain of command as Noah (and God) define it. Her
primary value is the preservation of her relationship to the gossips. Uxor's
thinking is relational and lateral; "higher" and "lower" have no meaning
in her company of women. To the dramatist, this is a serious violation of
domestic order in that the gossip relationship represents an alternate woman-
centered value system replacing duty to God and husband. Imagine, implies the dramatist, a new creation derived entirely from gossiping women;
what an absurd reversal of natural order that would be! It is impossible
that the gossips be allowed to survive among, or, worse, instead of, the
righteous Noah family. Finally Uxor is pried from her gossips and carted
aboard the ark by her sons; the gossips presumably meet a watery death
befitting their sinfulness. Their destruction is treated as trivial; Uxor's love
for her woman friends is just one of her silly ways, to be stamped out by
force so that the serious work of the world might proceed. Relational thought
(disorder, rebellion) is crushed; hierarchical thought (order) is restored.
Converted into a proper submissive wife, Uxor loses all individuality, and
Noah likes her better that way.

Unlike the "Noah" playwright, Chaucer takes the gossip relationship
more seriously. His disobedient wife, Alisoun of Bath, draws strength and
independence of mind from her community of women. Her close relationship with her late gossip, also named Alisoun, apparently outlasted the
Wife's five marriages and continues into the afterlife, as she prays for her
dead gossip's soul. She speaks of her gossips with fond nostalgia. When
husbands are away, gossips provide companionship. The Wife's visits to
the house of her gossip, going "fro hous to hous" in violation of domestic
enclosure, get her out of her own house, to see and be seen, to show off
"gay" attire (III.D., 545), "to heere sondry talys" (III.D., 547). Because
medieval women used their gossips' houses as gathering places, it is inevitable that Alisoun of Bath will meet the other Alisoun's boarder. With her
gossip's collusion, she is able to spend officially chaperoned but in fact
private time with Jankyn, during which she strikes the bargain to marry
him when she "were wydwe" (III.D., 568). With Alisoun, of course, she
shares her "privetee," her secrets and those of her husbands. The gossip
knows her friend's heart better than does her confessor, for it is to her that
she "biwreyed . . . [her] conseil al," whether trivial or life-threatening.
To her and "to another worthy wyf" and to her kinswoman (note the
widening circle of revelation), she tells her husband's "conseil," to such an

extent that he is embarrassed and castigates himself for violating the advice of the wise and foolishly trusting in his wife's discretion (III.D., 530–542).

With his instinctive understanding that speech is the bond between women, Chaucer describes concisely the special elements of the gossip relationship. The spiritual unity of close women friends is emphasized by their having identical names; they are as one person. The confessional nature of women's conversation means that a gossip knows a woman's secrets better than does her parish priest—confidentiality defines this relationship today as in the Middle Ages. Everyday details confided to the gossip (what men call trivia) describe every aspect of the marital relationship. Many a man then and now must feel "his face often reed and hoot / For verray shame" (III.D., 540–541) when he realizes how much of his life with his wife is bared to the gossip. Chaucer understands how universal is this relationship between women (and how unparalleled among men). He portrays the Wife of Bath as having ties to the world of women beyond the unique gossip relationship; he sees her as part of a group including "another worthy wyf," her "nece," a "norice," a "chamberere," and her "dame," her mother, who teaches her feminine "soutiltee" and "loore" (III.D., 536, 537, 299, 300, 576, 583). Chaucer seems to have understood that, despite prohibitions to the contrary, women would regard gossip as a psychological necessity, providing strength against the domestic authority of the husband. The "soutiltee" and "dames loore" passed along from woman to woman undercuts their submissiveness to their husbands, which was exactly why it was forbidden. Chaucer seems to know that this will always be true of women; he laughs at the feeble attempts of moralists to change women's very nature.

Medieval men deplored and medieval women adored gossip. So it is today. Twentieth-century analysts of women's speech-based relationships arrive at interpretations remarkably similar to those that apply to medieval literature. In her analysis of the significance of casual conversation in literature, Patricia Meyer Spacks calls gossip "a resource for the subordinated."[16] Its function in literature and in life is to support a community of women, which, in turn, strengthens individual women in relationships with men. Men do not understand the importance to women of same-sex relationships and therefore see the bond between women as not merely different from men's ways but hostile to men: "The women's intimacy depends on, or is reflected in, their discussion of their husbands. . . . They incite one another to insubordination. Their association violates traditional hierarchy."[17] To this day men disapprove of women forming such "social ties outside the institutions of male dominance," that is, marriage,[18] because such ties undermine that dominance.

Ray Oldenburg's *The Great Good Place*, on the significance of extra-domestic gathering places, defines the "third" place as an informal gathering place apart from home or work. In the twentieth century, it is mostly a male preserve. Men have always discouraged third-place associations for their wives while insisting on them for themselves. For medieval women, churches, taverns, and gossips' houses provided an alternative to the male-dominated family.[19] Gatherings of women in such places have always been perceived as potentially troublesome for men because, according to Deborah Tannen, men and women understand personalized speech differently. To men, women's "talking about a personal relationship to others is an act of disloyalty,"[20] a betrayal. To women, telling secrets is not so much directed against men as it is a means of bonding between women; it is "not only . . . evidence of friendship; it *creates* a friendship."[21] To women, being a friend means sharing secrets.

Men sense that women gain strength from the community of gossips and fear that the gossip relationship might supersede the marriage bond as the focus of a woman's primary loyalty. Women's persistent attachment to her gossip and to gossip itself undermines the very structure of a male-dominated culture. According to Katherine Rogers in *The Troublesome Helpmate: A History of Misogyny in Literature,* gossip is an expression of "self-assertion" in a patriarchal society. Women's "insubordination—disobedience, scolding, verbal or physical resistance, struggling for the mastery" is expressed in the

traditionally feminine love of talk which, especially when indulged with female cronies in the alehouse, was often an expression of independence of home and husband. Wives are constantly shown chattering in church, gossiping in the alehouse, babbling out all their husband's secrets, pressing fatal advice on him, and in general, in the contemporary phrase, clattering like a mill. . . . With these gossips, who were much dearer to them than husband or children, they exchanged every secret they knew, as well as hints for getting the better of men.[22]

Chaucer understood that a woman who has gossips is more likely to be an Alisoun than a Grisilde. Can we imagine Grisilde being so patient with Walter if she had confided in her gossips? Hardly, as gossips interfere in a marriage, encouraging rebellion against a tyrannical husband like Walter. A woman who is a gossip, encouraged in self-expression and armed with forceful speech rehearsed in gossip sessions, is very likely to become a dominating rather than a submissive wife: a shrew.

Jacques de Vitry, an early thirteenth-century preacher, tells the story of a man whose wife was

so contrary that she always did the reverse of what he commanded, and received in a surly manner the guests whom he often asked to dinner. One day he invited several to dine with him, and had the tables set in the garden near a stream. His wife sat with her back to the water, at some distance from the table, and regarded the guests with an unfriendly face. Her husband said: "Be cheerful to our guests, and draw nearer the table." She on the contrary pushed her chair farther from the table and nearer the edge of the stream at her back. Her husband, noticing this, said angrily: "Draw near the table." She pushed her chair violently back and fell into the river and was drowned. Her husband jumped in a boat and began to seek his wife with a long pole, but up the stream. When his neighbors asked him why he looked for his wife up the stream instead of below as he should, he answered: "Do you not know that my wife always did what was contrary and never walked in the straight way? I verily believe that she has gone up the current and not down with it like other people."[23]

The contrary woman, she who goes her own way, against the current and especially against the wishes of her husband, is a strong image of domestic disorder. "The stereotype of the shrew betrays the male fear that women in general (or their own wives or daughters in particular) may attain dominance within the family through verbal and behavioral aggressiveness."[24] The shrew appears in the mystery plays as a stock comic character—assertive, bossy, brassy, argumentative, and insubordinate. Her characterization, and the comedy of the dramatic situation in which she appears in the mystery cycles, depends on her blatant deviation from appropriate feminine speech behavior. As we will see, Chaucer draws on his audience's familiarity with the stock character of the shrew in creating the Wife of Bath. Described by an anonymous poet in an orgy of alliteration as "of tung intollerable," a "violent virago vennemouss,"[25] "stowte & bolde" in speech,[26] the shrew is a lively presence in a speech medium, the drama.

In "The Creation of Adam and Eve," the male-female relationship begins on the ambiguous note that is ever to characterize it: Eve is originally created as "feere" or companion (l. 136) to Adam, an expression connoting equality; but Adam names her as he does the animals, an act connoting dominance. If he is dominant, Adam should not subject himself to Eve. His unwisdom in following Eve's advice leads to the Fall. Behind every talking woman in the mystery cycles stands talking Eve, whose sin in talking to the serpent, thus inviting temptation, introduced sin itself into the world. Thereafter, every episode of domestic disorder reminds the audience of the original source of all evil, a talking woman.

Although Eve's silent antitype, Mary, cannot logically appear before her chronological place in salvation history, in the atemporal realm of the audience's perception Mary stands in contrast to Eve. In correct speech as in all other behaviors, Mary is the model, compared to whom all other women seem the more shrewish. Unlike Uxor, Mary is meek and humble, submissive to Joseph despite her clear moral superiority to him. Her characterization also depends on the wife's duty of compensating for the faults of a bad husband, with Joseph portrayed in this context. Decidedly unsaintly in his domestic behavior, he provides Mary with an opportunity to demonstrate her superior virtue as a guide to other women wed to morally inferior husbands. In the verbal interchanges between them in the "Joseph" play of the Coventry cycle, Mary restores household harmony through the use of conciliatory speech.

The dramatic action begins with what will emerge in the various cycles as a repeated ritual: the homecoming of the husband. If his realm is in the outside world, and that of the wife the home, the transition from outdoors to indoors is a significant event. One of Everywife's primary duties is to ease this transition with appropriate welcoming behavior. Conversely, a woman's failure to carry out the welcoming ritual properly is a sign of her deviation from an appropriate feminine role. In drama, an oral medium, the welcoming ritual must consist of speech, by which the wife's attitude toward her husband becomes clear. The "Joseph" play begins with Joseph knocking at his own door, returning from a long trip. Mary is within, with her maidservant; all is apparently as it should be. Joseph's extended absence calls up the misogynistic stereotype of the weak reed, in that it appears that his wife's virtue has collapsed in his absence. Joseph, a stock figure, the *senex amans,* was foolish to marry a young girl like Mary and then leave her unsupervised. While Joseph can be forgiven for his reasonable assumption of a human origin for Mary's pregnancy, his behavior even before he realizes she is pregnant marks him off as the wrathful husband who must be placated. He bangs on the door impatiently, allowing no response time and refusing to identify himself to Mary's maid. Mary recognizes his voice and, despite his rudeness, instructs her maid to open the door. A shrew would have responded with unkind and aggressive speech, but Mary behaves as if she were a dutiful reader of "The Good Wife Taught Her Daughter," in which a wife is advised to slake her husband's mood with just such sweet and patient words as Mary utters: "Well-come hom, myn husbond dere. / How have ye ferd in fer countre?" (ll. 9–10).

Mood unslaked, Joseph is surly. When he notices that his wife's "wombe to hyghe doth stond" (l. 26), his mood deteriorates further, and he accuses Mary of infidelity. Grilled about the identity of the child's father, Mary answers serenely: "This childe is Goddys and your" (l. 42). Joseph's wrath increases. God does not "jape so with may," and he himself never came "so nyh thi boure" (ll. 44, 46). Again Mary responds patiently. As in the "Clerk's Tale," a wife's tolerance under increasing provocation is tested. Even when Joseph threatens to abandon Mary to the harsh fate of the adulterous woman under Jewish law, Mary uses speech as the behavior manuals advised, to appease Joseph, to try to "a-mende [his] mod" (l. 63). But instead Joseph indulges in an anti-female diatribe, lamenting that he ever took a wife, planning (anachronistically) to take her before the bishop to be stoned to death. He does briefly allude to the tradition of the weak reed, admitting that he left his wife alone too long, neglecting his role as protector of her chastity. But mainly his thoughts are on himself, on the effect of her apparent actions on him. Joseph feels sorry for himself and looks to the male members of the audience for sympathy. Despite Mary's best efforts at using placating speech, despite her prayers that his suffering might be ameliorated (ll. 84–85), Joseph is becoming increasingly upset. In the battle between Wrath and Patience, Wrath is winning. For Joseph to play his allotted role in the supernatural drama, divine intervention is needed.

On the human level, this dialogue shows Joseph and Mary as on opposite sides of the virtue-vice seesaw. Joseph is self-concerned; Mary is concerned with Joseph. His speech aggravates the situation; hers appeases it. No matter how obnoxious Joseph becomes, Mary remains the perfect exemplar of a wife using the proper speech behavior. As a character in an oral medium, Mary can hardly be depicted as quite so quiet as she is in the sermons; so her trademark becomes correct speech: placating, other-directed, and brief.

Mary's ideal behavior stands as implicit contrast to the women in the cycles who emulate Eve. In the Towneley "Second Shepherds' Play," Mak's wife, Gyll, is associated with discordant sounds, the "unrest and noise" of sinful humanity, as opposed to the "peace and harmony" inaugurated by Christ's birth.[27] The play opens with lamentations on all sides concerning the disharmony in the cosmos due to Adam's sin. Fallen humankind, unredeemed by Christ, mourns its suffering. Gyll, fallen woman and shrewish wife, represents a special kind of pain.

Economic servitude and subjugation to sin are experienced by all humankind, but marriage is a further bondage. The Second Shepherd has great woe in marriage; his wife talks too much and is short-tempered ("As sharp as a thystyll, as rugh as a brere" [l. 101] with "a galon of gall" [l. 106]), unpleasant-looking ("browyd lyke a brystyll with a sowre-loten chere" [l. 102]); noisy and intemperate (when in drink, she sings her *Paternoster*); fat ("greatt as a whall" [l. 105]). Therefore, he warns young men to beware of marriage. The theme of the woes of marriage is reinforced by the troubles of Mak, who suffers from his wife's excessive fertility. She brings forth at least one child a year, so Mak is "eten outt of howse and of harbar" (l. 245). She is lazy (she "lyys walteryng . . . by the fyere, lo!" [l. 236]) and gluttonous (she drinks well and eats as fast as she can [ll. 237, 240]). He wishes he were rid of her, a widower; he would give all his money to "offer / Hyr hed mas-penny" (l. 252). The audience would have caught the relationship between Mak's wish for his wife's death and her fertility: death in childbirth was common, but apparently Gyll is the healthiest of breeders. Mak is likely to be in possession of his mass-penny for a good while.

The interaction between Mak and Gyll shows that Gyll has all the faults of the typical Uxor. Twice Mak returns home to an unpleasant welcome; Gyll calls the sounds of his homecoming a "dyn" (l. 297) and must be nagged to get up and open the door. Gyll's speech violates norms for wives. Even though Mak, like Joseph, is less than polite upon his homecoming, it is all the more Gyll's duty to emulate Mary and welcome him with conciliatory words. But Gyll is like Noah's Uxor, another shrew, and so greets her husband with a litany of housewifely complaints (ll. 415–421). A pattern begins to emerge in the mystery cycles concerning the homecoming ritual: a good woman greets her husband lovingly and placatingly, even if he is crabby; a bad woman seizes the opportunity to unload grievances and browbeat her husband. Written to celebrate the birth of Christ, the "Second Shepherds' Play" shows the cosmic dis-ease that needs healing in Christ. Cosmic is echoed by domestic as the problems of Mak and his wife occupy center stage for longer than might seem necessary in a play ostensibly about the Nativity. But if all suffering and disorder is a consequence of the Fall, so are marital difficulties. Each daughter of Eve must do her best to become a daughter of Mary, to control her speech in the interest of bringing her marriage into conformity with the ideal.

In the Wakefield "Noah," domestic problems involving Noah and his wife form the non-scriptural comic plot element, and, as in the "Second Shepherds' Play," they serve as an image of the chaos caused by disregard for hierarchy. God plans to destroy the universe because of man's insubordination; in the family microcosm, the rebelliousness of Noah's wife reflects this. All evil entered the world because of the disruption of hierarchical order; Lucifer, who "thoght hymself as worthi as hym that hym made" has to be put in his place, in "low degre" (ll. 19, 21). But Noah is saved, and his family with him, because he acknowledges God's authority. In the macrocosm, evil can only be purged by the cleansing violence of the flood. And domestic order similarly requires that Noah rule his shrewish wife; if violence is needed to restore this order, then so be it.

When God proclaims his plan for Noah, the patriarch's perfect obedience provides a model for proper hierarchical relationships. Noah accepts God's orders unquestioningly, even though, "old, seke, sory and cold" (ll. 60–61), he is an unlikely candidate for preserver of the human race. Noah's first thoughts upon receiving his mission are of the probable negative reaction of his wife, which immediately shows the disorder of their relationship. Even with Noah's conciliatory approach, Uxor is "tethee," "angre," and "wroth" (ll. 186–189). These adjectives characterize her, says G. R. Owst, as "the typical shrew of the sermons . . . an example of the disobedient wife, a disturber of domestic peace and charity."[28] The shrew is the opposite of the ideal wife in her refusal to accept responsibility for harmony in the home.

As might be expected, Uxor behaves badly during the homecoming ritual. Noah's brief greeting to his wife (accompanied in performance, no doubt, by suitably subservient body language), is followed by Uxor's long, complaining rejoinder (ll. 190–198, 208–216). Such excess of speech is a flaw in a wife, regardless of content. Then, the content of Uxor's speech is a litany of complaints, an uninterruptible anti-husband diatribe: How am I, you say? The worse for seeing you. Where have you been all this time? You don't make enough money to support me; I could die of starvation. Women (here no doubt she addresses the women in the audience, to the merriment of all) should beware of ill husbands. A wife is expected to be a tuning fork, to sympathize with her husband's moods, act as if sad when he is sad, wring her hands for dread. But at other times, with delight and guile, she gets back at him, gives him what he deserves. Noah's wife clearly knows what the rules are, but boasts of doing the opposite. Ironically, Uxor swears "bi Mary" (l. 209) that Noah is a bad husband. The humor of this is increased by the fact that the audience knows that Noah is the most virtuous man in the human race, chosen by God for its continuation. Good enough for God, Noah is not good enough for his wife. Order can only be restored by Noah's silencing this upstart, correcting her superfluity of speech: "Hold thi tong, ramskyt, / or I shall the still" (l. 217). Blows given and received follow.

Lest we interpret these according to legitimate twentieth-century concerns about domestic violence, we must factor in medieval ideas about corporal punishment. Such punishment, when inflicted by a superior on a subordinate, was considered not only permissible but necessary; God Himself is punishing the world for its sinfulness. Gratian's *Decretum*, a theological dictionary written at the beginning of the fourteenth century, ruled that "a man may chastise his wife and beat her for her correction; for she is of his household, therefore the lord may chastise his own."[29] Given medieval beliefs about marriage as a symbol of universal order, "a few cuffs on the ear given by a husband became a sign that a wife was being kept in her proper place. French and English sermons told of disobedient wives drowned, their backs broken, dead from poison, all because they had done what their husbands had forbidden."[30] Such sermon anecdotes should not be taken literally, however. Historian David Herlihy says that medieval law allowed discipline "but not to the point of maiming."[31] Tolerated in theory, wife beating was unacceptable in practice if it led to serious injury.[32] What is unquestionably wrong, however, is Uxor's reprisal. Noah is now more than ever obliged to assert his authority over his disorderly wife.

The arc of the plot is the movement from chaos to order in a universe now comprised of one family. While Noah is about the serious business of ark building, Uxor is setting herself to spin, an activity that stands as metaphor for all women's work. Women's work, especially in the laboring classes to which the Noah family seems to belong, was important to medieval people, necessary to survival. Spinning takes on in this context a triviality that was not attributed to it in life, when a woman's skills clothed her family. In the context of this particular plot, Noah's work—saving the human race—is unquestionably more urgent than spinning. When Noah explains God's plans to his family, the three sons acquiesce immediately, but Uxor, true to type, is "recalcitrant."[33] She doesn't like the idea of being shut up in such close quarters as the ark provides; she won't budge for either Jack or Jill until she has "spon a space" (l. 337), done her domestic routine. Her unmotivated stubbornness places her in the company of the contrary woman of Jacques de Vitry's sermon anecdote. A good wife would not question her husband. The playwright asks his audience to generalize about the stubborn rebelliousness of women from Uxor's behavior rather than from the docility of the three daughters-in-law, who, obedient though they are, never occupy center stage.

In the mystery plays, it is common for a character to solicit audience opinion. Noah threatens his wife with physical punishment, and asks for the agreement of other husbands that women's tongues should be controlled to ease domestic strife. The audience must have cheerfully joined in on both sides, making the problem's universality all the clearer. Uxor's annoyance with her husband, her desire to be a widow (she would like to offer a "penny doyll," a mass donation for the repose of his soul [l. 390]), sets up sympathetic vibrations among disgruntled wives in the audience. The Noah/Uxor conflict becomes a model for the proper resolution of marital disputes. In this argument, the stakes are high. Since Uxor stands in the way of Noah's accomplishment of his God-given task, Noah has no choice but to exert his God-given authority. Noah cannot simply leave his stubborn wife behind when she refuses to get into the ark. Just as the exact dimensions of the ark are important because they follow God's plan, so is the symmetry of its human and animal inhabitants; they must enter two by two, male and female. Therefore Uxor needs to be brought to a realization of her place in the authority structure, beneath Noah, even if this means she also needs to be "bete . . . bak and bone" (l. 407) to end the "stryfis" (l. 400). Just so, Noah tells the wedded men in the audience, must all wives be brought to heel. It is their husbands' responsibility to "chastice thare tong" (l. 398), to keep control of their speech. Only when Uxor is soundly beaten (ll. 413–414) does she enter the ark. Thus the world is saved.

Restored order is demonstrated in new, harmonious speech patterns. Placidly afloat, "no more . . . wroth" (l. 418), Noah and Uxor engage in equally peaceful discourse. Noah makes a statement ("this is a grete flood, wife" [l. 423]); she agrees ("so me thoght" [l. 424]). He prays for God's help; she echoes his prayer (ll. 426, 432). Captain of the marital ship as well as of his ark, he gives orders ("wife, tent the stere-tre" [l. 433]), and his mate obeys ("that shall I do ful wysely" [l. 435]). If she expresses any opinion at all, it is a truism ("Me thynk . . . / The son shynes in the eest" [ll. 453–454]). A reformed shrew becomes a tuning fork. Her personality reversal shows the radical opposition between disorder and order. So confident is Noah of his authority over Uxor that he ventures the risky business of asking for her "counsell" (l. 472) concerning which type of bird to send out in search of land. While accepting her (politely phrased) suggestion of the raven, he supplements it with his own choice, two doves, thus keeping firmly in control. Domestic harmony such as now prevails is the very image of a cosmos newly purged from sin and blessed by God.

The mode, timing, and content of women's speech, then, is seen in medieval literature as a major source of harmony or disharmony in a family. If, like Mary, a wife is obedient, accepting, meek, passive, orderly, peaceful, long-suffering, forgiving, and agreeable, such qualities will be reflected in her speech. If, as is more likely, she is disobedient, rebellious, feisty, aggressive, seductive, disorderly, wrathful, talkative, vengeful, self-indulgent, deceptive, and disagreeable, these qualities also will be reflected in her speech. Since speech is an expression of the self, the selfless woman will talk little, the selfish, much. One early fourteenth-century behavior manual sees silence as "a sign of modesty and chastity."[34] Conversely, then, copious speech signals sexual excess. When a good woman speaks, she does so mainly in the service of others, never to express personal preferences, or, worse still, negative emotions. While this is true of women in all estates of life, it is most important for married women, upon whom the peaceful functioning of domestic life depends.

Rules attempting to control women's speech are ultimately about husbandly dominance in marriage, a situation that was thought to mirror cosmic order. A husband has a right to exclusivity of affection, which not only precludes violations of chastity but also limits extramarital loyalties. No competing relationship, not even an asexual one involving other women, must be allowed to assume an important place in a wife's life, because such relationships threaten domestic privacy. Worse, gossip sessions rehearse rebellious speech acts.

As heresiarchs knew when they attracted women to their sects as preachers, speech is an act by which one lays claim to intellectual authority. To speak one's mind is to assert that one has a mind, has ideas of one's own. To have in addition the will to choose to express those ideas forcefully and well is to assert independence. In the little world of the household, rebellion must be discouraged. Gossips and shrews must be disempowered through mockery, and patient Grisildes must be held up for admiration and imitation as saints of wifeliness.

❧ 7 ❧

The Good, the Bad, and the Wavering: Women and Architectural Space

The female is an empty thing and easily swayed: she runs great risks when she is away from her husband. Therefore, keep females in the house, keep them as close to yourself as you can, and come home often to keep an eye on your affairs and to keep them in fear and trembling.

—Paolo de Certaldo[1]

When Jehu came to Jezreel, Jezebel heard it; and she painted her eyes, and adorned her head, and looked out of the window.

—2 Kings 9:30

Woman's place is in the home: this truism was only questioned in our own century. A more precise way of phrasing the medieval belief on the subject would be to postulate a close association between the idea of womanhood and the idea of a protected enclosure. In *The Song of Songs,* the beloved is described as a "garden enclosed," a walled garden, her sexual exclusivity expressed in an architectural metaphor. In Psalm 128 the good wife is in the recesses of her house; Jezebel looks out from a window. These famous scriptural images embody the idea that a woman's chastity is protected by architectural barriers; her proper position is not only in the house but in its most secluded areas. In contrast, the "loose" woman is associated with completely unenclosed or at least penetrable space. In their private domestic sphere, in the interior spaces of house and garden, women's chastity is safe.

The virtuous young maiden, wife, or widow demonstrates and preserves her virtue by living behind walls. Threats to chastity are represented by the house's apertures—doors, windows, and gates—and even more strongly by the open street or other undefined spaces. Lingering at the limits of protected space does not merely represent idle curiosity (serious enough in the medieval schema), but specifically sexual temptation. Moving entirely out of the enclosed space, a practice termed "wandering" when women do it, is severely criticized as connoting sexual availability if done voluntarily. If such wandering is done involuntarily, if a woman is ejected from her safe haven, that is a sign of a distorted relationship with her male protector. As we have seen, the virtuous woman remains within the house of her father until she is ritually conveyed to the house of her husband. Any disruption of this process is a threat to her chastity, possibly even to her survival. Thus the relationship between women and architectural space in medieval literature, as an extension of its usefulness as a metaphor for chastity, is also an indicator of her status with respect to her male protector.

In scripture, spatial imagery concerning the location of women situates them in terms of a walled city. The city gates are a place for men, a "place of public concourse" where "much of the legal business of the city was done,"[2] including bringing women's concerns to the attention of the city's elders there (e.g., Deut. 22:15, 25:7). While a woman generally stays away from so public a place, her reputation affects that of her husband there; if she is a good wife, her husband is "known" for it, her works are praised there, in the place where her husband "sits among the elders of the land" (Prov. 31:23, 31).

Within the gates are the streets of the city, where harlots wander. Only a bad woman appears in the public streets: "her feet do not stay at home; now in the street, now in the market, and at every corner she lies in wait" for the unsuspecting man who will succumb to her charms (Prov. 7:10–12). This strong image of the wandering woman becomes "the ground base of medieval attacks on women."[3] The phrase "within her father's house" describes a virtuous unmarried woman (e.g., Num. 30). A good wife bears children, is "a fruitful vine within [her] house" (Ps. 128:3); "within" is often translated "in the recesses of," stressing the idea of enclosure. Not only does the good woman stay home, she stays well within it. In contrast, the wanton woman "sits at the door of her house . . . calling to those who pass by, who are going straight on their way, 'Whoever is simple, let him turn in here!' " (Prov. 9:14–16). Such a woman lures a man from his "straight way" into the paths of sin, so he must be warned: "Do not go near the doors of her house!" (Prov. 5:8). One scriptural example shows that the door of the house symbolizes the limits of both paternal authority and protection. If a woman is cast off by her husband for not having been a virgin at the time of her wedding, she is brought "to the door of her father's house." Because of her transgression she is acceptable to neither husband nor father; thus she belongs nowhere, has no male protector, and is vulnerable to severe punishment: "The men of the city shall stone her to death with stones, because she has wrought folly in Israel by playing the harlot in her father's house" (Deut. 22:20–21).

Although it is also susceptible to complex theological interpretation, the story of the concubine in the Book of Judges is on its literal level an example of the scriptural association between female vulnerability and unenclosed space. A man releases his concubine to the "men of the city" (19:22),

and they knew her, and abused her all night until the morning. And as the dawn began to break, they let her go. And as morning appeared, the woman came and fell down at the door of the man's house where her master was, till it was light. And her master rose up in the morning, and when he opened the doors of the house and went out to go on his way, behold, there was his concubine lying at the door of the house, with her hands on the threshold. He said to her, "Get up, let us be going." But there was no answer. Then he put her upon the ass; and the man rose up and went away to his home. And when he entered his house, he took a knife, and laying hold of his concubine he divided her, limb by limb, into twelve pieces, and sent her throughout all the territory of Israel (19:25–29).

A stronger image of female desolation can hardly be imagined.

The valued woman, in contrast, has a safe enclosure provided for her by a male protector to whom the preservation of her virtue is a matter of the highest importance. Medieval people found in scripture justification for their belief in what we may call the principle of female enclosure. To be in the house is to be protected from harm and from sin. To be outdoors is to declare oneself, or be regarded as, sexually available. To find a virtuous woman, look indoors.

In the romance *Guy of Warwick,* a neat verbal contrast is established: "Knights sat in the hall / Ladies in the chamber all."[4] The great hall, the public space in a great house, is the domain of men; the chamber, the private space, is the domain of women:[5]

An open space, the hall was located close to the court and the gate, because it exerted considerable influence on the outside world. . . . A place for public acts, the hall was primarily a masculine preserve. Female relatives were admitted . . . because this was the place for festivities of all kinds. Their proper place, however, was the bedroom, where [their] fundamental function was carried out: reproduction.[6]

Due to the seriousness of this function and the need to protect its integrity, it must take place in the most secluded part of the house, reached only after a series of architectural barriers are penetrated. The medieval lady's chamber was not, however, only a bedroom; it also served as a "combination sitting-room and bed-chamber,"[7] where she and her women would receive selected guests. Thus they are depicted in literature and art. In Figure 2, Christine de Pisan is depicted presenting a copy of her book to Isabeau of Bavaria in the latter's bedchamber. With hostess and guest are a group of five other women, supporting, as do many other medieval images, the contention that the chamber is a *gynaeceum,* or "woman's space."[8] Women's space was private relative to the public areas in the great medieval houses. Access to women's space by men and egress therefrom by women are controlled in order to preserve female chastity.

The apertures of the house were the points of interaction between protected space and the outside world. From the twelfth to the fourteenth centuries, the window was a major feature of the great medieval house, designed to be "as large as possible and in as rich an architectural manner as the status of the building permits."[9] Often with an appealing window seat, the window was indeed a tempting locale, "richly decorated with panelled stonework, tracery and carving," a private place "to retire into for solitary thought or intimate conversation,"[10] a perfect locale for "secret encounters and less than honorable negotiations."[11] Curtains, shutters, and even iron bars on a window could add further to the sense of barrier, and thus assist in preservation of female virtue,[12] or, conversely, make the seduction process more alluring because more challenging. When "young dandies strutted up and down beneath the windows," when "girls were . . . not permitted to discover the world except through the window,"[13] these eyes on the world become the very symbol of the entrance of temptation into the maidenly fortress.

If windows are morally dangerous, similarly, of course, are doors and balconies. Allowing herself to be seen shows that a woman lacks humility.[14] A fifteenth-century moralist, Friar Cherubino of Siena, groups this behavior with other serious transgressions warranting corporal punishment:

You should beat her, I say, only when she commits a serious wrong: for example, if she blasphemes against God or a saint, if she mutters the devil's name, if she likes being at the window and lends a ready ear to dishonest young men, or if she had taken to bad habits or bad company, or commits some other wrong that is a mortal sin. Then readily beat her.[15]

Virtuous women are locked behind doors and chased from windows by centuries of behavior manual writers. "Decent women were supposed to lock the main entrance the moment their husbands left home,"[16] thus protecting themselves against their increased moral and spiritual vulnerability without a man's guidance. In Jankyn's "book of wikked wyves" (III.D., 685), a story is included of a man who left his wife because he saw her looking out of his door (III.D., 646). Jankyn might well regale his wandering wife with this cautionary tale.

The sexual significance of the garden is another commonplace in this tradition. One function of the medieval garden was to provide a setting for meditation enhanced by statuary depicting religious subjects. Thus, in Frank Crisp's *Medieval Gardens,* a comprehensive collection of visual images of

ee excellent de grant haulteffe
Couronnee poffant princeffe
Trefnoble royne de france
Le corps enclin bere bous ma dreffee

Pour ce liure cy que ie tiens
Bous prefenter ou il na riens
en biftoure nen efcripture
Que naye en ma penfee pure

Figure 2
Christine de Pisan presenting copies of her book to ladies in a chamber. Harley
4431 f. 3v. By permission of the British Library.

the garden from medieval sources, we find many examples of garden images of the Blessed Virgin. Often she is depicted with her infant son, in one case engaged in the mundane task of rinsing out the divine baby's diapers in the garden's fountain (Vol. I, Plate 90).[17] With that easy segue between sacred and profane characteristic of all medieval art forms, the garden is also seen as *locus amoenus*, earthly paradise. In gardens, Crisp's illustrations show lovers engaging in casual conversation (Vol. 2, Plate XLIV), cavorting in fountains (Vol. 2, Plate CCIII), sharing a snack (Vol. 2, Plate CCIV), and embracing in ways ranging from chaste hand-holding (Vol. 2, Plate CXXXIII) to aggressive breast-fondling (Vol. 2, Plate CXIV).

A semipublic space enclosed by a wall and accessible through a gate, medieval gardens often contained a smaller walled garden called the *hortus conclusus*. These enclosures within enclosures offered more privacy than the garden proper, which, in turn, was more private than the space exterior to it. In the larger garden area, some of Crisp's illustrations show loving couples paired off, strolling hand in hand, but sharing the garden space with many others (e.g., Vol. 2, Plates XLIV and LXVI), using the garden as a place for "social gathering, usually reserved for small groups, particularly of women."[18] In the *hortus conclusus*, on the other hand, the couple is afforded more privacy; therefore the sensual connotations of the space are stronger. In one illustration in the Crisp volume (Plate LXXV), a pair of lovers are in a *hortus conclusus* surrounded by a wall with a door, thus separated from the nine other inhabitants of the larger garden, itself subdivided by further walls and partitions, and finally divided from the outside world by a fence with foliage. Degrees of privacy provided within a garden are quite clear here. According to one commentator, the *hortus conclusus* was originally regarded as a tribute to the Blessed Virgin, so sexual use of it, as in Chaucer's "Merchant's Tale," is sacrilegious.[19]

The layout of the medieval garden, enclosed by walls within walls and accessible through sensuously appealing gates, provided a strong analogue of the barriers and obstacles that lent suspense to the courtship process. The thirteenth-century behavior manual writer Jacques d'Amiens, in his *L'art d'amors* (based on Ovid's *Ars Amandi*) calls attention to the role of architectural barriers in an illicit relationship. He advises the lady that, when she has arranged a rendezvous with her lover, she must make him wait outside, then let him enter by a little door opened slightly and shut quickly. If the rendezvous is in the garden, she must be sure to make him scale the wall or at least a hedge, probably as a demonstration of his determination. These things, d'Amiens opines, will increase his love.[20] Thus the process of seduction is envisioned as motion in space, past barriers, toward the ultimate inner space of the woman's body.

As in this garden image, architectural metaphors in medieval literature often refer to the biological structure of the female body. Women do not only *exist in* architectural space, they *are* architectural space; their bodies enclose inner space, and women are themselves enclosed for protection of that inner space. The concept of female body as enclosure had as corollary the idea that, if a woman is in her proper space, a safe, peaceful, static, enclosed space, her own inner space, her chastity, will be protected likewise.

The concept of woman as enclosure can be expressed with great dignity and beauty, as in Hildegard of Bingen's "Responsory for the Virgin," in which Mary's physical integrity is expressed in architectural metaphor, as inviolate interiority:

> Priceless integrity!
> Her virgin gate
> opened to none. But the Holy One
> flooded her with warmth
> until a flower sprang in her womb
> and the Son of God came forth
> from her secret chamber like the dawn.
>
> Sweet as the buds of spring, her
> son opened paradise
> from the cloister of her womb.
> And the Son of God came forth
> from her secret chamber like the dawn.[21]

Gates and chambers, however, more commonly formed part of the vulgar vernacular for the female genitalia. Most architectural allusions to the female body are to be taken as sexual double entendres. A late thirteenth-century translation of Andreas Capellanus by Drouart la Vache uses an architectural structure as an explicit chastity allegory. The sexual availability of the women is indicated by their position vis-à-vis the entrance to a palace. Courtesans "are always to be found wandering outside the threshold of the door," which shows that they are "promiscuous women who refuse no one; they admit all indiscriminately and are available for all men's pleasure." Chaste women, on the other hand, "remain behind closed doors, and observe nothing outside the boundaries of the palace," demonstrating their complete unavailability; they "open to no man's knock and refuse all men entry into the palace of Love." Between these two extremes lie the courtly ladies, who, though not totally unavailable, are highly selective; they "linger at the open doors and are for ever to be found on the threshold." Unlike the harlots, they are not wandering totally outside the palace, nor, like the chaste, are they completely within doors and secluded from the influence of the outside world. Rather they are in between, lingering at thresholds. No one intends to remain on a threshold indefinitely; it is by definition a passage, a point of decision: *in* or *out*. The courtly lady is about to make a choice. She will allow a select few "to enter the open gate."[22] The medieval analogy between architectural structure and sexual activity could hardly be more clearly expressed.

The Romance of the Rose is only slightly more subtle. To preserve the Rose, virginity's sacred flower, Jealousy undertakes an impressive building project, hiring masons and excavators (expensive then as now) to build fortifications: moats, walls, turrets, towers, battlements, portals, and, "within the enclosure's very center . . . a donjon thick and high." This fortress should prove invulnerable: "The walls would never crack / At stroke of any instrument of war." Even super-strong forts, however, must have entrances. Each of the four gates of the fort is guarded by allegorical guardians of chastity: Danger, Shame, Fear, and Evil Tongue. The extensive description of the protection against "villains" who "might purloin a rose or bud" shows the high value attached to virginity and how difficult it seemed to afford such protection.[23] The more barriers surrounding a woman, the stronger a male protector shows himself to be and, therefore, the greater the triumph for the man who penetrates those barriers to seduce or to rape.

The sharp differentiation between male and female uses of space must be understood, however, against medieval preferences for both sexes. Medieval men treasured enclosure for themselves, too, often interpreting it as inclusion within one's group. The romance knight concludes his adventure by returning to the shelter of a castle. Medieval cities were walled to provide a sense of communal identity as well as protection. Indeed, the enclosed space of the walled city was a feature of the medieval image of a crowded urban heaven: "The city promised urban security, if not prosperity. In heaven no one would be condemned to a precarious, hardworking peasant existence beyond the city gates."[24] Given the value attached to enclosure for both men and women, the difference lies in what is expected to happen when an individual leaves the protected space. Leaving can be positive for men; they can have adventures and return triumphant. For women, leaving has no positive connotations; it means threat without reward.

For this reason, Mary, as ever a symbol of womanly perfection, is depicted as enclosed. According to one homilist, Mary, "whenne the angel come to hure and fonde hure [was] inne a pryvy chambre and nouȝt stondynge ne walkynge by stretys."[25] No gadabout Mary. She stays at home, in her chamber. To stress this, in images of the Annunciation in the visual arts like that in Figure 3, Mary is found by the angel Gabriel either entirely enclosed within an interior space, or near a vaguer, but still sheltering, architectural structure—the point being that she is not in undifferentiated space.[26]

In this particular image, Mary's modesty is further stressed by her gesturing hand, lifted in warning against the intruding stranger. There is no biblical warrant for the assumption that Mary was indoors; the Lucan annunciation story (1:26–38) does not specify where Mary was when the

Figure 3
A fifteenth-century Annunciation scene.

angel appeared to her. Nevertheless, for medieval people, if she is pre-
sumed to be enclosed, claustrated, she is thought to be a better model not
only to maidens pure but also to good women of all estates. As Paolo da
Certaldo says: "Woman should emulate the Virgin Mary, who did not
leave her house to go drinking all over town, ogle handsome men, or listen
to a lot of idle talk. No, she stayed home, behind closed doors, in the
privacy of her own home, as was only proper."[27]

When Mary's sinful daughter leaves her enclosure, she is universally described in medieval didactic literature as "wandering." In *La Contenance
des Fames,* a didactic poem of the late thirteenth or early fourteenth century, women's desire to leave home, even her moving about within the
house, indicates emotional instability. She "Runs to the mill, then to a
neighbor, / Then to and fro and down the hall; / From room to room, she
fills them all."[28] Leaving the house can have no other purpose than to
invite male attention. In *The Romance of the Rose* the Jealous Husband
accuses his wife of wanting to leave the house to be seen by men, to

> waken the desires
> Of ribald lechers (who the harlots chase)
> When they accompany you on the streets
> And spy and ogle your bold-faced display.[29]

Thus the Jealous Husband must take the most stringent precautions to
keep his wife at home: "Without me never shall you leave the house /
Though I must clamp on you an iron ring / To make you slave at home as
you deserve."[30] Even if her intentions are purely virtuous (an unlikely
possibility), she can still be a cause of sin to any man who sees her.

Preachers caution virgins and widows to be "clos in hir house" as a
demonstration of their virtue. The biblical Dinah "walkede out" and was
"yravesched." Other "nyce [foolish] maydens" who "walketh aboute in
medes and in fayre places ledynge daunces and syngynge, as it were schew-
ynge hem self to lese her maydenhode,"[31] were demonstrating dissatisfaction with the estate of virginity. The *Speculum Laicorum* (thirteenth century) describes ignoble women as "roamers in the streets"; another preacher
castigates the "vagrant" woman, "not able to keep her feet within the house,
now she is without, now in the streets."[32] A fourteenth-century homilist,
the Dominican John Bromyard, sees a woman's "perambulation through
the town" as "inflam[ing] with the fire of lust—it may be—twenty of those
who behold her. . . . For this very purpose the Devil thus adorns these
females, sending them forth through the town as his apostles. . . . By a
single round of the town or one foolish appearance at the window she
converts many to the Devil."[33] Therefore, better not to go out at all; or
even be seen from doors, windows or balconies; or even wish to do any
of these.

Many homilists tie love of wandering to excessiveness in speech and sumptuousness in attire: the wandering woman gossips and displays her finery, thus committing several sins at once. The "vagrant" woman is thus also "garrulous," "loud," "impatient of quiet."[34] A woman also wanders to show off her clothing. As *La Contenance des Fames* puts it, "She will go stand at her door / To make sure she's not ignored."[35] Given all this moral opprobrium attached to the simple act of leaving one's home, then, it seems better to stay at home.

If a virtuous woman must leave the house for a serious reason, such as going to church or doing a charitable act, she must not only be suitably chaperoned but also carry a semblance of her enclosure with her. According to the Knight of the Tower, modesty requires that a woman walk with eyes downcast, being "stedfast in lokyng playnly to fore" her, turning her head neither to left nor to right, because "they be mocqued that so lyghtely cast their sight and hede and torne their vysage here and there."[36] Veiling herself and walking with small steps, practices often recommended,[37] have the desirable effect of causing her to occupy as little of the space around her as possible, to be modestly contained within herself.

These counsels against wandering apply with different force across the social strata. At the highest levels of society, where a woman's chastity secures the integrity of the lineage, the spatial safeguards apply most emphatically. At the lower echelons of society, women's lack of enclosure, though due to economic necessity, indicates also the lesser importance attached to their chastity and the powerlessness of their men as protectors. "At the bottom of the social scale," observes Peter Brown, referring to the early Christian era but in terms applicable to the Middle Ages, "the lower classes were not expected to be capable of protecting their womenfolk from exposure. The seclusion of one's womenfolk assumed power and wealth. The sexual vulnerability of poor girls was simply part of their general passivity to the powerful."[38] Therefore, the higher a woman's social station, the more enclosed she must be.

Women's position in space, as depicted in literature, is influenced by these cultural assumptions. Valued commodities are tightly enclosed. A woman's being voluntarily outdoors, or even near doors, connotes moral laxity, if not hopeless turpitude. A woman involuntarily wandering in unenclosed space is vulnerable because of the absence of a male protector to provide a proper enclosure for her. Unprotected, she is considered available for sexual purposes. Wandering from house to house in an uncontrolled fashion is conducive to a variety of sins. Because of the ideological correlation between women's bodies and architectural space, allusions in literature to a woman's position in space mark her off as good, bad, or wavering in her chastity.

Chaucer employs this complex of ideas much as his contemporaries do, as a way of describing his women, sometimes in passing, sometimes as a major element of a specific work. With his instinctive understanding of the rules circumscribing women's lives, he sensed that all the spatial control advocated in the didactic sources was not only limiting to women's lives but ineffective. Ami, the Friend, the voice of common sense in *The Romance of the Rose,* advises Amant, the Lover, that too much constraint kills love, that women like "the liberty to come and go."[39] Chaucer picks up this idea when he presents characters as rebelling against the norm of enclosure. This is a minor element in the character of May in the "Merchant's Tale," and a more significant one in the wandering Wife of Bath, whose freedom to move through space at will is a major component of the "maistrye" that women seek. In contrast, when a woman's proper relationship to enclosing space is violated against her will, as it is in the "Man of Law's Tale," the "Clerk's Tale," and the "Legend of Lucrece," the result is not freedom but vulnerability, often of a specifically sexual nature.

Physical or even visual access to the inner space, which is the realm of the female, constitutes, as we have seen, a stage in the seduction process, a kind of foreplay. This is particularly obvious in the complex sexual double entendres concerning locks and keys and garden gates in the "Merchant's Tale."[40] On the one hand, Januarie appropriately holds the keys to the garden gate in that marriage gives him exclusive sexual rights to his private *hortus conclusus,* May's body. At the same time, the key represents his attitude toward his wife as sex object, an attitude defined as sinful lust under canon law. A respected mistress of a medieval household would hold the keys of the house herself, as symbol of her important economic and managerial role in the household. A wife is a significant domestic authority, a holder of a respected job, not an object locked away for sexual use. To evaluate Januarie's behavior in locking May away, contrast the attitude of the Goodman of Paris, training his own young wife to take over her legitimate administrative function. Despite the provocation, May is guilty in violating the sacred meaning of the garden as private area and of marriage itself when she gives Damyan the "clycket" to the "wycket" (IV.E., 2117–2121). But May's adultery is at least in part a refusal to submit to being treated without the dignity properly accorded to a legitimate wife.

As a corollary of her lechery, the Wife of Bath is guilty of the moral flaw of *"instabilitas loci,"* a "fatal attraction to the outside world."[41] As wife and widow, she has always wanted to come and go as she pleases. The kind of husband woman love, she says, lets his wife do this, "ben at . . . large" (III.D., 322). When her husband is away, she perambulates through the town all the more—to the house of her gossip, to vigils, processions, preachings, pilgrimages, miracle plays, and weddings—"for to se, and eek for to be seye / Of lusty folk" (III.D., 552–553), all the while wearing her most garishly hued attire, her "gaye scarlet gytes" (III.D., 559). All this places her at risk of sinning or tempting men to sin. Jankyn belatedly learns from his books that Ecclesiastes cautions husbands to forbid their wives to "go roule aboute" like this (III.D., 653). Because, despite his prohibitions, his wife likes to "walke . . . / From hous to hous, although he had it sworn" (III.D., 639–640), this becomes a main area of conflict between them. Because of this common fault, the Wife's literary genealogy, says Lucas, "can probably be traced to [a] most distinguished ancestor,"[42] the evil woman of Proverbs, wandering in the street, spreading sexual temptation all about. Now, as widow, Alisoun should not be on pilgrimage. At the Council of York (1195), nuns' pilgrimages were criticized as giving unsuitable "opportunity of wandering."[43] For married women, pilgrimages are regarded as providing opportunity for adultery.[44] By Chaucer's day pilgrimage had become more an excuse for merriment than a religious event, and widows were supposed to be avoiding all occasions of pleasure, especially of the sexual variety. Widowhood only increased the desirability of enclaustration. Self-proclaimed seeker after new love, the Wife, in choosing to wander, boldly identifies herself with the misogynistic stereotype of the unsteadfast widow.

But women who wander involuntarily because of having been expelled from their proper space are pathetic. In the "Man of Law's Tale," Chaucer exploits the well-known connotations of a woman's wandering in undifferentiated space to heighten the pathos of Custance's plight. Both as virgin and as wife, Custance is subjected to spatial instability. Her sea journeys are forceful images of insecurity. Not only does she journey, but she journeys *alone*. Such travels as Custance's represent the sufferings to which an innocent soul is subjected by the forces of evil.

Custance, the very "mirour of alle curteisye" (II.B.,[1] 166), is associated with those married women saints who signal their holiness by their ability to convert the heathen, usually a highly placed heathen who brings "his baronage / And alle his liges" (II.B.,[1] 239–240) into the fold. Custance's father negotiates the marriage transaction with the pagan Sultan of Surry. Joseph E. Grennen points out the significance of the specific legal term used by the Man of Law to describe Constance's departure from her father's house. Poor Constance, the narrator apostrophizes. Leaving the house of her father for the house of her husband, she is unwittingly moving from safety to danger: "Thou knyttest thee ther thou art nat receyved; / Ther thou were weel, fro thennes artow weyved" (II.B.,[1] 307–308). Grennen shows that "weyve" is "a legal term referring precisely to the art of placing a woman beyond the pale, outside of any protection she might have had under the law."[45] In the period of transition between husband and father— too long here, involving (a play on words) the waves of the sea as well as the equally unpredictable elements in human relationships—Custance is without an official protector. Her father relinquishes his rights to and responsibilities over her too soon, before a husband is ready to pick them up. This hiatus in male protection is the eventual cause of Custance's woe.

At first all seems as it should be. Bishops, lords, ladies, knights, "and

oother folk ynowe" make ready "for to wende" with her (II.B.,[1] 253–
255), providing an entourage suitable for a woman of her position. Their
companionship not only adds to the solemnity of the occasion but also
eases the transition between father's kingdom and husband's. Not only is
Custance "compelled . . . to leave her parents and the folk among whom
she has grown up; but to leave Christendom for heathen land,"[46] to link
her life to that of a man she has never met. How painful this passage could
be for medieval women of high birth, often sent away at a young age,
probably for a lifetime, to an uncertain future, is suggested by Chaucer's
description of Custance's feelings:

> Allas, what wonder is it thogh she wepte,
> That shal be sent to strange nacioun
> Fro freendes that so tendrely hire kepte,
> And to be bounden under subjeccioun
> Of oon, she knoweth nat his condicioun?
> Housbondes been alle goode, and han ben yoore;
> That knowen wyves; I dar sey yow na moore.
> (II.B.,[1] 267–273)

Despite the threatening length of Custance's sea journey, she arrives safely
and is received into the Sultan's house with ritual solemnity and great feast-
ing. But as evil naturally hates good, the Sultan's wicked mother develops
an enmity for Custance and disrupts the transition. The particular form the
Sowdanesse chooses for her revenge on Custance is instinctively feminine.
If women are only secure in enclosed places, then the expulsion of Custance from such a place to the unconfined and therefore threatening space
of "a ship al steerelees" (II.B.,[1] 439) is an especially hostile act inflicted on
one woman by another.

Custance's retinue is dead and she is alone in a way no person of rank,
much less a woman, should be. No way exists to notify her father that he
must resume his protector role. When Custance, "woful" (II.B.,[1] 522),
"ful of care" (II.B.,[1] 514), is washed ashore in Northumberland, she is
taken under the protection of the constable and his wife Hermengyld. This
form of protection is weaker than that of a husband or a father, so she is
vulnerable to the lusts of the young knight who, by the vengeful murder
of Hermengyld, destabilizes Custance's life once again. The pattern emerges:
being in a man's house, under his protection, equals safety; being without
a definite male protector equals insecurity and specifically sexual vulnerability. In revenge for her refusal to submit to his advances, the knight tries
to frame Custance for the death of Hermengyld. Like Susannah accused
by the elders, Custance is brought before the emperor Alla, without a
champion (II.B.,[1] 631), standing alone (II.B.,[1] 655). A miracle proves
Custance's innocence and wins Alla's love.

Custance is wed "ful solempnely" (II.B.,[1] 691), that is, according to law and custom, not taken as a concubine as an unprotected, dowerless woman of no known rank might well have been. Stability and security prevail for a time. Deflowered in holy wedlock, Custance efficiently begets a "knave child" (II.B.,[1] 715), fulfilling her function. But again such perfection arouses envy. Alla, away at war, has delegated suitable protectors (a bishop and a constable), but no protection serves against the enemy within the house. Custance's mother-in-law, the vengeful Donegild, casts Custance once more adrift in a rudderless ship, this time with her child in tow. Again, threatened by the elements and by male lust, she is the very emblem of "wayke womman" (II.B.,[1] 932) unable to defend herself or indeed take any action at all. The narrator oddly compares her to David killing Goliath and Judith slaying Holofernes, both of whom, though weak, did take some initiative. But Custance's passivity is a corollary of her goodness; in Paul Ruggiers' words, she is "not so much acting as acted upon,"[47] like the heroines in *The Legend of Good Women*. Her situation can only be improved when her father, belatedly hearing of her misfortunes, dispatches his senator, who finds Custance haplessly bobbing about in her rudderless ship, reluctant for shame to explain who she is ("hire estaat") or why she is "in swich array" (II.B.,[1] 972–973). He provides her with safety, shelter, a home. Custance is safe again.

In Chaucer, female vulnerability leads to one of two possible male reactions: arousing either protectiveness (the Sultan, his constable, Alla, his senator, Custance's father) or lust (the young knight, the lord's steward). In this tale male virtue equals acceptance of a protective role with respect to women, and, conversely, male vice equals taking selfish advantage of woman's weakness. Ultimately, Custance "is protected by the triumphant Champion, Christ."[48] God's Son is woman's ultimate protector, and men are most like Him when they protect women.

The resolution of the story must then logically be the restoration of the fragile female to the shelter provided by proper protectors. Her identity revealed, she is restored to both husband and father, an occasion properly marked by a great feast. A happy and holy, if brief (II.B.,[1] 1143) married life is followed by a virtuous widowhood. At her husband's death, as a good woman should, Custance wends once again, this time to Rome, to her father's house, to the company and protection of her friends. Here, in a foreshadowing of heaven, she achieves her culture's definition of earthly bliss for a woman—that is, freedom from risk: "Now is she scaped all hire aventure" (II.B.,[1] 1151). "Aventure," which ennobles men even as it threatens, only threatens women. She settles into the prescribed widow's life: "In vertu and in hooly almus-dede / They lyven alle, and nevere asonder wende" (II.B.,[1] 1156–1157). If "to wende" or wander is a negative, then security is stasis, and ultimate security is never "to wende" again from the house of the Father. All humans are pilgrims in the journey from earth to heaven, but the smaller journeys within that larger arc are best left to men.

This interpretation complements V. A. Kolve's iconographic analysis of the "Man of Law's Tale," an analysis that focuses on the tale as an allegory of spiritual pilgrimage. What the reader remembers, Kolve says, is the "image of a woman in a rudderless boat, afloat on the sea."[49] If medieval people envisioned "life as a passage" through "a sinful world . . . like the sea, full of perils, tempests, and the risk of drowning,"[50] the destination, heaven, is the cessation of motion and turmoil. Ultimately the Christian soul "wends" alone, protected by faith alone from the "raising high and casting low" of fickle Fortune.[51] In the face of turbulence the proper Christian stance is resignation. Thus, given the complementary ideal of female will-lessness, the soul is perceived as female with respect to its Lord: "By refusing to will, by affirming God's governance and seeking no direction of her own, she allows God to become her steersman."[52] Journey's end is "joye" and "quiete" (II.B.,[1] 1131).[53] The feast that celebrates Custance's reunion with her father unites powerful images of security, the family, home and "communal dinner."[54] The end of Custance's journey is "a foretaste and symbolic pre-enactment of the joy in heaven that alone never 'changeth as the tyde,' " the Christian soul's completion of the " '*migratio ad Dominum*,' a journey of the soul to God."[55]

In the "Man of Law's Tale," then, Chaucer uses the idea of a woman in unenclosed space on an allegorical as well as a literal level: as the soul seeks its heavenly home, so Custance seeks an earthly one. His use of the theme of the unenclosed woman also stresses a related element of the tradition: the motion in space involved in a woman's transition from the house of the father to the house of the husband. As we have seen in examining the liminal state of the marriageable virgin, the successful completion of this journey is the one rite of passage women are expected to undergo. There, in stasis in her husband's house, her story should end. The true wife, like the clean maid, is virtuous by virtue of what she does not do. By remaining chaste, she should, in the right order of things, assure herself of safety and a home. But the house is a symbol of a husband's estate; his wife's is only a derivative of his. A wife's position in her husband's house is held only at his will and may be terminated for no cause, thus casting her from the structure that symbolizes the joy and quiet, the security and protection, which define married happiness.

Grisilde's movements between her father's house and her husband's reflect the changes in her status made by her marriage to, and undone by her separation from, the marquis Walter. On the day of Walter's announced wedding to an unknown woman, Grisilde is standing in the doorway of her house, on its threshold: a change in her domestic status is clearly imminent. In context, this pose does not carry the negative connotations of sexual availability but rather indicates her virginal state, her availability for marriage.[56] Because Grisilde is not a highborn lady, no moral opprobrium attaches to her sallying forth to fetch water from the well and lingering in the doorway upon her return. She is a virgin, but of low social status, so she is not as enclosed as a higher-status virgin might be. Her position in space as the tale begins, then, underlines her humility, but also the social disparity that will ever influence her relationship with her husband. An illustration in a 1395 manuscript (see Figure 4) depicts the ritual transmission of Grisilde to Walter. Grisilde stands between her husband and her father. Behind Janicula is his humble house; behind Walter is the retinue suitable for a man of his position. Grisilde faces Walter: she is going to a new life. But, though raised to higher estate, she remains the daughter of a peasant house, with every reason to be a perpetual subordinate.

As we have seen, Walter's speech patterns demonstrate his assumption of hierarchical superiority; so do his and Grisilde's respective movements in space. When Walter gets Janicula's consent to the marriage, Walter's body language shows his sense of his own superiority. Drawing his betrothed forth from her father's house, "forth he gooth with a ful sobre cheere / Out at the dore, and after that cam she" (IV.E., 366–367). He leads the way and will continue to dominate.

As we have also seen, the *domum-ductio*, or leading the bride from her father's to her husband's house, is a key element in the marriage ritual, so it is logical that the contrast between a woman's old life and her new one would be imagined in terms of houses. The house from which Walter leads her is vastly inferior to the one to which he will lead her. But Grisilde's innate moral superiority equips her to cope in both locations. Grisilde does not seem to have come out of her father's house; she has the qualities of nobility commonly found in a person of higher station:

> it ne semed nat by liklynesse
> That she was born and fed in rudenesse,
> As in a cote or in an oxe-stalle,
> But norissed in an emperoures halle.
> (IV.E., 396–399)

Houses, then, whether a humble cottage, a stable, or the hall of an emperor, symbolize families and indicate social status. But they are also supposed to represent security and protection. As Deborah S. Ellis explains, Walter's house is paradoxically an image of "domestic unease" and "vulnerability." Because of Walter's flawed character, his home is not safe for his wife. Because "Walter's palace [is] the unbending emblem of *his* will," it will only be a home for Grisilde as long as he wills it so. It will never be a true point of stasis, therefore happiness, for her, as she is too vulnerable there.[57] Walter's house remains his, never becomes hers; both the house

Figure 4
Grisilde being given by her father to her husband in marriage. From
Philippe de Mézière's *L'Estoire de Griseldis* (dated 1395). Bibliothèque
Nationale, fr. 2203, fol. 22 v. Courtesy of Service Photographique,
Bibliothèque Nationale, Paris.

and its contents (including the children and Grisilde herself) are Walter's chattel.

Grisilde is returned to her father's house. Resigned to this turn of Fortune's wheel, Grisilde acknowledges that she never felt herself mistress of her husband's house and is ready to resume her former station. But Grisilde's Boethian resignation to fate should not obscure the fact that this reverse transition is a disgrace that only the severest depravity on her part—a breach of chastity—could justify. Her pathetic journey from her husband's house to her father's house echoes the rejection of the unvirgin bride in the Old Testament (Deut. 22:13–21). It constitutes an unnatural inversion of the normal progression of women's lives from pure virgin to chaste wife. By remaining chaste, Grisilde has kept up her end of the marriage bargain, and she deserves in exchange peace, security, and stasis. She learns to accept her fate by redefining her role from faithful wife to steadfast widow, "clene in body, herte, and al" (IV.E., 836). Having so resigned herself, she is not allowed to remain peacefully in this role either. Again her life is disrupted by Walter's assertion of his will. Her dismal restoration to her husband's house as a domestic servant where she once was mistress underlines her degradation. When Fortune's wheel turns again and all is resolved, restoration of order is expressed by Grisilde's restoration to the position of mistress of her husband's house, resumption of residence in the chamber. Then she is led from the chamber into the great hall to be publicly acknowledged as secure in her rightful place once more. The reader cannot be as sanguine as Grisilde, however. The unnaturalness of Grisilde's life, forced from role to role in response to the whims of another, is the opposite of the steady and dignified progression that is the ideal for the virtuous woman. Order is restored because Grisilde is within the walls of a house again, acknowledged as its mistress. Though literary convention allows Grisilde's story to end happily, such violation as she has experienced, violation of all that a house means to a woman, means that her domestic security can easily be erased by yet another shift in Walter's mood.

The violation of Lucrece's right to a protective enclosure does not end even with the limited success of Grisilde's. Like that of the "Man of Law's Tale" and the "Clerk's Tale," the "woman-endangered" plot of the "Legend of Lucrece" rests upon men's failure in their duty to protect women. Understanding medieval expectations of the behavior of men and women with respect to the protective value of enclosure adds a further dimension to the predictably pathetic story of Lucrece. In this *legenda*, or saint's life, the honor of the true wife is conveyed by a combination of behavioral and architectural details. Colatyn's dereliction of his responsibility to defend his wife's chastity stands out in higher relief when the story is analyzed in terms of the spatial movements of the characters and the identification of the architectural structure with the male duty of protecting women.

Lucrece's situation is a typical one often described in the courtesy books:

the woman whose husband is absent. Behavior for such a wife, especially if her husband is away at war, is described in great detail. She is to behave as if widowed, to pray for her husband's safety, to dress simply, to look sad, and to lead a retired life.[58] Clear expectations, then, govern correct wifely behavior when a husband is away at war, and Lucrece adheres to them to the letter. However, "unfortunately for Lucrece, it is her perfect embodiment of 'wifhod' that causes her husband to boast and take Tarquinius to spy on her."[59] Lucrece's violation and death, ironically, result from her being too perfect a wife.

The action begins with a typical male-female role division: men at war, in undifferentiated outside space; women at home, in their protected inner space, waiting for the men's return. However, even wars involve down time. The siege lay "ful long . . . and lytel wroughten," the men languish, "half idel," accomplishing nothing. Bored, "Tarquinius the yonge / Gan for to jape, for he was lyght of tonge" (F., 1696–1699). The "jape," the game, is a contest: praising wives. In their desire to relieve boredom, the men are concerned only with their own amusement: "Lat us ese oure herte," says Tarquinius (F., 1704). For Colatyn to involve himself in this foolishness shows a deficiency in his sense of the seriousness of wifely chastity. It is not only women who get into trouble because of impulsive speech: Tarquinius is "lyght of tonge" (F., 1699), and Colatyn responds impetuously (he "up sterte" [F., 1705]) to short-circuit the game by offering proof.

As we read the account of Colatyn's entering his own house with Tarquinius to spy on Lucrece, we must bear in mind the house's protective function. Walls imprison a woman, preventing voluntary loss of chastity, but they also protect her from involuntary violation. Especially in wartime, when bored soldiers seek sexual relief against a woman's will, a man should be guarding his wife from such men, not exposing her to them. Colatyn is naive in his assumption that Tarquinius will respect his husbandly rights to Lucrece. Colatyn forgets that "the rule of the imagination is this: enclosing walls . . . connote not only strength and protection but also interdiction."[60] Colatyn introduces into his wife's private space just such a man as walls are built to exclude. His act violates his role as protector and renders Lucrece open to violation in her husband's house just as if she were in unprotected space.

Given the vulgar analogy between a house and a woman's body, Colatyn's entrance into his house with Tarquinius foreshadows the rape. Colatyn is master of the house and of its lady, and therefore has a right to enter "prively into the hous" (F., 1716), not only the structure but the body of his wife. But such stealthy entrance is dishonorable. Even assuming (given medieval notions of authority) that a husband has a right to spy on his wife, violating her privacy, it is a right that a truly loving husband would not choose to exercise. When Colatyn leads a potential rapist through an unsecured access route, where "porter nas there non" (F., 1717), he renders permeable, therefore meaningless, the architectural barriers protecting his wife's chastity. As master of the house of course he "knew the estris," or layout, the arrangement of the interior rooms, and therefore the way to Lucrece's "chambre-dore" (F., 1718). According to the description, the house's layout must be of sufficient complexity to require a knowledgeable guide. Therefore, Lucrece's chamber must be situated in the most intimate part of the house, the labyrinthine arrangement yet another means of protecting her chastity. Thinking in his soldierly braggadocio only of winning a foolish bet, Colatyn leads the way, serving both as pandar and coviolator.

What they find is a wife who is behaving exactly as she should be. One of Chaucer's sources, Boccaccio's *De claris mulieribus,* stresses the appropriateness of Lucrece's behavior. A group of men check up on their wives and find "the royal women enjoying themselves with their equals"[61]—that is, violating the rules of quasi-widowhood. But Lucrece, in the same situation, is as she should be: "weaving with her ladies and dressed without any ornaments. For this reason, everyone agreed that she seemed more praiseworthy than the others."[62] Chaucer picks up these details of appropriate wifely behavior and expands on them. Secluded in the innermost recesses of the house, she uses her chamber in typical medieval fashion, as a *gynaeceum.*[63] Surrounded by her ladies, who provide companionship and chaperonage, she is not expecting guests, as is shown by the fact that she is in casual attire. She keeps herself busy with a characteristically feminine activity: she "wroughte . . . softe wolle," thus avoiding "slouthe and idelnesse" (F., 1721–1722). Since sloth, a deadly sin, leaves a vacuum for other sins to enter, it must be assiduously avoided; for women, all sins exist on the slippery slope to unchastity. Mindful of the danger, Lucrece keeps not only herself but also her serving women busy, to avoid cultivating an atmosphere of sin in her household.

Her concerns are, properly, all for her absent husband. She inquires for his safety, prays for him, longs for the end of the siege. Crying, eyes downcast, she is the very emblem of the grieving wife: "Hyre contenaunce is to hire herte dygne, / For they acorde bothe in dede and sygne" (F., 1738–1739). When her husband suddenly enters, her welcoming behavior is too spontaneous to be anything but genuine: "She anon up ros with blysful chere / And kiste hym, as of wives is the wone" (F., 1743–1744). This last phrase, "as of wives is the wone," has a dual signification. On the one hand, it sums up the main point of the passage: Lucrece's appropriate behavior, both in the absence of her husband and on his return, makes her a model of wifely virtue. On the other hand, disloyalty of women in her situation is a staple of misogynistic lore. Given that Lucrece has done good and avoided evil in Colatyn's absence, she should be rewarded. This renders doubly ironic Colatyn's first words to her: "Drede the nat, for I am here!" (F., 1742). With her husband home, she should be safe;

but as events prove, he has rendered her more vulnerable than she was in his absence.

Perversely, Lucrece's domestic virtue arouses not admiration but lust in Tarquinius and impels him to destroy this perfect wife's perfect chastity. The description of the rape reprises the spatial motions of Colatyn and Tarquinius. Now Tarquinius, alone, penetrates the increasingly private spaces of Colatyn's house, through a "prive halke" (F., 1780), into Lucrece's chamber, into her bed (F., 1787), and finally into the most private recesses of her body. He performs this final act "maugre hyre" (F., 1772), in spite of her wishes, which, as we will see in the "Wife of Bath's Tale," is a key phrase embodying not only Chaucer's understanding of the mentality of a rapist but the definition of rape in law and theology. It is significant that, at the moment of violation, Lucrece lay "in a swogh"; she "feleth no thyng, neyther foul ne fair" (F., 1816, 1818). The heroine's swoon precludes consent to or pleasure in the rape. Anachronistically applying Christian casuistry to his pagan heroine, Chaucer exonerates her from guilt because unconsciousness precludes consent, the key element in medieval legal definitions of *raptus*.[64] This heightens the pathos of her self-blame and self-punishment.

No matter what they suffer due to masculine depravity, heroines in *The Legend of Good Women* "never get angry. . . . They are sad but not frenzied or vindictive, and at worst they weep and swoon."[65] A good woman, never does Lucrece blame Colatyn for introducing a serpent into the bosom of their household. She scarcely even blames Tarquinius, who, as the narrator apostrophizes, should obviously have acted more nobly, as "by lynage and by ryght" he is "a verray knight" (F., 1820–1821). Her public announcement ("in halle" [F., 1832]) of what has happened to her underlines the "trewe" quality of her character: it is not for her to conceal this act, as a devious woman might. It is likewise appropriate that she dies at home; a good woman is properly "immured in her home."[66] It is even appropriate that she die by the sword. According to the ancient Greek and Roman sources from which Chaucer and other medieval writers drew their material, use of "weapons that cut and tear, those that draw blood" is appropriate to a raped woman.[67] Ironically, her use of a male weapon tacitly acknowledges that she, avenging her rape, has in effect become her own husband. Chaste wife to the end, as she falls dead she catches her clothes, "Lest that hir fet or suche thyng lay bare / So wel she loved clennesse and eke trouthe" (F., 1859–1860). Unlike her husband and her rapist, she lives (and dies) according to the rules of her estate. Thus the death of the perfect *ensample* of wifely "trothe."

As Robert Worth Frank points out in *Chaucer and the Legend of Good Women*, a prime characteristic of the "good" women is a passive helplessness "set off against a threatening violence, malevolent and overwhelming."[68] If in the *Legend* helplessness is a female trait, violence is male. And it is the duty of a husband, in return for his wife's fidelity, to serve as a wall between her and the violence of all other men. Lucrece, then, is more helpless because her male protector has failed her. Walls mean nothing if one's own husband opens the door to the rapist. Colatyn's culpability, then, is an underlying theme set off against the virtue of Lucrece, and one of which Chaucer is well aware. Throughout the *Legend*, men are at best weaklings, at worst curs, failures in what was seen in Chaucer's day as a prime male duty: protecting women.

Architectural space, then, serves in medieval literature as metaphor for the integrity of the female body. In his observations of the block play of children, psychologist Erik Erikson noted a predilection on the part of little girls to construct and furnish interior spaces, which Erikson saw as reflecting the imaginative appeal to them of safe domestic havens. Boys, on the other hand, built what Erikson saw as more exciting structures— "buildings, towers, or streets." For our purposes, the issue is not the validity of Erikson's experiments nor his Freudian-influenced interpretations, but rather that this noted twentieth-century psychologist sees the relation of men and women to architectural structures much as medieval people did. To Erikson, " 'open' and 'closed' are feminine modalities."[69] So it is in medieval literature. The woman who "opens," violates enclosure, is unchaste. The chaste woman is "closed," maintains enclosure. But the act of being locked away has no moral value unless freely chosen; thus Januarie's locking May away does not make her a good woman (nor him a good man). The woman who is involuntarily placed in an "open" modality when she would choose to be "closed" is a victim of the negligence, ineptitude, or cruelty of a male protector, which permits an unnatural vacuum to develop in the system of protection rightfully surrounding her. In medieval life and literature it is assumed that the enclosed female has the right to expect that a wall will be built around her, provided by a male protector both physically and morally strong enough to make that wall an effective barrier.

An important element of the enclosure is that it is envisioned as being provided by a man for a woman; her role is neither to provide nor to maintain, but properly to use. These respective gender roles also apply to women's clothing. Men provide, women use. Whether clothing is used properly or improperly is another measure of a woman's character.

❧ 8 ❧

"Superfluitee of clothynge": Women and Sartorial Excess

So when the woman saw that the tree was good for food, and that it was a delight to the eyes, and that the tree was to be desired to make one wise, she took of its fruit and ate; and she also gave some to her husband, and he ate. Then the eyes of both were opened, and they knew that they were naked; and they sewed fig leaves together and made themselves aprons.

—Genesis 3:7

And why are you anxious about clothing? Consider the lilies of the field, how they grow; they neither toil nor spin; yet I tell you, even Solomon in all his glory was not arrayed like one of these.

—Matthew 6:28

Clothing, says a medieval preacher, is a result of sin. When Adam and Eve were innocent, they were naked. Their first garments, simple and natural, were made of the skins of beasts. But as time passed and humans degenerated to the corruption the preacher saw in his own age, lax morals were reflected in ever-increasing elaboration of clothing. Use of wool, then linen, then silk, each marked new stages of spiritual decay. Now, far from merely covering the body to hide its shame, clothing reveals deadly sins: pride and lust.[1] The preacher was not seeking to trace the world's moral history through Ages of Fabric. Rather he was elaborating on a homiletic commonplace: clothing as moral indicator.

For medieval Christians, the first and most important function of clothing was to hide the sinful body's shame. Lest lust be avoided only at risk of pride, the Christian ideal was simple clothing. The motif of a change of clothing from elaborate to simple was a common feature of the lives of high-born saints, of whom Francis of Assisi is the best known. But the human need to express both individuality and affiliation through clothing was perpetually at war with this high ideal. A woman's clothing, in addition to reflecting Christian humility and chastity, was expected accurately to signify her estate, not her individual personality. Because a wife's estate was derivative, her clothing was expected to reflect the estate of the dominant male in her life, being precisely attuned to his social status and, most importantly, his budget. Thus fashion would reflect the proper hierarchical relationship between the sexes, with men in control of the identity a woman presents to the world through her clothing. Imagery of women's clothing in medieval literature functioned to assess adherence to, or deviation from, strong social controls on her choices in this mode of self-expression. Again, Chaucer's patient Grisilde represents the ideal woman.

It must not be thought, however, that excesses in dress were regarded in the Middle Ages as a peculiarly feminine foible. The man in the gray flannel suit was hundreds of years in the future; his medieval ancestor was a veritable popinjay, and so came in for his share of criticism.[2] Chaucer's Monk, with his fur-trimmed sleeves, was violating not only sumptuary propriety but also his vow of poverty. Chaucer's Parson preaches against the pride of those guilty of the "synne" of "superfluitee of clothynge . . . as wel of man as of womman" (X.I., 416–420).[3] Christian detachment competed with the medieval love of "ostentation and display." Theirs was "a society in which a man is judged by what he wears upon his back. He knows he must be dressed well in order to be loved, feared, served."[4] When Francis of Assisi rejected his father's estate and all its trappings, he signaled his commitment to Lady Poverty by stripping naked before his father in the public square.

A key factor in understanding medieval people's attitude toward clothing is their belief in the function of clothing as sign. Ideally, modes of dress were accurate signifiers of one's real position in a structured hierarchy. Wearing inaccurately signifying clothing was considered sinful deception, an act in which, according to a thirteenth-century didactic poem, "On the Follies of Fashion,"[5] the devil delights. Clothing choices either reflected and maintained order or defied and destroyed it. The Deity's sartorial preferences were assumed to be knowable: God wants dress suitable to social rank. Luxurious dress, then, was suitable only to those born to high estate, "with a sliding scale of diminishing privileges from the royal families downwards."[6] How all-pervasive was this belief is illustrated in an eschatological problem discussed in Colleen McDannell and Bernhard Lang's *Heaven: A History*. The problem was this: what do the saved wear? Free from guilt and shame, like a prelapsarian Adam and Eve, they could well be naked. But this was not a congenial thought. So "medieval Christians . . . assumed that when the citizens of heaven enjoyed elaborate banquets they wore rich robes," just as nobility did on earth. "The higher the heavenly rank . . . the costlier and better the clothes."[7]

On the imperfect earth during the course of the fourteenth century, a major economic development was taking place, one that would not merely affect medieval clothing customs but alter the shape of society ever after. A redistribution of wealth was taking place, transferring economic power from the land-rich but cash-poor feudal nobility to the newly cash-rich groups, urban professionals like Chaucer's Physician and Man of Law, and craftspeople and tradespeople like his Guildsmen and Wife of Bath. This group was increasing in number and purchasing power to the point where they were able conspicuously to consume their excess wealth. These nouveaux riches could now afford garments once worn only by their social superiors. A revolution was at hand: the hierarchy of wealth no longer paralleled the hierarchy of birth.

In the good old days, before the unprecedentedly rapid socioeconomic changes of the fourteenth century, fashion had developed very slowly. Not only was clothing expensive, it was the very symbol of conspicuous expenditure.[8] Because they were so costly, garments were intended for use by more than one generation and bequeathed as valuable property.[9] A daughter, then, might wear not merely a similar but the identical costume that her mother wore before her. Fashion did not distinguish the generations, but linked them. Such continuity of dress had a socially stabilizing effect. Costume reflected a society in which rank was heritable, as were its outward signs. By dressing according to their rank, people demonstrated respect for hierarchy. By passing clothing along, they demonstrated frugality. When people "began to discard their costumes before they were outworn, this represented a new level of consumption,"[10] unacceptable because unprecedented. Sumptuary excess led to the repeated passage of legislation restricting the cost, composition, style, and decoration of clothing that could be worn by people in various strata of society. The sumptuary laws attempted to enforce a proportionality between consumption and rank, shoring up the crumbling social order by discouraging sartorial leveling.

The story of the sumptuary laws is a story of the futile attempt to stop the outward signs of an inevitable process. As Frances Baldwin points out in a 1923 study, which is still definitive on the subject, the basic assumption from which sumptuary legislation proceeded was that "government had the right to check extravagances and restrain luxury for the public good."[11] The public good was assumed to require visible signs of allegiance to the principle of hierarchical order. So a parliamentary meeting of 1392 petitioned the king to rectify a typical situation of sumptuary disorder: "Divers people of divers conditions use divers apparel not pertaining to their estate."[12] The pattern of complaining seen here is repeated by many critics of this trend: the lower seeks to be higher, the higher, higher still. But in an age of social and economic mobility, "a knight on the way down might pass an enterprising peasant on his way up,"[13] and the two representatives of the estates might be indistinguishable. This was unacceptable. In all classes but the highest, expenditure on fashion was defined as extravagance. The king's duty was clear: a law was passed to end "the outragious and excessive apparel of divers people against their estate and degree."[14]

Such sumptuary laws as this one of 1392 regulated styles, ornamentation, and types and cost of fabric, all according to rank. Yeoman and handicraftsmen, for example, were not to wear brooches or chains, nor silk, nor cloth of gold or silver, nor were their wives to wear fur, veils, or kerchiefs of silk, especially imported silk, "but only of yarn thread made within the realm."[15] The law was clearly designed to force compliance with what had previously been an informal system whereby expenditure matched social status.[16] An attempt was also made to control supplies so that plenty of humble fabric at regulated prices would be available to the lower orders, giving them no excuse for buying better. At the official enactment of this statute, the king and queen appeared, dressed in expensive, colorful, fur-trimmed fabric as befit their estate,[17] which now could no longer legally be imitated by their inferiors. Alas, in 1463, the House of Commons presented the king with the same complaint.[18] The human proclivity to express personality and social ambition through clothing rendered all attempts at sumptuary control through law futile throughout the Middle Ages.

Not only the state but the church felt it had a legitimate interest in regulating dress. In scripture, elaborate clothing indicated lust and pride. The prophet Isaiah warned that Zion's sinful daughters must forsake lavish attire at the time of the Lord's judgment: they must abandon

the finery of the anklets, the headbands, and the crescents; the pendants, the bracelets, and the scarfs; the headdresses, the armlets, the sashes, the perfume boxes, and the amulets; the signet rings and nose rings; the festal robes, the mantles, the cloaks, and the handbags; the garments of gauze, the linen garments, the turbans, and the veils. (3:18)

Such attire suggests other sins; the wearers "are haughty, and walk with outstretched necks, glancing wantonly with their eyes" (3:16). Because gifts of clothing can symbolize elevation of status, the Lord's loving generosity to His people is compared to that of a husband adorning his bride:

I clothed you also with embroidered cloth and shod you with leather, I swathed you in fine linen and covered you with silk. And I decked you with ornaments, and put bracelets on your arms and a chain on your neck. And I put a ring on your nose, and earrings in your ears, and a beautiful crown upon your head. (Ezek. 16:10–12)

Despite, or perhaps because, of this, the bride "played the harlot" (16:15). Elaborate clothing, then, signifies pride or lust in both Old and New Testaments, while plain dress signifies virtue. In Proverbs seductiveness is a woman "dressed as a harlot" (7:10). To reflect Christian humility, St. Paul advises women to "adorn themselves modestly and sensibly in seemly apparel, not with braided hair or gold or pearls or costly attire but by good deeds" (1 Tim. 2:9–11; cf. 1 Peter 3:3–6). Christ Himself linked clothing less with lust or pride than with detachment regarding worldly possessions. But the early Christian theologians firmly connected fashionable clothing to the iniquity of women. Certain types of dress compromised a woman's chastity all by themselves: "The virgin, adorned, Cyprian warns, is no longer a virgin."[19]

So derelict were medieval Christians in the matter of fashion that homilists' "outraged squawks" provide a major source of information for fashion historians.[20] Emulating the fashions of one's betters shows dissatisfaction with one's own estate, a sin in itself.[21] God would punish such behavior.[22] The well-dressed woman, says a preacher, is also guilty of pride and idleness: "Wommen settyn all here stodye in pride of aray of here hed and of here body, to lokyn in myrrourys, in kemyng here heed, in here hornys, in peerlys, in other riche aray abowte the heed, in ryngys, in brochys, in hedys, in longe trayles."[23] But most serious was the threat to chastity.

Preachers waxed eloquent upon the connection between the beautiful and the damned. Anything that makes women more attractive jeopardizes their salvation, and men's. Like the hawthorne, which has "many beautiful blossoms in open view, yet underneath . . . carries very sharp thorns," so women, "dressed up and decked out to provoke lust,"[24] conceal spiritual danger beneath a pleasing appearance. Women's bodies are "weapons of the Devil" to begin with, the more so when "whitened and ornamented" with cosmetics and fashionable dress.[25] Every detail of a woman's garment is "a spark breathing out hell-fire. . . . The garland upon her head is a single coal or firebrand of Hell to kindle man with that fire; so too the horns of another, so the bare neck, so the brooch upon the breast, so with all the curious finery of the whole of their body."[26] The combined motifs of lust and pride are shown in the image of *Luxuria* as a woman in elegant drapery and elaborate headdress inspecting the effect of her ensemble in a mirror. (See Figure 5.)

Another fashion sin of women is preoccupation with appearances to the detriment of the spiritual life. Like the wives of Chaucer's Guildsmen or his Wife of Bath, women attend liturgical events more to show off finery than to worship God. Homilists hate this:

Because, just as the sacristan makes more adornment of the altar at the greater feasts when more people come to church . . . so does the sacristan of Hell, Pokerillus, with regard to these women, saying to them—"To-day is a great feast; many folk will see you. Adorn yourselves, therefore, that you may be reputed

Figure 5
Lust as a well-dressed woman. Yates Thomson ms. 3 f. 172 v. By permission of the British Library.

beautiful and that those who behold you may delight in your loveliness." Lo! then, the Devil's altar, which is more gladly seen than God's altar.[27]

Religious services are thus perverted, becoming an occasion of sin for these women and for their beholders.

Cosmetics, a major element of the elaborate process of transforming a woman's appearance (a process probably mysterious to the celibate male homilist), compounds the mischief. "Paints" are artificial, unnatural. The cosmetics user is "a painted sepulchre in which lies a foul corpse."[28] This homilist's attitude had then, and was to have, a long history. Tertullian said that "women sin against God who annoint their faces with creams, stain their cheeks with rouge, or lengthen their eyebrows with antimony."[29] Since it is inconceivable that a woman would paint for her husband, who presumably knows what she looks like without paint, the painted woman is automatically suspect of a continuum of evils: "For a woman who is covered in make-up draws a sword to kill her neighbor; bears a flame to burn a home; carries poison for anyone who wishes to take; she uncovers a pit so that an animal may fall into it."[30] Women's use of cosmetics was to stand for centuries as image of their duplicity and instability of character. One didactic poem cites women's use of cosmetics as evidence of their "dowbylnesse," of their lack of "trowth" and "stedfastnes"; women are "chaungeabyll naturally," and, though they "feyne frendlynes," they "worchen treson."[31] Such practices exposed men, who were apparently prone to evaluating women by appearances only, to "mistaken judgments and disappointments" in the choice of a wife.[32]

Not least of the problems involved with dress and cosmetics is the cost of all this. A wife was expected to present herself to the public in dress appropriate to her husband's social rank.[33] But envy and pride stimulate fashion rivalry among women, with "disastrous effects on the economy of their husbands."[34] Inflamed by sinful desire to outdo her gossips, a wife violates her duty to conserve her husband's goods. St. Bernadino of Siena, sometimes a moderate on marital issues, counsels husbands to exercise "moderation in wife-beating," but sartorial excess, he believes, justifies "beating a wife 'with feet and fists.' "[35] "Underdressing" a husband's estate would presumably be inappropriate too, but this does not find its way into either homiletics or literature; it was a rare sin, and a cheap one.

In sum, to medieval people, fashion decisions were inevitably moral decisions. Lust, greed, envy, pride, deception: all can be committed by means of a clothing choice. Because fashion choices loomed as important enough to affect the fate of the immortal soul, homilists were inspired to great detail in their fashion commentary; their habit of elaborate description influences imagery of fashion in medieval literature.[36] The import of fashion descriptions in literature is, in general, this: the more detailed and elaborate the, description of the garments, the more sinful the wearer; conversely, sartorial simplicity coexists with virtue.

No feature of medieval garb was so severely criticized as the headdress. Exposure of hair, especially long hair, was considered erotic. In the visual arts, "long hair tends to be equated with strong sexuality, short hair with moderation, and shorn hair with celibacy."[37] Hence the ritual tonsure for clerics, and, at the other extreme, the depiction of "Eve, the supreme temptress . . . with long hair."[38] Long-haired women represent lechery or prostitution in the carvings on medieval churches, the coils of their hair associated with serpents and thus the devil.[39] A medieval monk describes the harlot as not only having sensuous hair, which is bad enough, but, worse, decorating it and herself, for which depravities she will be punished: "She who was wont to part her beautiful hair with golden combs, who painted her brows and face, who bedecked her fingers with rings, has become a prey to worms, and the food for serpents; a serpent winds itself around her neck, and a viper crushes her breasts."[40]

Veils and headdresses were originally meant to cover the hair in Christian modesty. The Virgin Mary usually is depicted as veiled. However, the simple veil of the nun, the widow, and the laboring-class woman was elaborated by upper-class women, and those who imitated them, into the headdress, a fashion accessory that grew so lavish as to defeat the original purpose.[41] Impractical, the headdress marked its wearer as idle and frivolous. Expensive, it demonstrated un-Christlike attitudes toward money. In a sermon anecdote, "a knight takes from the poor in order to buy his wife a fancy head-dress; a large toad fastens itself upon her head . . . and kills her."[42] Thus die the ungodly. The single-pointed headdress, the hennin, its point draped with a veil, has found its way into popular depictions of medieval women. A common variation, the double-pointed, or horned, headdress came in for particular censure because of the verbal association with the horns of the cuckold. Reasoning from etymological similarity, it was clear to critics that a woman thus horned must be intending to horn her husband.[43]

"Horns" were often paired with "tails," trains, in homiletic diatribes, and both are associated with man's lower nature. "Tailed and horned dames . . . insult God's special creation by degrading themselves to the level of brute beasts," says a preacher.[44] Trains are evil too because of their wasteful use of fabric, " 'clothing' the earth with precious raiment and caring nothing for the nakedness of Christ in his poor folk." So, says a preacher, women wearing trains "ought to be very afraid lest a devil may be sitting at rest on their tails."[45] This image of a devil (albeit a little, harmless-looking one) riding on a train appears in a contemporary woodcut and is featured frequently in fashion criticisms.[46] The devils had plenty of riding space, because, in the matter of trains, more was better. Some trains were so long that they required the services of "pages or maids of honor" to carry them.[47] Requiring as they did a stately pace, plus attendants to carry them, trains could be a way of aping the manners of one's betters, as do the wives of Chaucer's Guildsmen, all dressed up in gowns with long trains "roialliche ybore" (I.A., 377). Train length could clearly cause confusion with regard to the social status of the wearer, so sumptuary laws attempted to regulate this particular excess,[48] described by one incensed preacher as a "great sign of the ruin of the world."[49]

However, like all other aspects of the sumptuary laws, the attempt to control train length failed. Fashion evolved during the Middle Ages in the direction of using more fabric per garment and wearing more layers of garments at once. Some of this was a practical measure, affording protection against chilly medieval houses; but more important was the status message conveyed by voluminous use of expensive cloth.[50] Like trains, sleeves became longer and longer. Going about swathed in enough cloth to render the wearer incapable of useful activity demonstrates leisure and affluence. In *Seeing through Clothes* Anne Hollander traces the history in the visual arts of the "symbolic connections between draped cloth and lofty concepts or between the idea of nobility and the wearing of loose, flowing clothes": wearing draped garments had always been considered an upper-class prerogative, "a necessary display of raw luxury." When garments came to be cut and sewn rather than draped, maximum drape was retained to suggest maximum dignity. However, excess drape worn by the wrong person was pretentious. In Hollander's understatement, "drapery has a limited role among the poor,"[51] who must move around freely to earn their bread by the sweat of their brow, and have no discretionary income to invest in excess fabric. The affluent bourgeoisie could, however, demonstrate their earning capacity and leisure by parading lots of cloth, thus reaching for the status associations of drapery.

As if capaciousness and luxuriance in the main garment were insufficient, expensive trim[52] and bright color served further to raise the cost of garments. Medieval people loved "decisive, unequivocal" colors.[53] But brightly colored clothing was considered suitable only for the upper classes, while peasants were expected contently to garb themselves in the dull grey or russet considered suitable to their humble rank.[54] Dye cost money, as did the use of embroidery. Both were, of course, very popular. So was expensive fabric and fur trim and embroidered belts, all the more a conspicuous expenditure for being so fleetingly displayed. A major development in fourteenth-century dress was the wide neckline, often enhanced by elegant fur trim. A style like this was clearly an incitement to lechery; one early fourteenth-century source graphically compares such a neckline to "the hole of a privy."[55]

An illustration supplied by Herbert Norris in *Costume and Fashion* depicts the homilist's worst nightmare in the person of a fashionably dressed noble lady, circa 1450–1460, whose costume represents the logical culmi-

nation of developments well under way in Chaucer's day. She wears a high
hennin covered by an even higher and elaborately structured veil, decoratively trimmed. Her dress is cut low, leaving "neck, shoulders and back
. . . bare." Expensive fabric ("silk, velvet and brocade") in sumptuous
quantity (full gathered skirt, "very long train . . . lying on the ground in
front as well as behind"), assertive color (green), lavish trim (ermine), and
expensive accessory ("a very rich waistbelt of goldsmith's work, made of
jointed plaques set with jewels") complete the fashion statement.[56] The
lady violates every homiletic injunction in one outfit, surely an achievement of sorts. A fifteenth-century tapestry in the collection of the Metropolitan Museum of Art in New York shows that not only were women
prone to such excess; so were men. (See Figure 6.) Both sexes enjoy the
lavish display of fabric, trim, and jewels; both wear elaborate headgear;
and, while the women's decolletage is relatively innocuous, the men wear
the short garments criticized for their scantiness by Chaucer's Parson.

In contrast to the seductive display of court clothing, the widow's garb
is the ultimate in modesty and self-effacement. The mid-fourteenth-century widow would wear a veil, simple in style, simple in fabric, on her
head, a wimple on her forehead, a barbe or stiff neck-covering on her neck
and chin. Thus only her face appears, with no hair or forehead showing.
An even more copious hooded garment would be worn at a funeral. Her
ordinary garments are less voluminous in fabric than were those worn by
women in other estates, and they are not gathered in front to suggest a
fashionably rounded belly. They are simple in style and cut, devoid of
decorative elements, and, of course, dark in color. Asexuality is the fashion
message,[57] complemented by the serious expression and prayerful pose of
the widow in Figure 7.

As the public forces of church and state marshalled their resources to
control women's clothing choices, so too did the informal controls provided by the conduct books. They reinforced the concept of fashion as
reflector of a proper level of expenditure, balanced with modesty and generosity in almsgiving. St. Louis, writing in the mid-thirteenth century for
his daughter, cautions her against having too many clothes and jewels; the
money should be given to the poor, the time to good works.[58] The Knight
of the Tower, writing for his daughters, discourages competitiveness in
dress as being disruptive of domestic peace; when one woman has a new
garment, others want it, and the result is that "ryote and noyse shalle all
day be at home."[59] The true purpose of fine clothing is, the Knight says,
to honor God and to be a credit to one's husband. Good clothing should
be worn on "hyghe festes and holy days," to honor God, not to impress
"men of estate." Do not, he tells his daughters, whine and complain for
"noueltees" or "newe raymentis," new clothes in new styles, but be content with the old. The Knight is typical of his peers in counseling moderation in dress: "Good is to holde the myddel estate."[60]

Figure 6
Elegantly dressed courtiers in elaborate headgear. A fifteenth-century
tapestry.

Figure 7
An unknown widow (c. 1340–1350). Anonymous English
sculptor. Reprinted from Margaret Scott, *A Visual History
of Costume: The Fourteenth and Fifteenth Centuries*
(London: Batsford, 1986), 32. By permission of B. T.
Batsford Ltd.

The concept of estate is, as usual, crucial; conduct books take the same position as the sumptuary laws in discouraging the aping of one's betters through lavish attire. The bourgeois Goodman of Paris urges his young wife to dress neatly and appropriately "according to the estate of your kinsfolk and mine." The good wife, of humbler station, tells her daughter the same thing: do not envy the "riche atyir" of your neighbor's wife; do not use fashion as a mode of social climbing—"With ryche robys and garlondys, and swiche þinge, / Ne countirfete no ladijs as þi lorde were a kyng." To do so is "mekyll pride" and causes your lord to lose his manhood.[61]

All of these assumptions about women and clothing provided a shorthand method of characterizing women in medieval literature, assessing their adherence to or deviation from accepted estate norms by means of clothing details. An example of this is William's dream in Langland's *Vision of William Concerning Piers the Plowman,* where imagery of women's clothing is used as a vehicle of social criticism as well as to explore the larger issue of the deceptive nature of appearances. The peasant laborers in the "feir feld ful of folk," the producers, "swonken ful harde," only to see "wasturs in glotonye distruen" the fruits of their labors. The wasters are the nobility, their extravagance and pride signified by their mode of dress.[62] Holy Church is a woman simply clad "in linnen,"[63] set in opposition to Lady Meed, "a wommon wonderliche clothed,"[64] who, according to E. Talbot Donaldson, represents "reward, recompense, the profit motive."[65] She must also be sensual, prideful, wasteful, slothful, as she is clad in styles deplored by preachers and conduct book writers as evidencing lavish expenditures on the self rather than charity to the poor: an elegant fur-trimmed gown, "the ricchest vppon eorthe," and a "coroune" better than the king's.[66] Since she is not even the king's wife, much less the king, she is in clear violation of the sumptuary laws in aping court style with her expensive fur trim, her jewelry, the fine fabric and bright red and gold of her clothing. Since such lavish dress is usually a sign of alliance with a powerful man, William naturally wonders "what is this wommon . . . thus wonderliche a-tyret."[67] If she is not dressed to reflect her husband's estate, if she is indeed an unmarried woman, her attire, so sensually appealing, marks her off as sexually promiscuous. But Langland's main point in the fashion images is economic: Lady Meed's clothing is a sign of the profligacy of her social class.

In *The Romance of the Rose,* clothing imagery is used for purposes including, but more complex than, simple social satire. The usual misogynistic commonplaces are rehearsed, both from the viewpoint of Jaloux, the jealous husband, who discourages fashion foibles, and from that of the Duenna, the old bawd, who encourages them. The use of fashion imagery by these two characters is entirely conventional. Jaloux says that women's clothing arouses lust,[68] costs too much, makes women "vain and proud," is all outward show, to deceive men.[69] But the Duenna sees "dainty dress" as helping women to conceal Nature's omissions and emphasize Nature's gifts.[70] The Duenna advises a woman to behave in all the ways forbidden in the courtesy books and sermons. Never stay at home, she says, go to as many social and religious events as possible to attract men: "To church she should oft go, and visits pay, / Attend all weddings, all processions see, / View festivals, and plays, and carolings."[71] There, she should walk seductively, "sway her shoulders and her hips,"[72] lift the train, show the foot, display lavish trim and rich decoration on her clothes. "To show her precious, golden-gleaming locks,"[73] she should frequently turn her head. For maximum effect, then, she should break all rules of virtue. All this is standard boilerplate typical of misogynistic satire. The Pygmalion incident, however, is different. It explores, with considerable psychological sophistication, the relationship between clothing, sexuality, and power.

In love with his creation, Pygmalion clothes her with his own hands as a fine court lady, in lavish costumes made of the finest fabric, colored with the "freshest dyes," trimmed with "squirrel, ermine, fox, and other fur." Then he transforms her into a woman of more "modest countenance," wearing a "guimpe" and a "kerchief." Still another time he strips her naked, decorating her body "only with ornaments," scarves, earrings, hair brooches, necklaces, a belt with an alms-purse. Yet another time he dresses her as a bride, hair adorned with the flowers of virginity, and marries her.[74]

To understand medieval men's attitude toward women's clothing, the Pygmalion story has several important elements. First, Pygmalion creates his love exactly as he wants her. To a dominating man, a statue is in many ways a perfect woman, even more will-less than Grisilde. The clothing with which Pygmalion adorns the statue epitomizes his total control over her. He ornaments her, and strips her, as he desires. Given that virtuous medieval wives were not supposed to be seen naked even by their husbands, the image of the bejeweled nude is strikingly erotic. But the lust aroused by a woman's clothing, against which preachers repeatedly cautioned, is in the Pygmalion story controlled by the man. The statue incarnates many erotic images: elegant lady, modest wife, whore, virgin bride. But the transformations wrought through manipulation of clothing, which so confuse men as to the underlying character of women, are wrought by Pygmalion. Because she is incapable of independent thought, she cannot deceive him. She cannot use the clothing, which represents his largesse, to wander the streets to be beheld of other men. She is the ideal woman with respect to clothing: a blank slate upon which Pygmalion can write his own lewd tale.

In the Pygmalion story, the masculine power to control a woman's clothing choices has as its corollary the desirability of having a women malleable enough to submit to such control. Assertive clothing choice is, conversely, an unruly behavior, akin to other forms of the fight for the breeches like rebellious speech behaviors. A situation in which clothing is associated with female power is found in Boccaccio's *Corbaccio,* a diatribe spoken by a ghost to his widow's new lover. As Anthony K. Cassell's careful notes to his translation prove conclusively, it summarizes antifeminist lore on the "thousand foul passions"[75] of women. Through attractive clothing and cosmetics women "set traps for men's liberty," presenting themselves in many guises until they achieve their goal, marriage. Having done that, they use the fine clothing which husbands can buy for them as a way of achieving power over the husbands:

Thinking they have climbed to a high station, though they know they were born to be servants, they at once take hope and whet their appetite for mastery; and while pretending to be meek, humble and obedient, they beg from their wretched husbands the crowns, girdles, cloths of gold, ermines, the wealth of clothes, and the various other ornaments in which they are seen resplendent every day; the husband does not perceive that all these are weapons to combat his mastery and vanquish it. The women, no longer servants but suddenly equals . . . contrive with all their might to seize control.[76]

Clothing choices are part of a larger pattern of controlling behavior. The wife also wants to take over the collection and disbursement of household finances and the selection of food for the household.[77] Clearly, this is a woman who wants what the Wife of Bath calls "governaunce" or "maistrye." But to her husband, this is a violation of divine order. Man, not woman, is "made in the image and semblance of God, a perfect creature, born to govern and not to be governed."[78] The first step in governing her is controlling her dress, and the speaker's failure to do this, it is inferred, contributes to his untimely death.[79]

Like his contemporaries, Chaucer uses imagery of clothing to characterize his pilgrims, both male and female.[80] Clothing precisely signifies the character's adherence to or deviation from estate norms. The Knight's tunic, stained by rust from his coat of mail, shows that he has "late ycome from his viage" (I.A., 77); the Squire's floral embroidery marks him off as a typical courtly lover (I.A., 89–90); the Yeoman is clad in correct trade garb, "cote and hood of grene" (I.A., 103). Deviation from type occurs, in both clergy and laity, in the direction of excess. The Monk's sleeves, trimmed with finest squirrel fur; his gold pin; his supple boots—all are unsuitable for a humble man of the cloth. Scholars are "thredbare" (I.A., 260, 290), but corrupt churchmen dress well. The nouveaux riches, the Franklin, the Physician, and the Guildsmen, show prosperity in their rich and colorful clothing (I.A., 378, 439–440). The women, the Guildsmen's wives with their long trains, the Wife of Bath, and the Prioress, are guilty of the same excesses, but no more than the men. These clothing details show that Chaucer closely observed clothing customs.

In the "Parson's Tale," Chaucer shows himself aware also of homilists' commonplaces on fashion (X.I., 415–440), although, characteristically, he refuses to assign guilt to women only. The Parson sounds the recurrent themes: economic waste and inducement to lechery. "Superfluitee of clothynge" makes it "deere, to harm of the peple." The Parson criticizes the immoral features of medieval clothing such as embroidery, ornamental holes, fur trim, "daggynge of sheres" or slit clothing, and, of course, trains, "trailynge in the dong and in the mire" cloth that should by rights be given to the poor. Excessive use of fabric is one extreme; the other is "the horrible disordinat scantnesse of clothyng," even in men's fashions, which featured jackets too short in front to "covere . . . the shameful membres of man," too short in back to conceal "the hyndre part of hir buttokes." Women, too, are guilty of violations of modesty: "Now, as of the outrageous array of wommen, God woot that through the visages of sommme of hem seme ful chaast and debonaire, yet notifie they in hire array of atyr likerousnesse and pride." The fictional Parson, like his peers in the pulpit, sees clothing as a signifier, its function to "notifie" onlookers as to the true character of the wearer. Extremes of "superfluitee" or "disordinat scantnesse" convey a sinful message. But, in addition to the typical association of lavish clothing with lust and pride, Chaucer also understands women's clothing as an expression of individuality and a symbol of the balance of power in marriage.

A minor component of Chaucer's characterization of the Wife of Bath concerns clothing; it is minor, because, as we will see, the Wife has other, more important, ways to assert herself. As a clothing consumer, the Wife is a stock character. She knows that rule-makers hate lavish dress in women, because it encourages "wandering"; she knows that homilists preach abstemiousness in dress as a counterbalance to the lusts of the flesh. She has obviously heard many a sermon on the topic:

> Thou seyst also, that if we make us gay
> With clothyng, and with precious array,
> That it is peril of oure chastitee;
> And yet—with sorwe!—thou most enforce thee,
> And seye thise wordes in the Apostles name:
> "In habit maad with chastitee and shame
> Ye wommen shul apparaille yow," quod he,
> "And noght in tressed heer and gay perree,
> As perles, ne with gold, ne clothes riche."
> After thy text, ne after thy rubriche,
> I wol nat wirche as muchel as a gnat.
>   (III.D., 337–347)

She knows all this, and does the opposite. She goes to church to show off her clothes. She accuses her husbands of miserliness, which results in her being less well dressed than befits her estate and their, less well dressed than her gossips: "Why is my neighebores wyf so gay? / She is honoured overal ther she gooth; / I sitte at hoom; I have no thrifty clooth" (III.D., 236–238). A deplorable state for a cloth-maker, this. Now, widowed, on pilgrimage to Canterbury, she expresses her expansive personality in her flashy clothes: ten pounds of finely textured coverchiefs, "hosen . . . of fyne scarlet reed," "shoes ful moyste and newe," a large wimple, a big hat, a capacious "foot-mantel" or overskirt (I.A., 456–457), in all, "a flamboyant and provocative rig."[81] All this amplitude of garb shows amplitude of wallet as well. The complete traveler in this outfit, she is nevertheless noteworthy for what she does *not* wear, that is, correct garb for a woman of her age, and a widow; that is, the costume worn by the widow in Figure 7. But her sartorial violations are, as we will see, the least of her deviations from the feminine ideal.

In contrast again to the Wife of Bath, Chaucer's patient Grisilde serves as perfect *exemplum* of desirable female behavior in the matter of clothing. In her important article on this subject, "Array in the *Clerk's Tale*," Kristine Gilmartin notes clothing's function in the tale as an indicator of "the social distance between the splendid Walter and the simple Grisilde."[82] Grisilde's garments function as precise indicators of the status of her relationship with her husband. When Walter decides to wed Grisilde, he assumes sartorial control. Because she is a peasant's daughter, she cannot be expected to own garb suitable to the wife of a marquis. So, before asking her to marry him, Walter prepares a wardrobe:

> this markys hath doon make
> Of gemmes, set in gold and in asure,
> Brooches and rynges, for Grisildis sake;
> And of hir clothyng took he the mesure
> By a mayde lyk to her stature,
> And eek of othere adornements alle
> That unto swich a weddyng sholde falle.
> (IV.E., 253–259)

Like the husband in Ezekiel 16 adorning his bride, so the Lord lavishes blessings on His people. In his generosity to his bride, Walter is like the Lord. On the other hand, in medieval society, the giving of largesse was a sign of power over the receiver. The giver of gifts can withhold or take away. Then, too, like everyone else in medieval society, Walter sees "rich array as a sign of high rank."[83] Walter's giving gifts of clothing to Grisilde reinforces the analogy between God and the husband and stresses Walter's higher rank and consequent power over his wife. Unlike the bride in Ezekiel, whose rich garments led her to harlotry, Grisilde's virtue stands out in higher relief in that these adornments do not alter the basic structure of her character. She accepts the clothing with submission and detachment and wears it only to fulfill her wifely duty to dress according to her husband's rank.

Grisilde's metamorphosis is indicated by the new garments:

> this mayde bright of hewe
> Fro foot to heed they clothed han al newe.
>
> Hir heris han they kembd, that lay untressed
> Ful rudely, and with hir fyngres smale
> A corone on hire heed they han ydressed,
> And sette hire ful of nowches grete and smale.
>   (IV.E., 377–382)

Her hair, untressed—that is, not elaborately arrayed—does not represent her new estate; it must be changed. Her simple attire, her lack of jewelry, must be remedied. There is no need, says the narrator, to "make a tale" of her "array" (IV.E., 383). Medieval people would have known the kind of attire appropriate to the consort of a marquis and seen the contrast between a woman thus clothed and a humble peasant's child. This is surely a translation (IV.E., 385).

Grisilde's new clothes signify the change in her social status because of, and totally contingent upon, her relationship with Walter. She has no hereditary right to them; elaborate clothing, gems set in gold, and brooches and rings are not the lot of a poor man's daughter. Grisilde understands the clothing to signify her acceptance of her husband's will;[84] his desire that they have "one will between them"[85] is fulfilled in her dramatic change of appearance, as she replaces her father's estate with her husband's. But even in her new clothes she can never be her husband's equal; she will always be a peasant. Thus she is depicted "more as a servant to the marquis than as a wife deserving status in the household," and she, sharing this concept of her self, "views herself more as a servant than as a wife . . . a lowly servant responding to a highborn lord."[86] Everything she has is a gift from Walter, even the children.[87]

A *topos* dear to medieval hearts was the contrast between nobility of birth and nobility of character. Grisilde's character expands to match the challenges of her new estate, and, because she is so virtuous, she does not succumb to the character failings typical of the nobility. As Grisilde carries out all the expected duties of a woman in high position, she measures up. Busy and virtuous in her new role as helpmeet, she does not concern herself with clothing; this is an important indication that Grisilde does not become an idle rich woman obsessed with her appearance. So, when Walter rejects her, Grisilde is humbly grateful for the temporary use of trappings that she knows were never her birthright. Unlike the materialistic ladies criticized in the sermons and satires, like the ideal Christian of the Sermon on the Mount, she is detached from house, jewels, clothing. She is ready to leave them all behind and resume her former estate and the clothes that signify it.

Grisilde's old clothes have their own symbolic function as an indicator of status inferiority. When Grisilde is conveyed from her father's house to Walter's:

> And for that no thyng of hir olde geere
> She sholde brynge into his hous, he bad
> That wommen sholde dispoillen hire right theere;
> Of which thise ladyes were nat right glad
> To handle hir clothes, whereinne she was clad.
>
> (IV.E., 372–376)

So contemptible is her "olde geere" that, when Walter orders it removed, the ladies who undress her are loath to touch it. Equally contemptible was the estate her clothing signified. So Grisilde must abandon any vestiges of her identity as daughter in her father's house when she comes to her husband's house, even though, paradoxically, that life was so admirable that it made him desire her as a wife. The loss of identity is hard to remedy. When it is time for Grisilde to resume the garments of her old self, it is "hard now for to fynde" (IV.E., 851). Hard, but not impossible, since cloth was so valuable that even "olde geere" was put to use.

Being detached from worldly possessions as a good Christian should be, she is prepared to resume her old garb and return all her rich clothing to Walter. She no longer holds the social status that it signifies, the "translation" is over, so she leaves behind the fine clothes and jewels so beloved by women.

> My lord, ye woot that in my fadres place
> Ye dide me streepe out of my povre weede,
> And richely me cladden, of youre grace.
> To you broghte I noght elles, out of drede,
> But feith, and nakednesse, and maydenhede;
> And heere agayn your clothyng I restoore,
> And eek your weddyng ryng, for everemore.
>
> (IV.E., 862–868)

This scene, as illustrated in a 1395 manuscript of a play based on Philippe de Mézières's translation of the Grisilde story (see Figure 8). Grisilde is returning her elaborate dress to Walter, in the full public view signified by three onlookers; in this image, she remains in her simple "smok." But in her speech to Walter, Grisilde describes her "nakednesse." Since she brought no dowry from her father, and apparently received no dower rights from Walter, Grisilde seems to think that Walter will send her home with nothing, entirely naked. The image of a naked Grisilde has no erotic impact; it is not like Pygmalion undressing the statue. Rather it is an image of humiliation, taking away everything, even the minimal garment, the "smok." Grisilde's claim to a "smok" to cover her nakedness is based on the Germanic custom of *Morgengabe*, morning-gift, an irrevocable bequest "paid the day after the marriage in recognition of the bride's surrender of

Figure 8
Grisilde returning her clothes to Walter. From Philippe de
Mézière's *L'Estoire de Griseldis* (dated 1395). Bibliothèque
Nationale, fr. 2203, fol. 46 v. Courtesy Service
Photographique, Bibliothèque Nationale, Paris.

virginity and the groom's acquisition of sexual rights."[88] In other words,
she deserves the smock in return for her maidenhead.

What is this garment that Grisilde requests? It is glossed in *The Riverside Chaucer* as a "simple garment," a "shift, undergarment" (note to III.D.,
783). There is some ambiguity here. On the one hand, the term as used in
the "Wife of Bath's Prologue" indicates a basic garment without which one
would be entirely naked, which, remember, is unacceptable even in the
marriage bed, much less parading through the streets. On the other hand,
the term as used in the description of Alisoun in the "Miller's Tale" indi-

cates that it is a decorated but revealing outer garment (I.A., 3238). In the context of the "Clerk's Tale," it seems that the smock must be construed in the first sense, as being a humble garment, and also as close to nakedness as it was possible to be in medieval clothing. She only gains the use of such a garment by appealing to the custom of *Morgengabe* and to Walter's sense of shame that the "wombe in which youre children leye / Sholde biforn the peple, in my walkyng, / Be seyn al bare" (IV.E., 877–879).

Reduced from her former splendor to appearing in public in her smock, Grisilde is an emblem of humiliation: "Biforn the folk hirselven strepeth she, / And in hir smok, with heed and foot al bare, / Toward hir fadre hous forth is she fare" (IV.E., 894–896). She has lost the attendants who would undress a marquis' lady, lost the clothes and jewels and headdress and foot coverings symbolizing her husband's love. Naked she came out of her father's house, and naked she returns (IV.E., 871–872). Arriving at Janicula's cottage, he expresses sympathy and the meager protection he can offer by restoring to her "hir olde coote," made of rough cloth as befits a peasant and older by many days than it was at the time of her marriage (IV.E., 913–917). Could Chaucer be indicating by this detail that Janicula sensed his daughter's translation to be temporary, and so kept "hir olde coote" at the ready?

When Grisilde is recalled yet again to Walter's palace to prepare for the feigned wedding, she is dressed as a peasant. Annoying as ever, Walter offers to excuse her "badde and yvel biseye," bad and evil-looking attire (IV.E., 965). Even in her reduced status as a servant, Grisilde's "array" violates medieval custom. A lord's wealth and power is manifested in largesse, generosity, to his menials.[89] Grisilde's dress discredits Walter in the eyes of his people, who marvel at her "povre array" (IV.E., 1020); upper servants were usually better dressed than she is. Her clothing reflects discredit not on her but on Walter.

As would be expected, Grisilde's final restoration to wifehood is again described in images of clothing. Like the suffering Job, she is finally rewarded for constancy, having "established the complete suitability of rich array to the innate nobility of her character."[90] So she gets back the ladies who dress her, the gold cloth, the jeweled crown. Once again she is "strepen . . . out of . . . rude array" (IV.E., 1116). Once again, Walter reinforces his hierarchical superiority by controlling the dressing and undressing. Once again, changed attire must not change her. Rich attire is conferred by another; it belongs to that other; Grisilde's only real possessions are the qualities of mind and spirit which at least some of the medieval audience would have found admirable.

For medieval people, clothing, ideally, is a true signifier of one's place in a divinely ordered hierarchy. For medieval women, estate is predicated upon family relationships. The message a woman sends to the world through her clothing is supposed to be about her father's or her husband's estate. Be she peasant or marquise, a woman is a contingent being, dependent on male approval, which is granted or withheld with as much comprehensibility as the turning of Fortune's wheel. The ideal woman, like Pygmalion's statue and patient Grisilde, is will-less. She will thus have no clothes that have become genuinely her own by virtue of her choice of them; her husband will have to provide her clothing, and in so doing he will create her in his own image. This indicates his superior status and power. Instead of being subject to what men perceived as the mutability of woman, a man who clothes his wife is in control.

On the other hand, a woman's drive for economic power and psychological self-expression can be exhibited in rebellious clothing behavior. She can disgrace her husband, overdress his estate, grow lustful and prideful, ruin the family finances. Control of clothing choices is about control of money and, ultimately, control of the wearer's sense of self. The woman who selects her own clothes and pays her husband's money for them, but disregards his preferences, is making a statement about power and individuality. Her behavior places her husband at a disadvantage and arouses fear of "woman on top," out of control. Misogynistic diatribes against women's clothing were attempts to bring the unruly sartorial behavior of a subordinate being under control, thus preserving the domestic hierarchy.

Because so few medieval women preserved their thoughts in writing, little information exists on how medieval women in secular estate thought of their own relation to clothing. A sixteenth-century writer, Louise Labé, provides an insight into women's use of clothing as self-expression, a trait for which they were criticized in medieval sources. Labé shifts perspective on the issue by posing an analogy between clothing acquisition and education: "And if any woman becomes so proficient as to write down her thoughts, let her do so and not despise the honor but rather flaunt it instead of fine clothes, necklaces, and rings. For these may be considered ours only by use, whereas the honor of being educated is ours entirely."[91]

Labé's insight clarifies the role of clothing and individuality suggested in the medieval sources. Labé wants women to acquire learning, not clothing, that they might cultivate a higher art form—writing. Like a medieval homilist castigating vain women for gazing in mirrors all day, Labé assumes that the purchase and exhibition of clothing are activities so time-consuming as to divert women from worthier goals. But for this sixteenth-century woman, the choice is not a moral one; rather it is a matter of self-actualization. A well-dressed woman has devoted herself to an endeavor that is ultimately futile. According to the legal concept of *usufruct*, to which Labé alludes in her term "use," goods acquired during a marriage were retained in the patrilineal family. Thus a woman's "fine clothes, necklaces and rings" belong in law not to her but to the man who pays for them. Therefore, though women think they are seizing power and expressing individuality through dress, Labé knows that only qualities of mind and spirit are truly "ours entirely."

❧ 9 ❧

"Wel at ese": Widowhood

Let a widow be enrolled if she is not less than sixty years of age, having been the wife of one husband. She must be well attested for her good deeds, as one who has brought up her children, shown hospitality, and washed the feet of the saints, relieved the afflicted, and devoted herself to doing good in every way. But refuse to enroll younger widows; for when they grow wanton against Christ they desire to marry, and so they incur condemnation for having violated their first pledge.
—2 Timothy 5:9–12

I am myn owene womman, wel at ese.
—*Troilus and Criseyde* (II., 750)

When the bachelor of the "Wife of Bath's Tale" seeks to learn what women most desire, one suggested answer is that women love to be widowed and wed. Here Chaucer shows his awareness of the desirability of the estate of widowhood in the Middle Ages. As Arlyn Diamond says, "widowhood must have seemed in some ways a highly attractive state for strong-minded women."[1] Eileen Power sees widowhood as enabling a medieval woman to be, in private life at least, "on a par with men."[2] Such power could be wielded by a widow that it could truly be said that the "death of one partner was the legal liberation of another."[3] The Wife of Bath's privileged situation illustrates how sweet it was to be a widow in the Middle Ages, how preferable to the other two estates. As "clene maydenes," marriageable young girls, women were under their fathers' control, as "trewe wyves," their husbands'. But in widowhood, a woman indeed became what Criseyde called her "owene womman" (II., 750). Although the widow was urged to "conform to the traditional male ideal of the female,"[4] she was not obliged to do so; finally, she was "no longer forced to accept the authority of another."[5] Because of age disparity between husbands and wives, this estate did not necessarily come to a woman in old age, but often in her prime. If her husband had been affluent, she would also be economically comfortable, "wel at ese" like Criseyde (II., 750).

Coexisting with the economic and social phenomena that enhanced the estate of widowhood in the Middle Ages are other strands of less positive traditions concerning widows. One element, ultimately derived from scripture, is the depiction of widowhood as a pathetic state. Another element is the view of widowhood as a new opportunity to deny the flesh and rededicate one's life to God. Yet a third is the conflicting assumption of lecherousness in widows. During the fourteenth century, the experience of widowhood was being influenced by social, economic, and demographic changes in the direction of becoming a time of positive experience for women. Medieval attitudes about widows, as affected by all of these, form the backdrop for Chaucer's characterization of the recurrently widowed Wife of Bath, the young widow Criseyde, and the young wife and potential widow May in the "Merchant's Tale."

Usually grouped with orphans and sometimes strangers, the widow in the Old Testament is the personification of vulnerability. Treatment of this poor creature is a spiritual litmus test to distinguish the good man from the bad (e.g., Exod. 22:22–24). Job sees cruelty to widows as a sign of evil in the universe (22:9, 24:3); Ezekiel sees it as one of the greatest crimes of unfaithful Jerusalem (22:7). One of Yahweh's main roles, and that of his loyal followers, is to protect these helpless ones (Prov. 15:25). When a being so needy helps another in greater need, miracles result: a poor widow, possessing for food only a "handful of meal in a jar, and a little oil in a jug," shares her and her son's meager meal with the prophet Elijah. When she does so, jar and jug are wondrously replenished, saving both widow and orphan (1 Kings 17:10–16).

Besides vulnerability, the widow personifies grief and loss. Her function is to act as chief mourner (Job 27:15), to "raise the dirge" for her husband (Ps. 78:64), to act as a living memorial. Therefore she is a useful image of the sufferings of God's chosen people. Yahweh's sorrowing people in Lamentations 5 are widowed, degraded, losing their inheritance to aliens, their homes to barbarians. In Lamentations 1, Israel, she who "was a princess among the cities," has become "like a widow" (Lam. 1:1). Like women treated as spoils of war, Israel has become as a slave, an exile; her previous position as a respected wife is no more, and "all who honored her despise her" (1:8). But such loss is the human condition, not to be denied. The spiritual complacency of the "daughter of Babylon" is shown in her belief that she will never be a widow (Is. 47:8), never experience this commonplace catastrophe. On top of all her suffering, the widow is also impure: a Levitical priest cannot marry her; in this context she is even classified with harlots (Lev. 21:14; cf. Ezek. 44:22). She does not even achieve independence to offset her loss; the childless widow is returned to her father's house (Lev. 22:13).

In general, then, the portrayal of widows in the Old Testament is bleak. Especially if she is childless, the widow is a problem to be solved by re-marriage. In Genesis 38, Judah arranges two subsequent marriages for his childless daughter-in-law Tamar; finally, in a case of mistaken identity, he impregnates her himself. Upon the discovery of her pregnancy, he orders her to be burned, relenting only when his role is revealed. Impregnating the childless widow is a duty rather of her husband's brother. Onan, one of Tamar's brothers-in-law, wasted his seed not out of fondness for the solitary practice named in his honor, but "lest he should give offspring to his brother" (Gen. 38:9), and it is for this dereliction of brotherly duty that Yahweh slays him. The one positive thing about Old Testament wid-ows was that they could make vows not subject to annullment by a hus-band (Num. 30:7–10), a privilege suggesting some slight increase of auton-omy.

New Testament widows hardly fare better. Jesus, following Old Testa-ment rules for the good man, is kind to widows, as His followers must be (Acts 6:1; James 1:27). Jesus condemns scribes who hypocritically "devour widows' houses and for a pretense make long prayers" (Mark 12:40; cf. Luke 20:45–7). Several of Jesus's parables show His sympathy for widows. He praises the poor widow's small donation above that of the wealthy (Mark 12:41–44; Luke 21:1–4). Christ's parable of the unscrupulous judge and the importunate widow casts the widow in the role of the lowliest of mortals whose pestering prayers move the Almighty (Luke 18:1–8). In the miracle stories of the Gospel, widowhood becomes a plot element to ren-der situations more pathetic: one who is defined by loss has lost even more. Jesus raises the only son of the widow of Nain (Luke 7:11–17), and His disciple Peter raises Tabitha, a woman beloved by widows (Acts 9:36–42). Jesus's own death is rendered more poignant by the fact that He is a wid-ow's only son.

The main point of divergence between Old and New Testaments on widows becomes extremely important in the characterization of widows in medieval literature, that is, the issue of remarriage. Mainly because of the ascetic bias of St. Paul, an emphasis on perpetual widowhood emerges. Paul says that to marry is better than to burn (1 Cor. 7:9), but implies that to do neither is better still. If marriage is a sop to man's lower nature, having so yielded once, presumably in flaming youth, is moral compromise enough. While the lofty state of virginity cannot be regained, the widow has a new opportunity to reject her previous wallowing in bodily pleasures and devote herself to God.

Paul's enormously influential discussion of the subject is in effect the first behavior manual for widows in the Christian era and so sets the pat-tern. Paul is full of advice on how to treat a "real" widow, she who is "left all alone, has set her hope on God and continues in supplications and prayers night and day" (1 Tim. 5:3, 5–6). Apparently this ideal was often honored in the breach; hence Paul's distinction between the "real" widow and others who could not be "enrolled" officially and therefore could not be recipients of the charity of the Christian community at Ephesus. Unlike the Old Testament authors, who describe the behavior of widows in general terms (clad in mourning garments, they mainly weep), Paul is specific about what behavior during her married life qualifies a woman for virtuous widowhood as he defines it (see opening epigram to this chapter). Such a paragon of wifehood was rare, however; she was also exceedingly old by the standards of the time, sixty at least. Young widows should not be accepted into the company of enrolled widows because some cope with their loss all too well. Paul's negative attitudes toward women shape his interpretation of the behavior of the widows of Ephesus. Young widows, as Paul describes them, seem to be living a cheerful, leisurely life at Ephesus, visiting friends, involving themselves in community life, sharing opinions with groups of other women, and, in general, doing exactly as they please. To Paul, this makes them idle gadabouts and meddling gossips, lost to salvation. His desire to marry them off seems rooted less in concern for their souls than in discomfort with the ways of women living too easy a life free from male authority and domestic responsibility. Lest scandal ensue, it is best to keep them busy with a new husband, children, and home.

In addition to its relationship to Christian asceticism, the glorification of widowhood in early Christianity was also a consequence of Christ's inversion of earthly values as enunciated in the Sermon on the Mount (Matt. 5:6). Like the other lowly of the earth, widows shall be first in heaven. Encouraging widowhood as a permanent estate, however, did involve the risk that some widows might become first on earth. Demographers agree that, in general, the situation that prevails today, with women outliving men, has always prevailed. By the sheer weight of numbers, then, widows could become a significant element in any group. In the early Christian centuries, according to Peter Brown, "an 'order' of widows sprang up in all churches." These "helpless creatures" at first conformed to scriptural stereotype in being "only too glad to receive food and clothing from the hands of the clergy." But, as their numbers grew, widows became a powerful, controversial, group[6]—an institutional annoyance. According to historian Georges Duby, by the early Middle Ages popular acceptance of Paul's ideal of reconsecrated widowhood had taken second place to approval of Paul's fallback position, remarriage, due to a reluctance to have large numbers of women "without a man to watch over and correct them."[7]

Virtuous widowhood, however, continued to represent the ideal. St. Jerome's formulation sums up the principle involved: "The widowed state ranks as the second degree of chastity."[8] The theological principle is beau-

tifully expressed in the poetry of Hildegard of Bingen (1098–1179). Hildegard's central metaphor is the *Symphonia*, the heavenly orchestra, in which
each instrument plays in harmony with all the others. Widows have their
own special song,[9] different from (and inferior to) that of virgins, because,
through marriage, widows once freely chose Eve's specifically feminine
punishments, subjection to a husband and pain in childbirth:

>   we
> raced after her, embraced
> her exile, made her pain
> our own.

Now, in widowhood, they recommit themselves to Christ (whom they
neglected earlier for the sake of husband and children):

>   for you we left
> marriage, turned from fertility:
> we embrace you in charity
> like the people of heaven,
> O child of the virgin:
> When you wed us in the spirit
> you divorced us from our flesh.

Widowhood rejects the flesh and puts on the spirit. Unlike the virgins,
who have always so dedicated themselves, widows must undergo a last-
minute change of heart: "Now we race / after you with our final effort, /
delighting in penance." Penance is needed because marriage is inferior to
virginity. The widow's position in heaven is therefore permanently inferior
to that of the virgin, but, Hildegard implies, it is superior to that of the
remarried.[10] The principle here was stated less tactfully by St. Jerome in
Adversus Jovinianum: "For it is better to know one husband, although a
second and a third is permitted, than many: that is, it is more tolerable to
be prostituted to one man than to many."[11]
    Coexisting alongside this tradition of possible renewed dedication to cel-
ibacy in widowhood is a comparably strong tradition that asserts the sexual
voracity of widows. That such dichotomous attitudes existed in medieval
thought should be no surprise to those familiar with the Eva/Ave motif in
medieval art, which aligns women either with the worst or the best of their
sex.[12] Instead of walking the path of virtue, the widow misses sexual pleasure and is, therefore, vulnerable to seduction. Consider, for example, the
well-known and oft-repeated story of the Widow of Ephesus, from Pe-
tronius's *Satyricon:*

A certain Widow of Ephesus, not satisfied with the usual rites of mourning for
her husband, insisted on weeping over his body in its tomb until she should die

also. "There was but one opinion throughout the city, every class of person admitting that this was the one true and brilliant example of chastity and love." But nearby there was a soldier, guarding the bodies of some executed robbers. Seeing the light in the tomb and hearing the lady's groans, he went to investigate, and on understanding the situation, brought his supper into the tomb and tried to console her with the usual platitudes. At last she contented to share his supper, and after further persuasion "the conquering hero won her over entirely."[13]

This *exemplum* of feminine weakness was well known to Chaucer's audience. The stock character of the lusty widow was based on the notion that the delights of marriage were too wonderful to sacrifice.

Like most extremes, these two, of the totally virtuous or wildly lecherous widow, probably attracted fewer adherents than the middle path: widows who failed to measure up to the ideal in less theatrical fashion than she of Ephesus, widows who refused to conform dutifully to type. For these erring daughters of Eve, instruction was readily available in the form of didactic treatises. Ideally, all the virtues practiced by any woman are to be practiced the more fervently by a widow, since she "maintained her reputation by her modesty, her chastity, and by her acceptance of the authority of others."[14] But in reality, conduct book writers found continuing occasion to remind widows of their responsibilities to behave as exemplars of sorrow, to devote theselves to religious duties, to weep and to pray, to fast, and to give alms. Certain activities were clearly unsuitable to widows: "wandering" and its concomitant speech excesses, violations of clothing customs, and remarriage. The conduct books speak with one voice on these rules of behavior for women.

For the widow, use of speech must be confined to prayer, and prayer requires confinement at home or in church. According to the fourteenth-century *Book of Vices and Virtues,* the ideal widow should be like the scriptural Anna, constantly "at chirche in devocion and in teeres wepyng." When not in church, widows should be at home. Enclosure limits the habit of gossip and protects against sexual temptation. The widow, like Judith, must lead a retired life, "in hire chaumbre y-schut with hire maidenes."[15] Widows who are "idel & besy to go alday hider and þider & iangelode [chatter] & speke to moche" violate estate rules. Citing St. Paul on the matter, the author of *The Book of Vices and Virtues* reminds the reader that little has changed in the wicked ways of "thes ȝonge wommen widowes" since early Christian times.[16]

Appropriate garb was strict mourning. *The Book of Vices and Virtues* says that a widow's clothing must be "meke"; she must wear "no grete arraye ne riche robes ne queynte, as bi þe ensaumple of Iudith, þat lefte hire riche robes and noble atire whan hire lord was ded and toke cloþinge of widowhode, meke and symple, that was more tokenyng of wepyng and sorwe þan of ioye or of veyne glorie."[17] She must avoid cosmetics and false hair.[18] Such efforts to exude sex appeal, if successful, make a woman into a "wanton widow"; if unsuccessful, into an "old hag."[19]

Remarriage is a moral failing for a woman, but not for a man. Liturgical custom bears this out: the nuptial blessing was omitted in the case of a widow, but allowed in the case of a widower marrying a virgin.[20] Despite official disapproval, second marriages were tolerated to avoid the even greater scandal that might ensue from a widow's lasciviousness. Philip of Novarre considers remarriage appropriate only if a woman's parents recommend it. Similarly, the Knight of the Tower advises his daughters not to marry "for playsaunce ne for loue," but rather for family advantage and with family approval.[21] If a widow does choose to remarry, Barberino feels that she should do so no more than three times (a liberal number), and he regards the second-time wife as freer in her choice of a marriage partner than is a young virgin.[22]

By the fourteenth century, then, the ideal of celibate widowhood existed in tension with two other competing patterns of behavior. Remarriage of widows placed these potentially volatile creatures within a stable patriarchal structure and gave families new opportunities to form alliances. At the same time, developments in demographics, inheritance laws and customs, and economics were making permanent widowhood an attractive estate, for reasons unrelated to the spiritual ideal of renewed chastity.

Demographically, despite abysmal health conditions and the risks of childbirth, a married woman, like her modern counterpart, was likely to outlive her husband.[23] Historian Barbara A. Hanawalt reminds nonstatisticians that the low life expectancy figures cited in studies of medieval population patterns were caused mainly by high infant mortality rates. Therefore we should not think that "because life expectancy was about thirty-three years of age there were few old people."[24] Old people there were, but then as now there were more old women than old men. Demographers studying the Middle Ages agree that women were likely to outlive their husbands, even perhaps several husbands as did the Wife of Bath. While widowhood was an estate and the widow a stock literary figure, it is difficult for historians even to establish the existence of widowers, much less to trace their behavior, since the category "widower" is not an official one in public records.[25] Proper behavior for the widower was not described in didactic sources. A main reason for this is that the psychology of grief was perceived differently depending on whether the bereaved was male or female.

A literary example of contrasting norms for widows and widowers is in Chaucer's *Book of the Duchess*. The poem includes two grieving spouses: Alcyone, in the romance that the Dreamer reads; and the poem's central character, the Man in Black. As a wife, Alcyone is "the beste that mighte bere lyf" (64); therefore, when her husband is lost at sea, her behavior is ideal. She fasts, she swoons, she weeps; she is nearly mad with sorrow.

She prays to the goddess Juno for the only possible consolation, knowledge that he is truly dead. When Ceyx's spirit appears to her, it brings a message of consolation: "Let be your sorwful lyf" (202). But this advice shows the husband's good character post mortem; it is not meant to be taken literally, because Alcyone's following it would mark her as a bad widow. A good widow experiences a grief that is all-consuming and inconsolable, indeed fatal: Alcyone dies "within the thridde morwe" (214). The Man in Black, however, is "left with a grief he must not die of but survive."[26] His psychological healing is the point of the elegy. At first, his grief is so extreme that he loses all interest in life, indeed wishes himself dead. The Dreamer reminds him that those who "for sorwe mordred" themselves (724) are damned. Of his examples, four of five are women. Self-destruction for love, as in *The Legend of Good Women,* is a female behavior. The heroics of grief are for women only. Having mourned, a man must accept his loss, then, as the Man in Black does, "strake forth" (1312), return home, to normal life.

Normality was remarriage. Widowerhood was not an estate because men whose wives had died were likely to remarry, and promptly. In the aristocracy, a continual backup supply of heirs was needed. In the lower classes, the economic contribution of the wife was essential, especially if there were young children to be cared for; "an old peasant proverb noted that the household could survive without the husbandman but not without the good wife."[27] Widowerhood, then, was seen as very temporary. Also, no set of behavior rules developed for the widower mainly because men's estate was not predicated upon his relationship to a woman; there is no male analogue to the virgin/wife/widow formula.

Besides women's longevity and the prompt remarriage of widowers, another factor that may have contributed to the large supply of widows in the Middle Ages was the age discrepancy between the marriage partners. Historians debate the typical marriage age in the Middle Ages. David Herlihy traces a trend to later marriage ages for men, even "intergenerational marriages," from about the year 1200 on.[28] Other historians believe that there were variations in typical marriage ages depending on social class. The marriages of very young children permitted at the time by canon and civil law seem to have been characteristic of the highest strata of medieval society as a means of cementing political alliances. These prepubescent pairings were not characteristic of medieval society in general, however. Among the laboring classes, when people had to earn a stake in land or money, or wait for an inheritance, or learn a trade before marriage, marriages in the late twenties were common. The wife in such a household needed domestic skills which could only be acquired over time.[29] Barbara Hanawalt calls marriages among the medieval peasantry "partnerships"; an unskilled wife would be of little use in such a situation.[30] A young woman like the twelve-year-old Wife of Bath at her first marriage, or May in

Chaucer's "Merchant's Tale," is a luxury item, a form of conspicuous consumption. Chaucer, as we will see, treats marriage to such a woman as a piece of male foolishness, guaranteeing unhappiness for the husband and a merry widowhood for the wife.

Because of economic and legal changes during the course of the fourteenth century,[31] a widow's situation could be very good. Since Roman times, widowhood had conferred *sui juris* status, making a woman a legal person in her own right, and the concept influenced medieval law.[32] The economic status of the medieval widow was enhanced by the transition then in progress from a land-based to a money-based economy. Under feudalism, because land grants were made in return for military service, male heirs who could fulfill that service were preferable, women inherited only in default of the male line, and, if they did, they could find such an inheritance so burdensome as to compel remarriage.[33] But when no land or military obligations were involved, as in the case of increasingly affluent tradespeople, women could more easily operate on their own. A tradeswoman like the Wife of Bath could make money by operating as a *femme sole* in her husband's trade, a route often followed by medieval widows who trained in a trade by helping their husbands. Such widows enjoyed privileges (and responsibilities) comparable to those of men, some of which could be passed along to fortunate second husbands.[34] In general, English inheritance law favored the widow. She was likely to inherit at least a third of her husband's property by law and maybe more by custom.[35] She would regain control of her dowry, the goods she brought to the marriage. She would receive her dower, the goods settled on her for her widowhood by her husband at the public "chirche dore" ceremony. If she availed herself of the type of marriage contract newly devised in the late thirteenth century known as jointure, she could inherit all the property owned jointly by herself and her husband in his lifetime.[36] Doing this sequentially pyramided wealth.[37]

Undoubtedly some medieval men, like Januarie, disliked widows for the increased knowledge and assertiveness that came with all this power (says he, widows "konne so muchel craft . . . / That with hem sholde I nevere lyve in reste" [IV.E., 1423, 1425]). Warnings to men to avoid marrying widows, who, as a result of their period of independence, made too-feisty wives was to continue as a theme in misogynistic lore.[38] A prudent man might well prefer a young maid, who might be less her own person, maybe even, as Januarie supposes, as pliable as "warm wex" (IV.E., 1430). Seen from women's perspective, however, such comments mean that widows were stronger persons than were young virgins.

Indeed modern historians bear this out; they can hardly find enough positive things to say about medieval widowhood.[39] Widows often controlled money and property. Even peasant widows experienced "a variety of new options and new independence, both economically and emotion-

ally, that women could not achieve in any other phase of their life cycle."[40] So, as R. H. Hilton observes: "We must not picture the widow in
the late medieval village as a poor cottager or small holder on the edge of
the village community but as frequently the tenant of a full holding, living
an active life near the center of things."[41] One modern commentator calls
this "widow power," but cautions the modern reader that it varied consid-
erably from one social class to another: "Status with respect to men varied
roughly in inverse ratio to wealth and social standing."[42] A bourgeoise or
even a peasant could be more her "owene womman" than a knight's lady.

In general, then, the audience of a work of medieval literature would
have seen a widow not as pitiable but as powerful, even threatening.
Nevertheless, despite contradictions, the several themes involving widows
could be called up as the demands of characterization required. The image
of the widow could connote renewed dedication to chastity, or sexual in-
satiability; weakness, or strength; power, or vulnerability. So when Chaucer paints a scene like the one in which the newly widowed Wife of Bath
follows her fourth husband's corpse to burial, he has a mass of background
information at his disposal.

> Whan that my fourthe housbonde was on beere,
> I weep algate, and made sory cheere,
> As wyves mooten, for it is usage,
> And with my coverchief covered my visage,
> But for that I was purveyed of a make,
> I wepte but smal, and that I undertake.
>   To chirche was myn housbonde born a-morwe
> With neighebores, that for hym maden sorwe;
> And Jankyn, our clerk, was oon of tho.
> As help me God, whan that I saugh hym go
> After the beere, me thoughte he hadde a paire
> Of legges and of feet so clene and faire
> That al myn herte I yaf unto his hoold.
> He was, I trowe, twenty wynter oold,
> And I was fourty, if I shal seye sooth;
> But yet I hadde alwey a coltes tooth.
>
> (III.D., 587–602)

Alisoun knows the proper behavior: weep, look sad, cover the face in
heavy mourning. That is usage, custom. But she weeps only a little, because she is already provided with a new husband, one with good legs and
feet. She is a lecherous widow as Ovid described in his *Ars Amatoria*:
"Often a husband is sought for at a husband's funeral; it is becoming to
go with dishevelled hair, and to mourn without restraint."[43] Similarly
Matheolus: "I know that a woman who on the outside weeps over the
body of her husband rejoices and sings in the inside. She would not hesi-

tate to brag about her new husband even when she is wearing her black dress."[44] The indecorousness of the Wife's behavior is the more pronounced because of her advanced age. At forty, she is a dirty old lady by medieval standards.[45] For men, *senectute* was held to begin at forty, an age at which, according to Pope Innocent III, "generally man's energy to live is completely spent."[46] For women, old age was thought to begin even earlier. Surely by age forty a woman should be ready to "prepare . . . for a dignified, Ciceronian senescence,"[47] to "lapse into decorum, piety, and silence,"[48] all the more if she is a widow. Alisoun, ogling a twenty-year-old, is grotesque. The only way in which she does act the part of the dutiful widow is in her brief prayers for a husband's soul (III.D., 826–827, 501, 525). Her violation of all estate norms is obvious. More subtle, more decorous, but equally in violation, is Criseyde.

The Scots poet William Dunbar (born c. 1460) writes, in "The Twa Mariit Wemen and the Wedo," of a widow who is "weill . . . at ese," whose "mynd lauchis," who conceals under her traditional mourning garb a "courtly and ryght curyous . . . corse."[49] Here Dunbar might well be echoing the language of Chaucer's description of the widow Criseyde, who, like many medieval widows, is thoroughly comfortable, "wel at ese" in her new estate. While far more complex a creation, Chaucer's Criseyde, like Dunbar's "Wedo," exists against the background of estates rules for widows. Living the genteel life of a comfortable medieval widow, she is enjoying newfound freedom. Her concern for her reputation appears to differentiate her from the stock lecherous widow. But events will prove that in reality she, like Dunbar's lusty widow, has a right curious body ready for love. At the same time, Chaucer maintains audience sympathy by associating Criseyde with the idea of the widow as *persona miserabilis*. These conflicting elements of her character—violation of estates rules, on the one hand, yet the role of exigent circumstance on the other—exist in tension in Criseyde. Like a good confessor, Chaucer judges Criseyde's sin, but also considers how circumstance mitigates guilt.

As the story begins, Criseyde's external behavior conforms to her role. She is in full mourning garb, "widewes habit large of samyt broun" (I., 109). In other words, she looks like the widow in Figure 7. Presenting herself thus to Hector, she identifies herself as weak and helpless. Chaucer uses this stock situation for similar effect in the "Knight's Tale," when the procession of widows approaches Theseus. Kneeling in the highway, two by two, dressed in mourning, the "compaignye of ladyes" raises the dirge without cease until they capture Theseus's attention (I.A., 898–947). Their black garb, their tears and complaints, their swoons, their pleas for "mercy," "socour," "pitee," all identify them as the most "wrecched wommen" on the earth, tossed down from high position by Fortune's wheel, and thus worthy objects of the ruler's charity. Criseyde presents herself in the context of this tradition when she seeks aid from Hector: "On knees she fil biforn Ector adown / With pitous vois, and tendrely wepynge, / His mercy bad" (I., 110–112). Conforming to social expectations by behaving properly, Criseyde is rewarded by proper treatment. Hector, like Theseus, shows his "pitous . . . nature" and his "goodnesse" (I., 113, 116) by charity to a widow, and grants her refuge in Troy. Thus Criseyde's story begins with a vivid dramatization of her vulnerability; she is a pitiful object of charity like the widows in the Old Testament.

In the normal course of events, a young widow like Criseyde would revert to the protection of her father, Calkas. When Calkas the traitor leaves Criseyde in Troy, it is all the more a "false and wikked dede" (I., 93) in that he leaves behind an unprotected daughter. Much has been made of Criseyde's timidity: the narrator describes her as "the ferfulleste wight / That myghte be," so much so that she "wel neigh starf for feere" (I., 449–451). Some modern commentators even seem to think of Criseyde as unusually fearful by nature. One sees her need for a male protector as "aris[ing] from the concept of woman as chattel of some man," and regards it as one of the "obstacles to her liberation."[50] That is an ahistorical interpretation. Chaucer's audience would have seen Criseyde's fears as well grounded. All women are more vulnerable in wartime than at other times, and widows are most vulnerable of all. Therefore Criseyde is behaving both according to type and realistically reacting to what is indeed a fearful situation. To be "ful sore in drede" is a reasonable response for a woman who was "bothe a widewe . . . and allone / Of any frend" (I., 97–98), especially in wartime. As David Aers notes, because Chaucer "wants his audience to take Criseyde's social situation seriously," he "emphasizes her isolation in Troy, her danger as daughter of a traitor in a long war, and the aspects of her widowed state that meant she lacked a male protector."[51] This crucial factor—Criseyde's lack of a male protector in wartime—motivates her behavior but mitigates her guilt, thus allowing Chaucer to maintain sympathy for Criseyde, despite her violation of her estate's rules.

Having played a conventional virtuous role and elicited a conventional virtuous response, Criseyde resumes life as a proper widow under Hector's protection. Details of that life suggest that she is more the comfortable and easy widow well known in medieval life than the grief-stricken, pitiable creature who knelt before Hector. She lives appropriately to her "estat," with enough attendants to maintain her reputation, observing all externals. However, it soon becomes obvious that she lacks the interior disposition of mourning. While as a pre-Christian Criseyde cannot be held to the duty of praying for her husband's soul, a practice that assumes belief in the doctrine of purgatory, it is significant that she doesn't even think of him. The fact that Criseyde shows no attachment to her dead husband helps to explain the famous "slydynge . . . corage" (V., 825), construing it in modern terms as wavering commitment. For Criseyde, mourning can be cast aside with the "widewes habit blak" (I., 170).

Hints that widow Criseyde is ripe for new love permeate the description of her watching the procession in honor of Palladion. No widow should be involved in activities proper to a wife or a virgin, to a "lady fressh" and "mayden bright." These women might appropriately attend spring festivities, "ful wel arayed . . . bothe for the seson and the feste" (I., 166–168), and visible to "al the prees" (I., 173); Criseyde, however, must not only wear her widow's garb but also seclude herself. Despite the strong cultural prohibitions against these two behaviors, Criseyde has placed herself in a location where she can be seen from the street:

> And yet she stood ful lowe and stille allone,
> Byhynden other folk, in litel brede,
> And neigh the dore, ay undre shames drede,
> Simple of atir and debonaire of chere,
> With ful assured lokyng and manere.
>
> (I., 178–182)

Some elements of this important description do conform to prescribed behavior. Criseyde's isolation within her house is supposed to reflect her sorrowful indifference to the outside world. Humble, quiet, and alone, standing behind other people as if for additional shelter, taking up as little space as possible as if in recognition of the degradation involved in her reduced estate, properly clothed in simple attire, Criseyde seems the proper widow. At the same time, she is near the door, her position a well-known vulgar image of sexual availability. Her attire, though simple, does not conceal but rather enhances her beauty, as all the crowd notices. In choosing her widow's weeds, Criseyde has used the art that conceals art; she looks good in black and knows it. In manner, she is no longer grief-stricken as she was before Hector; she is gracious in disposition, but, more importantly, "ful assured," completely confident. She clearly has no intention of dedicating herself to asexuality. On the contrary, she is the very essence of femininity: "alle hire lymes so wel answerynge / Weren to wommanhod, that creature / Was nevere lasse mannysh in semynge" (I., 282–284). This feminine appeal is contrast to the somber message of her widow's clothing (see Figure 7).

The combination of elements in this passage shows simultaneous adherence to and deviation from behavioral norms for widowhood. At a psychological threshold, Criseyde vacillates between availability for new love and reluctance to violate the widow's prescribed social role. As David Aers says, she assumes "the posture of contemplative withdrawal from the life of the world and the overcoming of natural instincts," but nevertheless "does not claim this is what she positively wants, only that it would be decorous."[52] Her body language says that she wants to leave the house and join the spring procession, but dares not make the public statement that this behavior would involve. In this ambivalent mood she sees Troilus.

Were Criseyde not on the threshold of abandoning her widow's life, she would not have reacted to Troilus as she does. Troilus can only see her because she allows herself to be seen, standing in the doorway. At this juncture, the appropriate thing for her to do would be to cast her eyes down, then retreat with dispatch. Instead, watch Criseyde's eye movements: she "let falle / Hire look a lite aside in swich manere, / Ascaunces, 'What, may I nat stonden here?' " (I., 290–292). While she does let fall her look, as behavior manuals prescribe, she does it "aside," not down—a significant difference. Her manner is at once flirtatious and assertive, holding her ground under Troilus's gaze, as if to say: this is my house and I'll stand in the doorway if I want to, despite the rules! Her manner here combines the self-assertion and sexuality that medieval people would have associated with the feisty, lusty widow.

Pandarus senses and plays upon this disparity between Criseyde's appearance as steadfast and her reality as lusty. When he visits Criseyde to plead Troilus's case, he finds her reading, in the company of two other ladies "withinne a paved parlour" (II., 81). Reading would associate her with prayer—secular reading was scarce as well as inappropriate to her estate. The architectural detail connotes affluence; usually parlor floors were made of clay and covered with rushes, not paved.[53] Criseyde, then, lives as a proper widow, in above-average accommodations, with suitable accompaniment. Though she seems an *exemplum* of chastity, Pandarus feels free to test her commitment by attempting to persuade her to put away her book and to abandon the conventional garb of her estate: "Do wey youre barbe, and shew youre face bare!" (II., 110), he says. The widow's barbe, "a piece of white pleated linen passed over or under the chin and reaching midway to the waist,"[54] is an essential element of the "mourning habit."[55] To abandon it would be a fashion statement indeed, a clear signal of availability, and Criseyde reacts to this suggestion conventionally, with horror: "Is that a widewes lif . . . ?" (II., 115). At no point does Criseyde abandon her widow's weeds; for the duration of her relationship with Troilus, she looks like the pious widow in Figure 7. The incongruity between Criseyde's dress and her behavior is the more apparent if the downcast eyes and prayerful bearing of that image are kept in mind.

In one of Chaucer's sources, Boccaccio's *Il Filostrato*, the analogous character, Criseida, refuses Pandarus's suggestions on the grounds of mourning her dead husband.[56] Chaucer's Criseyde, significantly, does not say that she is in mourning but, rather, that she should be leading the widow's life, that is, observing customs: "It satte me wel bet ay in a cave / To bidde and rede on holy seyntes lyves; / Lat maydens go to daunce, and yonge wyves" (II., 117–119). Not that she is indeed reading saints' lives, however; she is reading the "romaunce . . . of Thebes" (II., 100). She knows that a widow should encloister herself to pray and meditate. The lives of holy saints, she knows, teach no greater lesson than the necessity of chastity. Criseyde knows all the conventions of her estate, but the content of her reading shows that she is observing them less than diligently, as does the retention of the outward show of mourning—the clothing, the pious practices—once its spirit has been abandoned. Sensing her lack of genuine commitment to her estate, Pandarus seizes upon clothing images:

> "But yet, I say, ariseth, lat us daunce,
> And cast youre widewes habit to mischaunce!
> What list yow thus youreself to disfigure
> Sith yow is tid thus fair an aventure?"
>
> (II., 221–224)

Laying the groundwork for a sexual "aventure," he suggests activities connoting sexual license. Eventually he persuades her to appear with him in that semi-public and romantic setting, "sittynge / At some wyndow, into the street lokynge" so that Troilus, passing by, "maystow us salue" (II., 1014–1016). This action shows her protestations to be hollow. In her widow's attire, she violates enclosure by exposing herself to the gaze of a man. And, when she gazes back, she sees that man in a very desirable image: Troilus triumphant.

"So fered" of Greeks that she could "deye" (II., 124), she must weigh the risk that love poses to the independence of widowhood, as against a widow's need for security. Pandarus has told her that he (her "em," her only male relative in Troy) will die if she does not accept the love of Troilus. She is already fearful, and would be even worse off without Pandarus. When Criseyde says, "myn estat lith in a jupartie" (II., 465), she means that either she must compromise her widow's life by accepting Troilus's love, or she must undergo the increased threat to her security resulting from the possible death of her sole kinsman in Troy. Criseyde is caught between a need for independence from men and an equally exigent need for protection by them. A traitor's daughter could easily lose a ruler's support, so a more personal relationship would be better. But "the problem of having a male protector as husband was that whatever measure of independence she had, however risky, would be quite lost as soon as she married, since she would immediately come under the absolute rule of the husband."[57] What she needs, ideally, is not a husband but "a loving protector willing to leave her identity and widow's status intact."[58] She will decide that Troilus fills these needs, but only after due deliberation. Criseyde is no romantic, but a pragmatist.

Given her "estat," what is significant about Criseyde's interior monologue is what she does *not* consider in making her decision to accept Troilus's love. Criseyde's careful reasoning process[59] shows her to be calculating, self-concerned, and amoral. She never considers adherence to the high code of ethics applicable to widows. Instead, in a habit of mind that prefigures her later betrayal of Troilus for Diomede, she gives greatest weight to personal advantage. Chaucer's audience, evaluating Criseyde through the filter of Christian moral absolutism, would have perceived her pagan ethical system as inferior. She holds herself to a lower standard, "mesure," moderation (II., 715), than would be expected of her Christian counterpart. With instinctive and complete self-concern, she ignores what medieval people believed to be the cardinal principles of woman's moral life: service to others, self-abnegation, suffering. Instead, she sees the loss of her husband as a gain to her in personal autonomy and contentment. While, as we have seen, such was the practical effect of widowhood in the Middle Ages, it was not appropriate to express it in so open, indeed so self-satisfied a way, even in interior monologue:

> "I am myn owene womman, wel at ese—
> I thank it God—as after myn estat,
> Right yong, and stonde unteyd in lusty leese,
> Withouten jalousie or swich debat:
> Shal noon housbonde seyn to me, 'Chek mat!'
> For either they ben ful of jalousie,
> Or maisterfull, or loven novelrie."
>   (II., 750–756)

This paean to widowhood captures in brief the advantages of the estate to medieval women. Criseyde is free of the adversarial game-playing of marriage in which, no matter how well a woman plans her moves, her husband wins. Not subject to her father, Criseyde is now as much her "owene womman" as it was possible for a medieval woman to be, and she is entirely comfortable in that estate. Like a previously restrained animal now untethered in a pleasant pasture, she enjoys her freedom. No longer must she deal with the arguments, the petty jealousies, the limitations, the infidelities, and the struggle for mastery in marriage. Criseyde enjoys independence and sees no reason to make her life unhappy by needless self-sacrifice. Casually, proclaiming that she is "naught religious" (II., 759), she sets aside what the medieval Christian audience would have seen as the special moral obligation of widows to remain chaste.

Criseyde's reluctance to sacrifice the independence of widowhood explains why she and Troilus do not marry. Marriage allows men to dominate women, and Criseyde wants to avoid this: "Allas! Syn I am free, / Sholde I now love, and put in jupartie / My sikernesse, and thrallen libertee?" (II., 771–773). "Jupartie": Criseyde has now used the term twice in deciding what course of action to take. On the one hand, she is "fully alive to her vulnerability to male coercion," on the other hand she "fear[s] . . . losing the liberty from male control which she currently enjoys."[60] To maintain the advantages of widowhood while at the same time achieving a greater sense of security, Criseyde enters into a secret relationship with Troilus. To marry would have the dual effect of compromising Criseyde's freedom and reducing the *grand amour* to banality. Under the courtly love tradition, Criseyde has the upper hand. Troilus is in her service, she can command him; he is under her "yerde," her authority (III., 137), and has pledged not to seek sovereignty (III., 169–175). This means that, in the eyes of society and in her own eyes, Criseyde is still a free woman, given to no one, taken by no one. For the privilege of retaining her status, she sacrifices the security of marriage. This decision backfires when she is seen primarily as her father's daughter, thus a good choice for a hostage exchange. The wife of a son of the ruling house would clearly not be thus regarded.

As the relationship develops, Criseyde's security needs are fulfilled so well by Troilus that she begins to lose her competing need for independence. She begins to trust Troilus, to cling to him as a vine does to a tree (III., 1230–1232). She sees him as her "knyght," her "pees," her "suffisaunce" (III., 1309). That is, she has allowed him to take the role of the male protector:

> wel she felte he was to hire a wal
> Of stiel, and shield from every displesaunce;
> That to ben in his goode governaunce,
> So wis he was, she was namore afered.
> (III., 479–482)

Yet Criseyde's wall of steel is ultimately vulnerable. As the medieval audience knew, Troilus is doomed and Troy will fall through penetration of the gates of the city. Also well known is the common association of images between violation of a gate and rape. Criseyde knows, everyone knows, that the bodies of women are the spoils of war. If Troy falls, concubinage to a victorious Greek would replace a freely chosen alliance. Thus Criseyde, alone in the Greek camp and accustomed now to a male protector, will need a new wall, a new shield.

Criseyde has no motivation to remain aloof from a new love, since her valued independence was lost when she was traded for Antenor. A young widow, returned to the custody of her father, resumes the role of daughter. Criseyde's plan to beguile her father and return to Troy would have been doomed even if she had maintained her determination. As Troilus knows, once she is in Greece her father will resume his appropriate role and, as fathers do, urge or even force a new marriage to "som Grek," using traffic in women to solidify his relationship with his new allies (IV., 1471–1477). She will not be as strong in this father-daughter relationship as she was as an independent widow. No longer well at ease, she has suffered a decline into two powerless states, hostage and daughter.

The departure of Criseyde to the Greek camp is to be read against this background, as well as in terms of the threatening quality of undifferentiated space for an unprotected woman. Cast from the walled city into nebulous space outside, Criseyde is vulnerable, and Diomede her only safety. Imagine the scene cinematically: Criseyde, alone as no medieval woman of rank would ever be alone, separating from Troilus, moving through emptiness to Diomede, who, in a gesture more protective than imprisoning, gently leads her horse away "by the bridel" (V., 92). Considering what could happen to Criseyde, Diomede's gesture is full of positive resonances. To fulfill her own security needs, Criseyde will commit herself to their provider. What are her alternatives? Rape? Concubinage? An arranged, and possibly uncongenial, marriage? Better to take Diomede.

Once unfaithful to her late husband's memory, Criseyde is now a second-time traitor. Such widows as she represent all that is undependable in life. The steel image, which has represented the role of male strength in the relationship, recurs in a different context in Troilus's lament upon hearing of Criseyde's exchange:

> "O ye loveris, that heigh upon the whiel
> Ben set of Fortune, in good aventure,
> God leve that ye fynde ay love of stiel,
> And longe mote youre liff in joie endure!"
> (IV., 323–326)

The two rhyming words, "whiel" and "stiel," call attention to the logical impossibility of Troilus's prayer being answered. Fortune is a wheel, by nature unstable. There can be no permanence, no "stiel" about this wheel. In the tale's analogue in Guido delle Colonne's *Historia Destructionis Troiae*, the abrupt change of fortune is echoed in the abrupt change in Briseyde's behavior. At her separation from Troilus, she drenches her clothes with tears, to the point where they could be wrung out; she mutilates her face, gashing it with her nails. But despite the histrionics associated with widowhood, she promptly betrays her lover. Just so, Guido says, are all women inconstant.[61] Unfaithful Criseyde, then, is the sign and symbol of the transitoriness of all human bliss, the mutability of all earthly things, not the permanence of the estate ideal. But Troilus should have known all this, considering that Criseyde abandoned chaste widowhood for him.

Criseyde's fall is the more blameworthy given her awareness of that ideal. At first, she is devastated, retreats to her chamber, tears her hair, wrings her hands, vows observance of the conventions of a new "widowhood."

> And, Troilus, my clothes everychon
> Shul blake ben in tokenynge, herte swete,

That I am as out of this world agon,
That wont was yow to setten in quiete,
And of myn ordre, ay til deth me mete,
The observance evere, in youre absence,
Shal sorwe ben, compleynte, and abstinence.

                    (IV., 778–784)

She tries to avoid Diomede's courtship by portraying herself as a stock widow: she once had a lord who is now dead; she never loved another; she is now intending to be the very model of her type, "unto my deth, to pleyne and maken wo" (V., 985). But she is too much the pragmatist to endure the suffering this entails. She hedges her bets: if indeed Troy is defeated, she says in effect to Diomede, try me again; if I love any Greek, it will be you (V., 990–1001). Compared to her yielding to Troilus, her capitulation to Diomede is so abrupt that Criseyde knows she has ruined her reputation forever. Poor Troilus, sorrowing but trusting, watches at the gate, makes excuses for her, rationalizes, does everything possible to justify Criseyde's behavior. In contrast, Criseyde writes lying letters concealing her own new arrangement and callously retains a lover on both sides. It is suitable that, unlike Troilus whose spirit mounts to the empyrean, the ultimate realm of the true and steadfast, Criseyde remains earthbound. She is, after all, "wordly vanyte" (V., 1837), in which man can place no lasting faith. But though her behavior is reprehensible, most readers also feel that Chaucer has somehow maintained sympathy for his heroine.

Chaucer does this by placing Criseyde in the context of the unprotected woman, the widow in wartime, and showing how the exigencies of that situation contributed to her failure to live up to the highest estate ideals. A sophisticated Chaucerian, E. Talbot Donaldson, describes Criseyde as "a conventional damsel-in-distress, for whom we are to feel sorry because she is alone, 'With wommen fewe among the Greekes stronge.' It is for this reason indeed that she is feeling sorry for herself."[62] Donaldson does not seem to understand, as Chaucer surely did, the degree of insecurity for a woman in this situation. Criseyde goes to the Greek camp all alone, without even the women companions who would customarily attend her. There are very few women in the camp, and many sexually deprived men, their violence fueled by acts of war. Any woman who has been alone in a dangerous situation can understand Criseyde's feeling here. If Criseyde needed a "wal of stiel" in Troy, she needs it even more here. Diomede's appeal to Criseyde is too courtly to mention the specifically sexual threat implicit in her situation and her urgent need for a new protector, but both know her danger.

In The Legend of Good Women, pagan heroines accept torture and death rather than compromise their chastity. All suffer, some die for this princi-

ple. Suffering with and for others is expected of women. Therefore Criseyde is expected to suffer for the loss of Troilus. In accepting Diomede,
Criseyde avoids this suffering. Yes, she lacks the moral courage needed to
sustain her through suffering; as Nevill Coghill says, she "only had the
qualities appropriate to a secluded garden, for life and love in a protected
world."[63] But men built gardens, and castles and moats and keeps, to protect just such women as Criseyde. Such women are very appealing to men
who like the protector role, men who are, like both Troilus and Diomede,
good men. In *The Legend of Good Women,* good women suffer for the
love of bad men. Criseyde, not so good, attracts two good men to protect
her. Life is unfair, that good women die martyrs to chastity while an unsteadfast woman has such good fortune.

Another dimension of Chaucer's characterization depends on a theological development: medieval people's increasing awareness of what Mary
Flowers Braswell terms the "psychology of sin."[64] As she explains in *The
Medieval Sinner: Characterization and Confession in the Literature of the
English Middle Ages,* the canon-law requirement of confession of sin "lay
the groundwork for the interior probing of character by fourteenth-century poets."[65] The penitent must undertake detailed self-examination, and
the confessor must try to "take into consideration the motive behind the
deed" and the "circumstances surrounding the sin," that he may better
"adapt the punishment to the individual sinner."[66] Examination of con-
science prior to confession required self-analysis and introspection. By requiring this practice, the Church, though unintentionally, also contributed
to penitents' increased understanding of their own motivations. The medieval audience, in consequence, grew sensitive to psychological complex-
ities and were ready to understand medieval writers' more nuanced creations. They learned from their own self-examination that no sin is committed
in a vacuum; a welter of circumstances surround, and exacerbate or mitigate, the seriousness of any single moral choice. Whether they imagined
themselves as penitent or confessor, they were increasingly able to understand, if not to condone, sin.

The mental stance of the reader toward Criseyde is that of a charitable
confessor balancing all the factors that surround her action. Objectively
she is doubly guilty—first in her illicit relationship and then in its abandonment. But subjective factors mitigate her objective guilt. She is "in a
strange place, friendless, indifferent to her father,"[67] without the social
supports that women regarded as theirs by right, without the physical capacity for self-defense that a man might have. Moderns can most readily
sympathize with her threatened situation; but for medievals, a major additional factor is that Criseyde is not a Christian. Natural woman, she is
not the beneficiary of supernatural assistance. Unredeemed woman, of course
she is "an opportunist" whose practical choices enable her "to make the

best of things,"[68] on earth if not in heaven. Her behavior would show the medieval audience how patently inferior were the ethics of natural man compared to their own, giving them a smug sense of the rightness of their own faith. Natural woman naturally fails at heroic virtue; she "does exactly what any other person *of her type* would do in similar circumstances."[69] She cannot rise to the sanctity of the holy martyrs. So while the medieval audience would surely fault Criseyde's lack of steadfastness, they would also understand how, bereft of the guidance of Christian moral instruction, she might well fail to suffer enough, and instead look out for her own self-interest.

By selfishly disregarding, even perverting, the high ideals of her estate, however, a woman can often ensure her own financial well-being. When a healthy young woman marries an older (and richer) man, Chaucer's medieval audience would have viewed that marriage with the cynicism of the worldly wise as an interlude, preparation for a longer (and happier) widowhood, and assumed that the young wife could manage her marriage so as to ensure her own prosperous future. In his comic characterization of May, Chaucer depends upon his audience's awareness of the legal and therefore economic benefits accruing to a widow, and on their beliefs concerning male potency and female fertility in a May-Januarie marriage insofar as these biological matters affect inheritance. May's economic interest is best served by securing the patrimony to herself, by excluding the possibility of an heir, and by wearing Januarie out in the sexual excess he so enjoys. Then, she could, like the Wife of Bath, live happily ever after, with or without a Damyan. But May's behavior shows her to be as blind in her own way as Januarie is in his. She is too much the sensual animal to act in her own best interest. A lecherous creature, she impetuously and foolishly risks all for the interlude in the tree.

A May married to a Januarie can look forward to many advantages in widowhood. She is a girl "of smal degree" (IV.E., 1625) who has achieved upward mobility through her marriage, and she will retain that higher social status in widowhood. Her role as a wife is to bear a child who will secure the patrimony to the lineage. May's capacity to "engendren . . . an heir" (IV.E., 1272) is one of the rationalizations that Januarie uses to convince himself of the rightness of his decision to marry a young girl, not an old, sterile widow more like himself. By common custom, in addition to gaining control of whatever share of the property fell to her, May would also have jurisdiction over the inheritance of a child in its minority. But without a child, she might well inherit all. So one of the key comic ironies of the story becomes Januarie's loss of self-control in promising to secure the entire patrimony to May whether or not she bears an heir and May's corresponding loss of self-control in risking her total inheritance for a brief adulterous liaison.

In evaluating May's situation, the economics of marriage and widow-hood must be considered. The Merchant narrator, quoting Theophrastus, regards taking a wife as an expensive venture:

> "Ne take no wyf," quod he, "for housbondrye,
> As for to spare in houshold thy dispence.
> A trewe servant dooth moore diligence
> Thy good to kepe, than thyn owene wyf,
> For she wol clayme half part al hir lyf."
>   (IV.E., 1296–1300)

Justinus also cautions Januarie that he would be much better off with a good servant than with a wife, because a wife can be a "wastour of thy good" (IV.E., 1535). These two passages clearly show that a medieval wife had a great deal of access to and control over her husband's property: she could claim half of a man's goods all her life; she could waste both that half and his half. All wives cause economic problems, but May's situation is unusual in that she has an even more favorable economic situation than most wives. Given her low station in life and concomitant lack of a dowry,[70] May receives a wildly disproportionate dower agreement. The narrator refuses to bore the reader with a recounting of the legal boilerplate, "every scrit and bond" by which May was "feffed in his lond" (IV.E., 1697–1698). But the point is that May was legally endowed not only with Januarie's movables and money, which would be a common practice, but also with his land, the basis of medieval power. Later Januarie, blind and jealous, in effect bribes May to remain faithful by agreeing to "maketh chartres," still more legal agreements, which presumably go even further than the "scrit[s] and bond[s]." These will be written according to May's own specifications ("as yow leste"), giving her "al" his "heritage, toun and tour" (IV.E., 2172–2174). The typical medieval bequest to a wife was not all of one's possessions, but one-third.[71] If Januarie offers "al" now, the implication is that her dower was less than "al" before, probably the typical third, so May's situation is improving, which is not bad for a girl of small degree. As Jill Mann notes, these legal details show that May, "so far from being forced into wedlock . . . has willingly married this old fool for his money, trusting that she will not have to wait too long for it to come into her hands."[72]

The tradeoff is that Januarie expects May to behave as a proper wife and widow:

> For neither after his deeth, nor in his lyf
> Ne wolde he that she were love ne wyf,
> But evere lyve as wydwe in clothes blake,
> Soul as the turtle that lost hath hire make.
>   (IV.E., 2077–2080)

In other words, he is bribing her to behave in ways routinely expected of women. But even as her potential inheritance waxes, her fidelity wanes. Since Januarie is old and hoar and daily debilitating himself in sexual excess, the period of fidelity should not be long.

Januarie promises that these charters will be drawn "to-morwe" (IV.E., 2174), even before May has provided him with an heir. The medieval audience would have seen Januarie as grossly negligent in his legal neglect of that heir; by giving May all, he has failed to secure the patrimony to his son, which is, after all, the point of having children for medieval landholders. This places May in an absurdly favorable situation. She has only to be faithful for one more day, and then outlast Januarie, to be a wealthy and independent woman, her own woman, well at ease.

She would be even more wealthy and easy if there were no heir at all, especially since Januarie has not made any part of her inheritance contingent thereupon. Leaving aside the physical risks, May would be financially and legally much better off if she does not become pregnant. One of the ambiguities Chaucer plants in the story is whether May is pregnant when she climbs into the tree (she uses food cravings as an excuse for a boost from Januarie), or whether she might be pregnant when she climbs down.[73] The medical beliefs of the Middle Ages concerning conception must influence the interpretation of the story here. It has been well known since the work of W. C. Curry that Chaucer, like his own Doctour of Phisik, was familiar with much of the scientific and medical knowledge of his day. As I have maintained elsewhere,[74] Chaucer was capable of using medical minutiae for an offhand joke. To decide whether May is lying when she implies that she is pregnant, it is necessary to consider what medieval people might have thought about Januarie's ability to impregnate May.

Medieval people's attitudes toward the decline of male potency with age is reflected in the *senex amans* theme.[75] The old man's difficulty in satisfying a young wife is so common an idea that Januarie feels the need to reassure Placebo and Justinus that he is still a lusty man, well able "to do al that a man bilongeth to" in marriage (IV.E., 1459). In fact, he sees himself as so well able to do "al" that he truly needs marriage; his lust imperils his salvation. But his self-proclaimed virility is undercut by his use of aphrodisiacs and creative modes of sexual stimulation. The medieval Church considered such practices sinful, even within matrimony.[76] Januarie does not know his theology: a man may indeed sin with his own wife.[77] Bad enough that he sins, and at a time of life when he should be turning his thoughts to God, but he is unlikely in the process to accomplish the only unsinful goal of the sex act, procreation. Old age dampens potency; medieval people knew this from both experience and authority.

On their wedding night, May "preyseth nat his pleyying worth a bene" (IV.E., 1854). The fact that the bride takes no pleasure in the sex act was believed to reduce her chances of conception. Here Chaucer alludes to a

Galenic belief of his time on the relationship between female pleasure (moderns call it orgasm) and conception. Galen's theory was formulated in opposition to that of Aristotle. In *Generation of Animals*, Aristotle expressed his belief that "the female state" was "a deformity, though one which occurs in the ordinary course of nature."[78] Galen, reacting to this, is concerned to defend women from Aristotle's charge that they are defective men, "female in account of an inability . . . to concoct semen." Although, like men, women "sometimes derive pleasure" from sex and "also produce a fluid secretion," Aristotle believed that this did not constitute a female contribution to conception.[79] Galen argued, on the contrary, that one "ought not to think that our Creator would purposely make half the whole race imperfect, and, as it were, mutilated." So he came up with the idea that females were not mutilated but inverted, "men turned inside out."[80] Though inverted, women's bodies contained anatomical organs which performed functions analogous to men's.

Proceeding from this premise in *De Semina*, Galen describes the emission of "female seed" in intercourse, and this hypothesis was widely accepted in Chaucer's day. Medieval theologians, accepting Galen's biological theory,

are convinced that there is a female seed and that its release coincides with orgasm. They believe that there is a parallel between male ejaculation and pleasure and female ejaculation and pleasure. Cajetan, for example, speaks of the pleasure for a woman in emitting seed as an indication that nature put the pleasure there to stimulate the reproduction of the species. By the theologians "female semination" is used to designate both what they believe is the discharge and what they believe is the pleasure accompanying the discharge. As late as 1750, for instance, [St. Alphonsus] Liguori says of "female seed" that "according to all, it contributes greatly to the perfection of offspring. . . . It is necessary, or at least very helpful, to generation."[81]

Avicenna agrees: "When the woman does not emit any sperm, conception cannot take place."[82] Albertus Magnus believes that "female sperm" is discharged in orgasm; therefore infertility can be caused by "the man's failure to achieve near-simultaneous 'emissions' with the woman."[83] How, to the medieval mind, can this impressive group of "auctores" be wrong?

Therefore, lack of female pleasure was regarded in Chaucer's day as causing sterility. When May finds Januarie's "pleyying" unpraiseworthy, this is more than a marital misfortune without practical consequences. Given the Galenic theory, no pleasure, no child. The very ineptness of Januarie's lovemaking, described in such graphic detail, would have sent a signal to the medieval reader that the marriage was likely to be barren. So medieval people would have suspected that May was lying to Januarie (as women do) when she implied that she was already pregnant by him when she asked for a boost into the tree. Januarie's believing this is part of his blindness. But May is blind too to her own self-interest in risking the much more likely possibility of being impregnated by a pleasurable young man.

Wearing Januarie out with sterile sexual excess is May's best shot at the inheritance. Familiar though Januarie was with Constantinus Africanus's *De Coitu* on the aphrodisiac effect of wine, he is blind to the contraindications to sex for the *senex* mentioned in that treatise. While Constantinus concedes that "nature . . . grows hot for copulation," he sees sex as a dangerous business in which "the animal spirit and the natural spirit are dissipated." Therefore "it is hardly surprising that someone who has intercourse too often will be weakened. . . . Many have died in this way, and no wonder."[84] Constantinus directs this warning to all men, but obviously the old are in more jeopardy, being weaker to begin with. His view is shared by an impressive roster of medieval thinkers. Andreas Capellanus observes that "by love and the work of Venus men's bodies are weakened. . . . I remember that I once found in certain medical books that because of the works of Venus men quickly grow old."[85] Andreas believes that because of a loss of "natural heat," old men cannot love at all.[86] Although some medical writers see intercourse as healthful, a strong tradition holds the opposite view, that, in the words of St. Bonaventure (c. 1217–1274), "every sex act helps to shorten one's life."[87] Similarly Albertus Magnus: "Too much ejaculation dries out the body. . . . When warmth and moisture are drawn out of the body, the system is weakened and death follows. This is why men who copulate too much and too often do not live long."[88]

Since everyone knows that, for old men, sexual restraint, even total abstinence, is in order, Januarie certainly should have known it too. His duty in his chronological estate, *senectute*, is to put aside the lusts of the flesh and prepare for death. St. Gregory says in his homilies that if a man "has not woken up to the ways of eternal life in maturity, he may at least come to his senses in old age."[89] So, according to authorities religious and scientific, Januarie is on shaky ground indeed. His soul is in danger; his body grows weaker; and he probably cannot father a child. His attentions to May will shorten his life and hasten her independent widowhood, heir to all Januarie's heritage, which will fall into strange hands with her remarriage: just the outcome Januarie said he wanted to get married to avoid.

In order to inherit "al," unencumbered by a heir, May should avoid pregnancy. Damyan, young and virile, is more likely than Januarie to cause May pleasure and thus impregnate her. The only hope for May's continued childlessness is that the rendezvous in the tree is not ideally suited to conception. Both Albertus Magnus and Constantinus Africanus agree that the woman-reclining position is most conducive to the purpose, and Constantinus prescribes a postcoital nap, which "preserves the semen better."[90] Obviously the position in the tree facilitates neither reclining nor napping. Worse is May's jumping down from the tree. Jumping is regarded by Avicenna and Albertus as a contraceptive practice: if "the woman gets up at once, and moves, or jumps . . . the seed, being slippery . . . passes out."[91] In short, according to medieval beliefs, for purposes of conception still and horizontal is better than active and vertical. Nevertheless, the brief encounter might be so pleasurable as to outweigh the negative factors, causing May to conceive. While Chaucer appears to leave the pregnancy issue unresolved by planting doubt as to whether one fertility factor added (female pleasure) balances out two subtracted (correct position and motionlessness), it seems that the humor of the situation requires that May not be pregnant when she climbs into the tree. The point seems to be that May, if she is smart, should know better than to risk pregnancy. May risks pregnancy; *ergo*, May is not smart. All the elaborate medical details concerning potency and fertility lead inevitably to this simple conclusion.

The medieval audience would have snickered at Januarie for his claim that he could indeed do "al" that belongs to a man. Deceived by her suggestion of pregnancy, and influenced by his ever-increasing anxiety about her fidelity, he tries to buy what really belongs to him already, May's fidelity, by promising her "al" his heritage. Her fidelity is the only contingency. "Al" Januarie's heritage will be May's if she can be a true wife, first, until the papers are drawn ("to-morwe"), and then, for the rest of Januarie's excess-shortened life. But silly, sexy May cannot keep her eye on the great goal: comfortable widowhood. If her adultery is discovered, she could lose her dower rights.[92] If she becomes pregnant by Damyan, even if she can play upon Januarie's hubristic belief in his own virility to cause him to accept the child as his, the inheritance will have to be divided with the child. She would have been better off with "al" than with some.

Chaucer is punning on the word "al": because Januarie cannot do all that a man should be able to do, May stands to gain all. His medieval audience would have laughed at blind May for not realizing this and taking advantage of it. Too lusty to scheme, she risks all the advantages of childless widowhood for an interlude of pleasure. Thus Chaucer uses contemporary legal practices and medical beliefs to make his May look just as foolish as his Januarie.

Throughout all the stages of her life, a medieval woman was expected to behave in specific ways, all somehow related to the preservation of chastity. Ideally, for the young virgin, the transition from father to husband marks the only significant rite of passage that she may experience. Safely married, she is expected to accept her subordinate position in the domestic hierarchy, demonstrating her acceptance by appropriate speech habits and clothing choices, and by stability of place. In this she is continuing habits of virtue formed while she was a daughter in her father's house. Should she become a widow, another point of liminality occurs, a point at which she was advised to choose a celibate life dedicated to good works and to the memory of her husband. Social and economic realities, however, made other choices likely: remarriage, or an independent and comfortable widowhood. If the latter choice was made, and if her economic situation permitted, a medieval widow could experience the greatest possible degree of self-determination possible to a medieval person. Free of father and husband, the widow was her own woman at last.

Such a deviation from prescribed behavior, however, was discouraged in all medieval didactic sources. If a woman decided to break all their rules at once, she would become very much like Alisoun of Bath. As we have seen, Alisoun is characterized in terms of the stereotype of the unchaste widow, the gossip, the wanderer; even her clothing choices violate estate norms. Chaucer can call up a complex web of associations with all these types in characterizing the Wife of Bath. Where the Wife goes far beyond the stereotype is in Chaucer's addition of a strong intellectual component to her character. The Wife of Bath is armed with the allied weapons of knowledge and rhetoric, which the medieval educational system traditionally offered to men only. So equipped, the Wife cannot be dismissed merely as shrew. Using her clattering—but educated—tongue to pierce male armor, she is a powerful force. Her sense of entitlement, her assumption that her words have authority, that her will shall prevail, sets her apart from all other women. The antithesis of the ideal wife, the will-less Grisilde, the Wife teaches the lesson that men must acknowledge and respect women's will.

✺ 10 ✺

Summa Feminarum: The Archwife

Let a woman learn in silence with all submissiveness. I permit no
woman to teach or to have authority over men; she is to keep silent.
—Paul, 1 Timothy 2:11–12

Prolix of speech, capacious of dress, unstable of place, disloyal, bold, bossy,
brassy, friend to woman, enemy to man, archwife Alisoun is a compendium of undesirable female traits, a *summa* of misogyny. While Chaucer
employs the received wisdom of his time on the faults of women, he went
far beyond that, developing her character "from archetype, through stereotype, and finally to the portrayal of a unique personality."[1] The methods
of her trade serve as a key to understanding how her character is developed. Weaving is "the stock metaphor for rhetorical activity (to weave a
poem, to spin a yarn; Latin *texere*, 'to weave, to compose')."[2] The rich-
ness of the Wife's Prologue and Tale is due to this "intricacy of intermin-
gling" based on the "techniques of weaving."[3] Interwoven are the conventional elements of the Wife's characterization, the stock misogyny, plus
the innovative elements that are Chaucer's unique contribution to the creation of a new kind of woman: economic independence and intellectual
authority.

Using her gossip relationships to strengthen her in the battle of the sexes,
she browbeats her husband into submission by shrewish speech. She defies
estate norms on clothing and enclosure. Staying home, grieving in her widow's garb, is not for her; she goes on pilgrimage, merrily arrayed, seeking
a new husband. Blended with these conventional violations are new elements of women's lives that Chaucer sees emerging. Now, not only is a
woman a virgin, a wife, or a widow, she is also a tradeswoman and an
heiress. New modes of economic thought and language among the rising
bourgeoisie permit discussion of the economic motives that govern mar-

riage. Civil law allows women independent control of money, whether earned or inherited. Canon law, though likely to enforce limitations on women's freedom, can often be ignored. Growing economic power leads to an increased assertiveness that cannot be dismissed as mere shrewishness. Alisoun does not merely use speech to make her will prevail, as the shrew does; she assumes that it will prevail, because she has mastered the art of rhetoric, long a part of men's education but withheld from women. While many women characters in medieval literature disobeyed the authorities who were supposed to instruct them, Alisoun has gone further than that: she speaks out, proclaiming herself an authority from whom others must learn.

The Wife of Bath's sense of entitlement is the result of a variety of intersecting developments affecting women. The fourteenth century witnessed increased opportunities for women through "traditionally male sources of power: literacy, the economy, and the law."[4] Not only is the Wife literate, she is educated, and in the subject she needs as an instrument of domination: rhetoric. Economically, she has benefitted from new opportunities for women in trade. To her own earnings she adds the proceeds from the sequential inheritances permitted by civil law, while pragmatically ignoring disadvantageous canon law. With education, legal rights, and money of her own, the Wife has a strong sense of self. While maids and wives were supposed to listen, as an experienced widow Alisoun assumes that she has finally earned the right to speak on her own authority. In "life," the marriages she describes in her "Prologue," her decidedly unfeminine speech habits lead to partial success and limited marital happiness. But in "literature," the idealized world of her tale, the authority of women's speech is completely accepted and results in perfect marital bliss for both husband and wife.

The courtesy books' advice to women on speech is, as we have seen, to restrict it. Aggressive speech is a form of rebellion for which old wives were famous. As "The Henpecked Husband's Lament" has it, this is a good reason not to marry old wives like Alisoun:

> Young men, I warn you every one,
> Old wives take you none;
> For I myself have one at home—
> I dare not speak when she says "Peace!"[5]

The henpecked husband has clearly lost control to a woman using speech as an instrument of power, just as the "Envoy" to the "Clerk's Tale" advises "archewyves" to do. In the length of the Wife's speech, its assertiveness, its refusal to brook interruption, its power imagery—in all ways she is a typical shrew.

In the first place, the Wife is not only guilty of what a medieval preacher called "over muche spekynge,"[6] she is proud to be "of [her] tonge a verray jangleresse" (III.D., 638). Her prologue is the longest by far in *The Canterbury Tales*. Such copiousness of speech is a sign of major character flaws in women. If in the behavior manuals silence is "a sign of modesty and chastity,"[7] the Wife is immodest and unchaste. Then, the content of her speech is self-centered and prideful. Even given the tale-telling situation, to monopolize the conversation as she does is to fail in the feminine virtue of concern for others. The Wife uses speech as a medium not only of self-expression but of self-glorification: "I" is her favorite pronoun.

Instead of using speech to restore domestic harmony, the Wife uses it to achieve the upper hand. Her language is the language of power. She "pleyned first" (III.D., 390), seizing the initiative by fomenting arguments. Often she invents issues, accusing her elderly husbands of infidelity, unleashing a barrage of accusations: men are miserly, lecherous, jealous, bigoted. When her husbands engage in this duel, she "quitte hem word for word" (III.D., 422). Her word choice shows her power drive. She wants the "bridel in [her] hand," she has her husbands "hoolly in . . . hond" (III.D., 211), she "governed" them (III.D., 219). No moral considerations apply; she can "swere and lyen" twice as "boldely" as a man (III.D., 227–228). On those rare occasions on which she "spak to hem faire" (III.D., 222), as behavior manuals advise, her husbands were downright grateful.

Such a person would hardly tolerate interruption. As Deborah Tannen notes, it is a commonplace of speech research that "men interrupt women."[8] Despite the length of the Wife's monologue, only one of the pilgrims dares to interrupt her, and he only briefly. The Pardoner interrupts the Wife early in her monologue ("Up stirte" he [III.D., 163]), and at about the time when she might have been perceived as having held the floor long enough. But she silences him only five lines later: "Abyde!" (III.D., 169). She does not allow the Pardoner to seize control of the speech situation. He tries again later (III.D., 184); again she swiftly recoups (III.D., 188), and so effectively that she is not interrupted again for the duration of the prologue and tale.

The length of the Wife's monologue must be appreciated in terms of its oral delivery. Not only is the whole of *The Canterbury Tales* spoken narrative, but the poetry would have been read aloud to its original audience. Thus the very duration of the Wife's share of the tale-telling contributes to its humor. Every member of the audience would have noted with amusement the contrast between the ideal woman's silence and the Wife's verbal prolixity. Her control of the speech situation as only one of two women in a group of men shows a remarkable degree of personal force. More masculine than feminine in her speech style, the Wife overturns the man-on-top system encouraged by the prescriptions of didactic literature urging women to be silent. The Wife lectures at length, usurping a male prerogative connoting authority and connected with male dominance in education.

Deborah Tannen says that, even today, women listen while men lecture.[9] The Wife's public self-aggrandizement is uncharacteristic of women who, Tannen says, usually "dislike putting themselves on display, claiming public attention for what they have to say."[10] The Wife has no problem with these prideful acts. She assumes that she has superior knowledge and demands the attention that knowledge deserves. That is, she sets herself up as "a woman whose opinion is authoritative,"[11] a person whose stance is: I talk, you listen. And learn.

Such independence of spirit requires economic independence. Even without her rich old husbands, the Wife has a significant source of income in the clothmaking industry. Weaving was always considered "the duty of the feminine estate, the task that Langland assigned to women in the division of labor—'Wyues and wydwes wolle and flex spynneth.' " So as a weaver, the Wife is involved in the "archetypal feminine occupation."[12] By the fourteenth century, however, weaving was not just a symbol of femininity, but a growth industry. The Wife's lucrative trade establishes her as a "woman of independent means with a strongly developed commercial attitude toward life." Although Chaucer does not specify whether the Wife's money is mainly earned income or inheritance,[13] readers must assume that Chaucer has given her not only a specific occupation but "the most lucrative trade possible" in her day[14] to show that she makes money at it. The "General Prologue" descriptions show that Chaucer is interested in money, the getting and spending of it. Alisoun's weaving does not signify that she sits at her distaff like a meek wife, but that she is an entrepreneur, rising with the tide of capitalism to a point where she need no longer identify primarily with the femaleness of her occupation. A study of women's economic role in fourteenth-century England, Martha Howell's *Woman, Production, and Patriarchy*, confirms that women were not only isolated in certain female-dominated trades, but increasingly involved in market competition against men, and that Alisoun's rivals in Ypres and in Ghent were in fact men. Such rivalry, Howell says, led to the characterization of the women involved in it as shrewish and sexually aggressive to boot,[15] probably accurately, as women in trade must speak the language of trade. These opinions on tradeswomen, which Howell says Chaucer knew, are reflected in the Wife's speech and behavior. Her "vocabulary of commerce"[16] reflects a mercantile mode of thought.

The Wife of Bath, then, is a new woman of her age, a woman of "business and enterprise."[17] At the same time, other, more traditional laws and customs allow her to retain the economic protection offered to her in her estate as a widow. Both these income sources, earnings and inheritance, are interwoven elements of her income. Alisoun has an absolute legal right to hold and control her dower from her several marriages "so as to gain for herself the greatest possible benefit."[18] She got the rich husbands to

the church door, so now as widow she has their money, and her own
income besides.

The Wife of Bath has taken advantage of every proviso of civil law; but
this would all be futile were it not for her ability utterly to disregard every
proviso of canon law that worked to her disadvantage. The laws of the
Church were intended to guide the Christian on his quest for spiritual
perfection. Since all Christians were called to sanctity, every law, however
trivial, represented an opportunity to test oneself against the Church's
standards for holiness. But, as the Wife tells her pilgrim audience, she has
no desire for perfection, to be the gold vessel in the household of the Lord,
but is content to be one of those which "been of tree, and doon hir lord
servyse" (III.D., 101). This logic is of a piece with her distinction between
commandment and counsel (III.D., 60–68). "Conseillyng is no comandement," theologically. A commandment is an order, a moral absolute for
all Christians, and violation is a sin. A counsel is a suggestion, a work of
supererogation for the pious, and violation is an imperfection. The Wife's
proclaimed goal is to be a passable Christian, a lesser vessel. However,
even if spiritual mediocrity were a worthy Christian goal, the Wife's least-
common-denominator approach to morality places her in a position of violating even the counsels. Christian widows are counseled to be steadfast
and not remarry; but even the widow who ignores the counsel and remar-
ries was not supposed to go about the business so aggressively as does the
Wife.

Now, widowed again, the Wife has another chance to take the moral
high road. But she is unrepentant, still rejecting counsel:

> For sothe, I wol nat kepe me chaast in al.
> Whan myn housbonde is from the world ygon,
> Som Cristen man shal wedde me anon,
> For thanne th'apostle seith that I am free
> To wedde, a Goddes half, where it liketh me.
>   (III.D., 46–50)

The Wife discounts the counsel of chastity in widowhood by using so-
phistical logic to justify her own preferences. Having distinguished between counsel and commandment, she blurs the issue by arguing not against
the remarriage of widows but against a separate issue, perpetual virginity:
"Men may conseille a womman to been oon [a virgin], / But conseillyng
is no comandement. / He putte it in oure owene juggement" (III.D., 66–
68). "Men," that is, theologians, counsel but do not command virginity.
She proves the obvious, that Paul's counsel to virginity cannot be universal
law, because Christianity would have long since died out were all Christians virginal. Since the Wife's "maydenhede" (III.D., 69) is long gone,

what is in question now is that renewed commitment to chastity expected of the widow. The Wife has cleverly deflected the argument from the real issue and assumed as proven an issue never addressed.

Having thus established to her own satisfaction her moral right to re-marry, the Wife of Bath defines for herself a new set of standards concerning a key canon law concept, the *debitum maritale*. The canon law concept of the marital debt seeks to justify the pleasures of marriage by finding legitimate motivations for performing the sex act. Each marriage partner has a right to the other's body; thus do they avoid adultery and conceive children. But, as James Brundage points out in *Law, Sex, and Christian Society in Medieval Europe,* marital sex was restricted as to time, place, manner, and season, so drastically as to harness rather than liberate the sex drive. "Marriage did not confer a license for unbridled sexual experimentation or lascivious comportment," says Brundage;[19] quite the contrary. Such frequency and intensity as the Wife of Bath describes were forbidden: "Myn housbonde shal it have bothe eve and morwe, / Whan that hym list come forth and paye his dette" (III.D., 152–153). The ideal, according to Brundage, quoting late fourteenth-century Dominican preacher John Bromyard, was "marriage as 'a lifelong curbing of desire,' punctuated occasionally by serious and solemn attempts to conceive a child."[20] Lust in marriage is lust still. The Wife says that marriage is a Christian vocation—an "estaat" to which "God hath cleped us" (III.D., 147)—but she behaves as if it were an admission ticket to an orgy.

According to Philippe Ariès, the marital debt concept evolved in response to the clerical assumption of a woman's sexual reticence. Since a wife was thought to be "too inhibited to . . . ask for what is owed her," the husband had a duty to "anticipate [her] desires."[21] If he did not, canon law recognized her equal right to demand payment of the debt; this was the one area in which "men and women enjoyed equal rights before the law."[22] But, although bilateral rights existed, it was still possible for one partner to "sin in asking payment of the sexual debt for wrongful reasons or at inappropriate times" or with excessive frequency.[23] It was assumed that the marital lecher would be the husband, not the wife.

Not only would the Wife's level of sexual activity and her assertiveness in demanding it be inconsistent with medieval canon law, it would also be considered that her motivation was questionable. The Wife of Bath's language shows that she uses sex not only from motives of lust (bad enough) but also to exert power (worse). Her husband is to be her "dettour" and her "thral" (III.D., 155); she is to have dominion over him, in violation of natural law and scriptural injunction: "I have the power durynge al my lyf / Upon his propre body, and nought he" (III.D., 158–159). The Wife's inversion of hierarchy corrupts a sacrament. Exercising her one legitimate canonical right in marriage, she nevertheless sins by doing so for all the wrong reasons, not only lust of the flesh but also lust for power. This naked declaration of aggression—I own your body—would have been considered highly offensive in the mouth of a man speaking of his lawful wife. Neither marriage partner could legitimately hold beliefs so inconsistent with the mutuality canonists envisioned in their construct of the marital debt theory.

But the worst violation of the spirit of canon law, if intentional, would be the Wife's use of sex to undermine the health of her old rich husbands. The common belief, as expressed by Albertus Magnus, has already been discussed with reference to the Merchant's Januarie. Similarly with the Wife's old husbands; too much sex debilitates them and hastens their deaths; and the Wife's inheritances. There is no evidence in the text that the Wife is a murderer, with sexual exhaustion the weapon. But if even unintentionally she has been careless of her husbands' physical well-being, she has neglected a prime duty of a wife according to the behavior manuals.

To the medieval audience, then, it would be clear that the Wife is a sexual sinner in marriage. The one redeeming motive that might mitigate her guilt—desire for procreation—is missing too, despite the Wife's justification of her sexual activity on the well-known legitimacy of using the "membres . . . of generacion" (III.D., 117) for the purpose for which God made them. Here we must address the vexed question of the Wife of Bath's fertility, because it bears on the Wife's violation of the canon law concept of the *debitum maritale*. Many critics are curiously certain that the Wife is childless. Mark Amsler attributes the Wife's assumed childlessness to Chaucer's desire to "focus squarely on the marital relationship" and not on her role as mother.[24] Beryl Rowland assumes sterility and attributes it to the lack of sexual enjoyment characteristic of nymphomaniacs, connecting both to the medieval belief in the necessity of female orgasm for conception.[25] Other critics debate whether contraception is to be added to her list of sins.[26] But textual evidence is lacking for or against the Wife's having children.

The question of the Wife of Bath's motherhood impinges upon an area in which medieval and modern assumptions clash. Moderns, childed or unchilded, consider the matter very important, surely important enough to mention. So to moderns "the absence of any mention of a child"[27] in the Wife's long monologue constitutes evidence of childlessness. But there are medieval precedents for ignoring children by historical figures known to have been parents. Margery Kempe leaves not only her husband John but their fourteen children to pursue her holy career, involving pilgrimages to far-flung shrines. She feels some conflict over her husband, and returns to nurse him in his final illness. But she never mentions her children after she leaves them, except for one son whose sinful life triggers Margery's ostentatious prayers for his conversion. Similarly, we know that Heloise and Abelard had a son, Astrolabe; but he is not discussed in their many letters, nor do medieval observers of the pair criticize them for their detachment.

If such behavior does not bespeak a "lack of emotional ties" to children,[28] it certainly indicates that medieval people did not express such feelings in ways moderns consider appropriate. Given medieval practices, then, the Wife of Bath's failure to speak of children is not conclusive evidence of childlessness; the point must be left unresolved. What is evident is that procreation is no priority for her, and so cannot serve as the one good among her many bad motives for demanding payment of the *debitum maritale*. Therefore, in citing procreative purpose as justification for sexual pleasure in marriage, she is following her usual practice of finding legal loopholes.

All her violations of canon law lead to the very situation in which civil law gives her so many advantages: widowhood. Combining the economic advantages of that estate with a lucrative trade gives her the confidence to impose her own will against those authorities secular and religious who seek to impose their collective will on her. Her sense of self is further strengthened by her assumption of all the privileges concomitant upon a medieval education. The new element is that the education the Wife of Bath has somehow obtained was for men only. The Wife violates ideal feminine speech patterns because she has abandoned traditional feminine thought patterns. This is a consequence of her assumption of prerogatives available only to those with a traditional "masculine" education.

Medieval formal education has been described as a "men's club constituted by a knowledge of Latin."[29] A study of fourteenth- and fifteenth-century wills shows that book ownership, even regular access to books, was rare among men, much less women, and mostly restricted to the "better-endowed," thus the Latin-literate clergy.[30] While some women could not only read but write,[31] literacy was in general low and largely a clerical phenomenon. The educational system was geared to mastery of the teachings of the great authors of the past, the classical *auctores,* and was accessible through knowledge of the classical languages. The knowledge thus gained was to be joined to the formal study of rhetoric for the purpose of excelling in the *disputatio*, "a formal discussion of a subject by two or more people, who take opposite or differing sides. . . . The basic process involved the statement of a question, then the offering of a proposition in reply to the question, followed by objections to the proposition. Finally a determination *(determinatio)* of the correct or approved answer must be presented."[32] Men's education, in short, involved memorization of authoritative statements for the purpose of argumentation.

In contrast, the informal, at-home training of women was limited to those accomplishments thought necessary to the estate of virgin/wife/widow. It was by no means assumed that women had to be literate, much less accomplished in the art of debate. Some theorists felt that a woman should know how to read, the better to assist her husband; but others thought that only young girls destined for the convent needed to learn how to read, as married women could ask their husbands—their own personal authorities—anything they needed to know, as St. Paul advised (1 Cor. 14:35). Even the courtesy books, so prolific in their advice to women, were not intended primarily for a female audience, but were written for men to use in the instruction of women.[33] Access to books and the ability to read them would mean "the beginning of the end of total dependence on male instructors,"[34] an outcome obviously to be discouraged.

Certainly no woman was expected to have the type of education men had, and from the Wife of Bath's behavior we can see why. For one thing, a woman was to have no public role. An educational treatise of the early fifteenth century says that women should not learn rhetoric as "it can only be properly used in courts of law and in government—all men's work."[35] In her domestic role, the knowledge of authorities meant to be used in public debate would make her a shrew. She might, as the Wife of Bath did, master the *disputatio* well enough to argue both sides of the question, then come to a *determinatio* by herself, all without allowing her husband a word on his side of the question.[36] Education equals argumentation, and no man wants a woman who is "a consummate debater."[37] While all educated women were attempting to raise themselves above what the fifteenth-century humanist Laura Cereta contemptuously described as "babbling and chattering women,"[38] a woman educated in rhetoric was clearly even worse, especially if she were physically attractive. As R. Howard Bloch says: "The seductiveness of the feminine is for the medieval Christian West virtually synonymous with the delusiveness of language embodied in rhetoric."[39] Because argumentation added to the already threatening sexual and linguistic power of women, all the more reason for excluding women from the formal education that would equip them with still another dangerous weapon.

Despite all official prohibitions, then, the Wife employs rhetorical techniques. In so doing she usurps traditionally male prerogatives regarding intellectual activity as manifested in speech behavior. According to Lee Patterson, the Wife "subverts an established order . . . founded on the 'auctoritee' not of class but of the 'lore' of 'lerned men.' " Claiming the right to speak, she becomes "a nightmare of the antifeminist imagination, a woman who not only exemplifies every fault of which women have been accused but preempts the very language of accusation" by employing "masculine modes of argument."[40] But her linguistic crimes do not end there. She encroaches upon two further areas of male dominance: preaching and glossing.

Patterson describes the speaking Wife's relationship to the interrupting Pardoner as that of "professional colleague[s]."[41] The Pardoner, who ought to know, calls her a "prechour" (III.D., 165), be it in mockery or grudging praise. Robert W. Hanning's analysis stresses the Wife's rivalry with clerical authority figures at all levels. Hanning sees the Wife's argumentative stance as an expression of frustration at being arbitrarily excluded from a role she is so well equipped to play, that of preacher.[42] In retaliation, she will silence not only the Pardoner but all other representatives of the hierarchy and do a better job of preaching than they can. And she can also "glosen" as well as men (III.D., 26). The interpretation of ancient writings was at its best an attempt at deeper understanding, at worst a manipulation of the text to the glosser's own ends. Robert W. Hanning describes glossing as a technique proper to education and preaching but which by Chaucer's century acquired a sufficiently bad reputation to become a "metaphor for all kinds of language manipulation."[43] Hanning further explains how, because men wrote the books and other men glossed them, women were reduced to a "human 'text' " to be glossed. Thus arose "a culture in which one half of humanity is defined not in its own words, nor by observation of its actual deeds, but by an autonomous, nonexperiential tradition of exemplary texts composed, handed on, and interpreted by a small elite drawn entirely from the other half of humanity."[44] Alisoun's speech attempts to correct this absurd situation. She creates her own text, glosses it herself, and preaches it to a congregation of attentive listeners.

But, though Alisoun commands the respect of moderns for claiming the rights to her own story, her concomitant claim to the right to gloss the ancient authoritative texts was, in medieval terms, innovation bordering on heresy.[45] Alisoun the intellectual rebel sets herself against the weight of important theological thinking. Concerned to "establish stable doctrine," St. Augustine cautioned that "no one, however learned, should set himself against 'the consensus of so many older and more learned men.' "[46] Tertullian, castigating the behavior of women in heretical sects, professes shock that they are "audacious enough to teach, to engage in argument."[47] According to Christian orthodoxy, then, scripture could not be approached directly by the believer, but is mediated to him through more *auctores*, great theologians like Augustine and Tertullian, filtered down from them to the learned clerics; and only then received by their humble flocks. All must submit to these layers of authoritative transmission. For women, another layer was added: the husband. When the Wife of Bath assumes the right to eliminate the theological, the clerical, and the domestic middlemen, she "deliberately challenges the Church's and the antifeminists' interpretive authority."[48] Since all authority comes from God, to challenge any authority is to challenge all; of such mental sets are heretics made. Like the sects against which Tertullian fumed, the Lollards allowed women to read scripture and to preach—areas restricted in orthodoxy to "well-read clerks of good understanding."[49] The heterodox Wife certainly claims the authority to make her own judgments on what she read and heard, and to convey her judgments to others. The whole tone of her discourse, especially her many "I" references, show a powerful ego coming at authoritative discourse without appropriate deference. In essence her preaching forms a "new and dangerous sect, whose principle was that the wife should rule the husband."[50] Its teachings are her words, and she is the only authorized glossator.

In addition to the theological rebellion, the Wife's foray into public speaking has radical social implications. In "The Subversive Discourse of the Wife of Bath," Barrie Ruth Straus explains how the Wife's public speech is subversive of patriarchal order. Public speech is a male prerogative, while women are "traditionally restricted to privacy, domesticity and silence." Therefore when the Wife speaks in public on any subject she chooses, she is also addressing "the entire issue of who may speak and who may not, and on what authority." She claims authority to add woman's voice to the discussion of marriage, in defiance of longstanding custom: "The pillars of male authority, the discourse of Church, government and the written word, depend precisely on sequestering women's experience to the domain of private talk among women." The Wife extends the boundaries of "women's talk" from private gossip to public discourse. Whether arguing with husbands or lecturing pilgrims, she seizes control of speech, a major element of male power. This theme, which Straus rightly stresses, will culminate in the "Tale," in which the knight's life is saved and his happiness assured when he learns to regard women's speech as authoritative, when he listens to his wife.[51]

The Wife's fictional creation, her knight, compensates for the countless arguments in her "real" life with husbands who fail to listen—that is, fail to acknowledge her authority. Like many marital disputes, the culminating argument between Alisoun and Jankyn is a synopsis of the trigger points in their relationship, especially the root conflict: dominance or "maistrye." Two subthemes emerge in this power struggle: money and knowledge. Knowledge is further subdivided into its two sources: authority and experience. For the Middle Ages, authority meant books, and books were written and read predominantly by men. Experience, the Wife claims in her "Prologue," is the basis of her claim to knowledge; but, as we have seen, she also has a good claim to the power of the book.

Like access to money, access to education leads to power in marriage, and, conversely, loss of power in either is loss of "maistrye." Young as he is, Jankyn is a traditionalist. He wants to preserve the conventional hierarchy of marriage and will resort to violence to do so: "By God, he smoot me ones on the lyst, / For that I rente out of his book a leef, / That of the strook myn ere wax al deef" (III.D., 635–637). Because books maintain male dominance, the struggle between Alisoun and Jankyn is bookish, involving "the power of authority, especially that of written texts."[52] As Robert A. Pratt shows, Jankyn's book was an authoritative source for Oxford students like him.[53] Thus it is fitting that the domestic argument culminates in a physical battle over the book as object, attacking the book itself, ripping it, burning it, destroying the offending arguments by force if argumentation cannot lead to agreement.

Alisoun knows her misogynistic lore; but with Jankyn, she locks horns with a man who knows the "book of wikked wyves" (III.D., 685) as well as she does. Since Alisoun and Jankyn are equals in book knowledge, Alisoun's strategy is to undercut the book's authority. Since all authors are clerks and all clerks are men, how can they know what they are talking about? It is impossible for clerks to "speke good of wyves" (III.D., 690), Alisoun says. Everyone knew that clerks in their oratories wrote as they did of women not from experience but "to persuade young men to embrace celibacy not merely with eagerness but even with thanksgiving."[54] If the authorities were women, says the Wife, things would have been different:

> By God, if wommen hadde writen stories,
> As clerkes han withinne hire oratories,
> They wolde han writen of men moore wikkednesse
> Than al the mark of Adam may redresse.
>   (III.D., 693–696)

Truth is subjective: change the authority and truth changes too. The Wife's charge is no trivial matter; it undercuts the entire medieval educational system, based on belief in the absolute truth of old words written in old books. The marital argument, as Ralph Hanna points out, engages the issue of the relative validity of the authority of speech versus the authority of writing. Women have always transmitted "oral teachings on the control of husbands," while men have employed "the modes of lettered production." Men wrote, women spoke; speech is evanescent, but writing, because of its "permanence," seems truer, more authoritative, and the book itself a "sanctioned artifact."[55] The rebellion against the book makes a larger social point, according to Elaine Tuttle Hansen. When the Wife denies the authority of the written word, she is simultaneously challenging "the power of male voices to control her own behavior."[56]

Ironically, Alisoun makes a mistake in the very area in which she has so much experience and authority. She began her marriage to Jankyn by conforming to one of the key principles of the conduct book writers and other authorities on marriage: a male-dominant financial arrangement. She so loved Jankyn that she endowered him at the church door:

> This joly clerk, Jankyn, that was so hende,
> Hath wedded me with greet solempnytee,
> And to hym yaf I al the lond and fee
> That evere was me yeven therbifoore.
>   (III.D., 628–631)

Land and fee: the terms are reminiscent of the terms used to describe Januarie's uxorious gifts to May. In both situations, the older, more affluent

marriage partner makes a tactical error. Alisoun had an absolute right to her money and had more economic experience. In endowering Jankyn, against common practice, she relinquished "her authority, her independence, and maybe her identity."[57] Momentarily besotted, she lapses into the "ideal of subordinate wifehood painted by the 'auctoritee' of clerical writers . . . and deportment-book writers."[58] Perhaps indeed she has some desire to be what her culture regarded as a " 'normal' submissive wife."[59] Soon, however, she regrets this. If "sovereignty is the power of the purse," then giving away money is giving away mastery, and the only logical action is to take both back.[60]

But Jankyn is a difficult opponent even for the Wife. In fact he is very much like his Wife, especially in his ability to use speech as a weapon. Armed with book-learning, Jankyn piles up *exempla* of bad wives, implicating her, as she tried to implicate her other husbands, in the collective evil of her gender. Like Alisoun too, Jankyn monopolizes the air waves, preaching, not allowing her to interject any opinions or defenses. Alisoun has truly met her match. Her main weapon, her tongue, is for once rendered impotent. This triggers violence:

> And whan I saugh he wolde nevere fyne
> To reden on this cursed book al nyght,
> Al sodeynly thre leves have I plyght
> Out of his book, right as he radde, and eke
> I with my fest so took hym on the cheke
> That in oure fyr he fil bakward adoun.
> And he up stirte as dooth a wood leoun,
> And with his fest he smoot me on the heed
> That in the floor I lay as I were deed.
> (III.D., 788–796)

By all the rules preached to women, Alisoun should be listening attentively to the wise advice vouchsafed her by the learned one from his lofty vantage point of higher rationality. To refuse to submit to his will is wrong; to resort to violence is worse. Not to mention that books were very expensive in the Middle Ages. So Jankyn, like Noah with his Uxor, is justified in attempting to quell this domestic uprising.

The greater, then, is the Wife of Bath's accomplishment in turning this occasion, in which she is so clearly in the wrong, to her advantage. She does so, as misogynists say that women will, by means of deception. She pretends to be dying: "And for my land thus hostow mordred me?," she whines (III.D., 801). This is rhetoric, since she has already signed over her land and property to him at their marriage (III.D., 630); he does not need to murder her to get it. Nevertheless, her accusation does make him feel guilty. As he kneels to repent, she "hitte hym on the cheke" (III.D., 808),

with one blow transforming him into the classic henpecked husband.[61] She gets her revenge and regains the upper hand in the relationship. He submits himself to her authority, and thus is marital harmony restored:

> He yaf me al the bridel in myn hond,
> To han the governance of hous and lond,
> And of his tonge, and of his hond also;
> And made hym brenne his book anon right tho.
> And whan that I hadde geten unto me,
> By maistrie, al the soveraynetee,
> And that he seyde, "Myn owene trewe wyf,
> Do as thee lust the terme of al thy lyf;
> Keep thyn honour, and keep eek myn estaat"—
> After that day we hadden never debaat.
>   (III.D., 813–822)

This marital argument has been about the power derived from control of money and knowledge, and the Wife has won, recapturing jurisdiction over her property, over her husband's speech, and over the source of his knowledge, the book. The fact that she visualizes this in terms of the image of the bridle shows her redefinition of the institution of marriage so as to accommodate her own strong power drive and sense of herself. Horse and rider were a conventional image of the control of passion by reason, the lower by the higher, the body, especially its "sensual appetite," by the soul, of women, especially in the sexual sense, by men; in other words, righteous order.[62] Inverted, the image is used in Matheolus to represent female power, the "dominating wife in debate."[63] The bridle image is also connected with women's speech excesses; Beryl Rowland describes a device called the "scold's bridle, an iron noose believed to date from medieval times, which was placed over a woman's head to hold down her tongue, [and] might even have a chain or ring attached so that the victim could be led like a horse."[64] The Wife, then, has used her powers of the speech, as the "Envoy" to the "Clerk's Tale" advised, to her own advantage. The archwife has taken a situation in which she was being controlled, and regained control.

But the degradation implicit in this image of the bridle, no matter upon whom it is used, calls into question the whole enterprise of seeking mastery in marriage. No human wants to be in the position of a bridled horse. Jankyn's situation is no more enviable than was his Wife's. Though Alisoun and Jankyn never thereafter had debate, the absence of argument can be the silence of a dead relationship rather than the peace of domestic harmony. The "Prologue," the story of the Wife of Bath's life, is domestic "truth," as opposed to the literary "fiction" of her tale. In "life," the quest for mastery can end in a standoff. In her "fiction," the Wife creates an

idealized world in which, as Lee Patterson says, "mastery is sought only that it may be surrendered, an abnegation that allows both spouses to escape from the economy of domination that blights marriage."[65] The resolution of the "Wife of Bath's Tale" involves a husband's acknowledgement of his wife's genuine superiority; her reciprocal act of generosity rewards him for his good judgment; and both live happily ever after.

It is a commonplace of critical opinion that the "Wife of Bath's Tale" reflects Alisoun's desire to retain physical attractiveness to men even though age has bereft her of her pith. And so it does, but to reduce the tale to that theme only is to operate on the assumption that male admiration is what women most desire. Granted that the Wife does feel that she can depend no longer on "physical attraction alone."[66] Preachers told their flocks as much, reminding them that old widows were so repulsive as to jeopardize their husbands' salvation:

Som had lever to take an olde wedow, though sche be ful lothelyche and never schall have cheldren. And, fro the tyme that he hathe the mocke that he wedded her for, and felethe her breth foule stynkynge and her eyen blered, scabbed and febyll, as old wommen buthe, then they spen a-pon strompettes that evyll-getyn goodes.[67]

Though beauty is certainly preferable to ugliness, the tale tells us that what women most desire is not beauty but mastery.

As we have seen, education, money, and legal rights are the main components of mastery in marriage. In the educational system, the "master" is the one who knows, the one who, through knowing, has authority. Chaucer uses the term in its sense of the holder of a university degree, a teacher, a master tradesman.[68] All are derived from the common Latin, *magister:* the "maister" of a school or the master craftsman is the authority in his field; the *magisterium* is the teaching power of the Church. The Wife of Bath has proclaimed in her "Prologue" that she too wants to be regarded as a *magister,* an authority in her field, which is women and marriage. Other women, her gossips, already accept her as such; to them she is, as the Clerk's term has it, an "archewyf." Men, however, tend not to see women as authorities on any subject. They look to other men, to the clerks who wrote the books, not to women or to the medium for the communication of women's experience, speech.

In the ideal world of the fiction, this deplorable situation will be corrected. Men's symbolic representative, the young knight, will learn about women by listening attentively to the spoken words of a woman authority. This takes incorporation of women into the educational system further than mere access to a male-constructed system that would train women to think as men do. It is to make women not only the educational authorities but also the curriculum. From listening carefully to a woman, listening as if his life depended upon it, a man can learn what it is like to be female, and, finally, to acknowledge and respect intellect and will, the highest of their common human faculties, in women.

The "Wife of Bath's Tale" begins inauspiciously, with the rape of a virgin by a "lusty bacheler" in the house of King Arthur. The description of the rape contains a phrase that is important to the interpretation of the tale:

> [It] happed that, allone as he was born,
> He saugh a mayde walkynge hym biforn,
> Of which mayde anon, maugree hir heed,
> By verray force, he rafte hire maydenhed.
>   (III.D., 883–888)

"Maugree hir heed": against her will. The phrase was used to define rape at law.[69] As we have seen, Chaucer gave much thought to the question of will and will-lessness in women. He has portrayed a *reductio ad absurdum* of feminine compliance in Grisilde, and her opposite in the will-ful Wife of Bath. Now, rape: the ultimate denial of a woman's will.

In the Wife's idealized kingdom, a "land fulfild of fayerye" ruled by an "elf-queene, with hir joly compaignye" (III.D., 859–860), the tribunal before which a rape complaint is made is a tribunal of women, to whom Arthur has given authority over this crime against women. Robert J. Blanch argues that Arthur's deed "subverts legitimate rule and order and jeopardizes the common good" by overturning the rule of law and encouraging the illegitimate power moves of both Guinevere and the loathly lady; order is restored only when "the transformed wife . . . chooses obedience to husbandly rule."[70] This interpretation may mirror legal and social reality in Chaucerian England, but in the Wife's fictional kingdom a reconstructed hierarchy accommodates women's needs for both protection and authority. In such an idealized criminal justice system, women are the exclusive judges of a crime uniquely against them.

For this particular rape, popular outrage is such that the ultimate penalty is demanded:

> For which oppressioun was swich clamour
> And swich pursute unto the kyng Arthour
> That dampned was this knyght for to be deed,
> By cours of lawe, and sholde han lost his heed—
> Paraventure swich was the statut tho.
>   (III.D., 889–893)

Such was the statute in England too. To understand this requires a brief excursion into the rape laws of England in the fourteenth century, a matter thoroughly investigated by legal historians.

Rape was one of only two complaints at law which a woman could lodge against a man, the other being the murder of her husband.[71] While in theory penalties included castration, blinding, and death,[72] in practice such severe punishment was rare to nonexistent. The system of complaint was dauntingly complex, embarrassingly public, and biased against the victim, whose motivations were assumed to include entrapment into marriage.[73] All rape was illegal, but the severity of the crime depended on the victim's estate, what moderns call her previous sexual history. The crime was considered more serious if the victim was a virgin, widow, or nun.[74] But whatever her estate, legal records show that "no woman succeeds through prosecution in securing a harsh punishment for a rapist"; "strong sanctions" existed in theory, but in practice they were a "dead letter."[75] Such facts must have discouraged reporting of crimes, since to do so would shame the victim and her family to little purpose.[76] Says Barbara Hanawalt: "Rape, although newly a felony in the fourteenth century, had already taken on the characteristics that have persisted to the present day: the character of the victim determined the indictment, and the crime was seldom prosecuted."[77]

Against this historical background, Chaucer's tale fits its female teller in taking the crime with the utmost seriousness. Some analysts of the tale assume that the victim is "a peasant girl," and therefore believe that the medieval audience would condone the crime based on the lenient interpretation of such a rape in the courtly love tradition.[78] For example, Bernard Huppé interprets the incident on the basis of Andreas Capellanus's opinion that "an outburst of violent passion" as "curative of any inclination toward romantic involvement" with a woman of unsuitable social status. Because of this loophole in the courtly code, Guinevere "acts to protect a young gentleman who has not necessarily committed a crime in her code of love."[79] Legal historians tell us that a man of higher estate than his victim was indeed more lightly punished: "The swineherd who ravished a duchess, if by some miracle he escaped mutilation and death, would be enslaved; the duke who ravished a shepherdess, if punished at all, could make compensation by providing her with a purse full of coins as a dowry."[80] But the flaw in this reasoning with regard to the "Wife of Bath's Tale" is that there is no evidence that a question of disparate social status is involved in the crime. The Knight's victim is described simply as "a mayde" (III.D., 886–887), a virgin; the narrator makes no social classification, but simply places her in her estate. That the victim's lost maidenhead is a matter of sufficient importance to draw the attention of the king and queen and to require significant punishment is thus linked not to her social status, high or low, but to her prior virginity. Thus Paul Ruggiers is closer to the mark: "Even a lusty bachelor-knight cannot, after his day of exercise, casually rape the maiden he encounters. Arthur's law demands the loss of his head."[81]

Capital punishment is the penalty for the rape of a virgin in "faerye" land, as in medieval England, yet mitigation of penalties is common in both countries. What is significant about the "Wife of Bath's Tale" is the psychologically sensitive nature of the mitigated penalty and its control by the community of women. In England, penalties for rape were often assessed on the basis of monetary compensation for a nonmonetary loss. The raped virgin has lost value to her father, the raped wife to her husband. So the male relative could claim damages, as the important point was "property consequences."[82] In *Ravishing Maidens: Writing Rape in Medieval French Literature and Law*, Kathryn Gravdal makes the case that medieval literature reflects medieval law in regarding rape as primarily a matter between men. *Raptus* violates the rights of a father or a husband; rape laws have as their primary aim "maintaining peace among men." In Arthurian romance, rape triggers a revenge plot featuring knightly derring-do: "Women must be attacked so that men can become heroes."[83] Here is Chaucer's innovation in the laws and customs of his land of Faerye: the raped woman is not regarded as a man's property, nor is she a pawn in a contest between men, nor is the rapist's punishment assigned by men. It is not the victim's economic value or her significant male's honor that has been violated, but her own will. The knight's crime is a radical disregard of a woman's will. He has inflicted a personal injury that cannot be healed. Even God cannot restore a lost maidenhead. In making this alteration, Chaucer is deviating not only from the context of medieval law but also from the Arthurian romance genre within which he is working. By removing the rape from the context of a matter between men, by eliminating all the men except the rapist, Chaucer makes the rape a personal injury directed against a woman, not a property crime directed against her husband or father. The only restitution that can be made is psychological. As an act of reparation to the community of women, the errant knight is subjected to "an educative process which will eradicate the male mentality that produced the crime."[84]

So, when, according to common practice, Guinevere and her ladies suggest a mitigating penalty, the capital penalty is waived only on the condition that the required psychological growth take place. The knight knows that, despite the fact that judge and jury are women, he will surely die for his offense against that same community if he cannot meet the stipulations set for him. The Wife is presenting women not in the image of the merciful Mary, but in the image of the avenging God. No one doubts that even gentle women will authorize the execution of a rapist. Under the threat of death, the perpetrator is highly motivated to rehabilitate himself, and the punishment is precisely designed to that end: "Clearly this particular knight, as a surrogate for men in general, needs to learn more about women, and the plot becomes a device for forcing him to do so, putting him in a position more familiar to women, who have to cater to male desires, and giving power to women from the beginning of the tale."[85] The penalty requires careful study of will in women. The rapist, resembling his nonviolent

brothers in incomprehension of women, must learn "what thyng it is that wommen moost desiren" (III.D., 905). He must explore the psyche of a creature whose needs seemed so irrelevant to him that he could disregard them entirely on a matter of great seriousness. The answer he finds must satisfy not the knight himself but the assembly of women. They already know the answer, so what they will be evaluating is his newly achieved psychological sensitivity. If this educative process fails, if the knight still cannot understand that women are creatures with wills and desires of their own, with the right not to be violated, then he is truly an incorrigible rapist, a permanent threat to all women, and must die.

The knight's task involves questioning many of his culture's assumptions derived from old words in old books. Readers of the book of wicked wives, like Jankyn, think they know women from reading the writings of men, and then, worse, they attempt to teach women about themselves from these same flawed sources. Therefore, misinformation abounds:

> Somme seyde wommen loven best richesse,
> Somme seyde honour, somme seyde jolynesse,
> Somme riche array, somme seyden lust abedde,
> And oftetyme to be wydwe and wedde.
>   (III.D., 925–928)

A canard of such lore is the idea that men should not seek the advice of women; thus Adam fell, by listening to the advice of his wife. But to save his skin, the knight must not only submit to listening to women's opinions but must actively solicit them. So he goes about seeking knowledge of women from women. It is a process of replacing the clerical, male-dominated written tradition with the female-dominated oral tradition. The knight's learning to listen prepares him for accepting the truth of what his "olde wyf" says (III.D., 1000).

Confident before an assembly of ladies representing all three estates, "ful many a noble wyf, and many a mayde / And many a wydwe," with "the queene hirself sittynge as a justise" (III.D., 1026–1028), the knight confidently asserts that "Wommen desiren to have sovereynetee / As wel over hir housbond as hir love, / And for to been in maistrie hym above" (III.D., 1038–1040). No one, "ne was ther wyf, ne mayde, / Ne wydwe that contraried that he sayde" (III.D., 1043–1044). He has learned well. Women most desire that the superior position that they enjoy in courtship should continue into marriage. The answer is obvious. What human, having once enjoyed power, would not prefer to retain it? Why does it take a year and a day and the threat of death for a man to learn this obvious lesson? Is the whole procedure Chaucer's sly way of acknowledging that women think of men as thick-headed, obtuse, unable to infer from hints and suggestions as women do?

Though the knight has saved his life, his process of education is not over. To accept the old wife as *his* wife, he must still learn to question even more cultural assumptions, those concerning qualities considered valuable in a woman. Youth, good looks, family background, wealth: are not these qualities what we still mean by a "good" match? By these standards the knight's wife is undesirable. The old wife admits to being ugly, old, of low birth, and poor. But she violates norms in still other ways. She is forceful in instigating an unwanted courtship and pressing her advantage. She does not allow a man's will to rule. She is argumentative. But she needs all these abilities to convince the knight that his culture makes superficial judgments about women.

So ashamed is the knight of his unsuitable mate and the disparagement of his rank that the marriage involves that he weds her "prively" (III.D., 1080), without the publicity that makes a marriage enforceable under canon law. This would suggest to Chaucer's medieval audience that he hopes to set the marriage aside. Another indication of this intent is that he tries to avoid consummating it, hiding himself "as an owle" the whole next day (III.D., 1081). When he is brought to bed at last, he shows extreme physical aversion: "He walweth and he turneth to and fro" (III.D., 1085). Undaunted, his old wife seeks payment of the *debitum maritale*, which under canon law would validate the private nuptial agreement and render the marriage binding. And the knight has no legitimate reason for refusing to pay the *debitum*.[86] The lack of free consent on his part already shadows the validity of this marriage;[87] the additional factor of nonconsummation would render this marriage null. Therefore it is in the old wife's best interest to get her knight, so willing to rape a maid, to bed his bride.

"Oold" and "loothly" (III.D., 1100), she cannot use the tricks available to a younger and more attractive woman, but must rely on her intellectual abilities—hardly regarded then or now as woman's primary source of erotic appeal. The old wife's long monologue to her mate, like the Wife of Bath's own, argues a point, but at the same time it expresses a complex set of emotional needs: that men would listen, carefully and without interruption, to what women are saying; that men would regard women as authorities who could educate them; that men would change their minds on the basis of what women say; that men would not only respect but genuinely love them for the force of their reasoning. If as Peggy Knapp says, "embedded deep in this story is the idea that men must learn from women,"[88] the length of the speeches, of both the old Wife and the "olde wyf," show how much teaching is required.

Listening attentively to his teacher, his *magister*, forms the last stage of the knight's education, as he learns finally to reject his culture's expectations of women. The old wife demolishes false beliefs one by one, to the point where the knight is ready to accept the idea of female sovereignty in

practice as well as in theory. This is not an easy lesson to learn; he "sore siketh," sighs sorely (III.D., 1228), before he acknowledges conviction:

> "My lady and my love, and wyf so deere,
> I put me in youre wise governance;
> Cheseth youreself which may be moost plesance
> And moost honour to yow and me also.
> I do no fors the wheither of the two,
> For as yow liketh, it suffiseth me."
>   (III.D., 1230–1235)

So complete is his capitulation that the old wife apparently must check her hearing: "Thanne have I gete of you maistrie," quod she, / "Syn I may chese and governe as me lest?" / "Ye, certes, wyf," quod he, "I holde it best" (III.D., 1236–1238). Having achieved what women most desire, mastery, *magisterium*, teaching authority, the old wife is magically metamorphosed into what men most desire. As Jill Mann says: "Miraculous as it is, this transformation is no whit more miraculous than the transformation of a rapist into a meekly submissive husband."[89] Nor more unusual, perhaps, than a husband who listens to his wife, listens carefully, thoughtfully, and without interruption, and then, *mirabile dictu*, changes his mind.

A major theme of both the "Wife of Bath's Prologue and Tale" is the need for men to listen to women. According to Deborah Tannen, men's tendency to "lecture" usurps women's authority to talk themselves and makes them into "an appreciative audience"[90] rather than possessors of expertise in their own right. The Wife begins her lecture by making an analogy between the education that clerks receive in their various schools—"Diverse scoles maken parfyt clerkes" (III.D., 44c)—that craftsmen receive under a master—"Diverse practyk in many sondry werkes / Maketh the werkman parfyt" (III.D., 44d,e)—and her own education in marriage—"Of fyve husbondes scoleiyng am I" (III.D., 44e). Having served her apprenticeship, she now assumes the authority of a master, and its privileges, the main of which is *to be listened to*.

The Wife uses this authority, makes a predominantly male audience listen to her, at excessive length, without interruption, on a subject of her own choosing (in fact, on herself). In her "Tale," the old wife not only lectures but gets even her husband actually to listen and to change his opinion based on her superior knowledge. Chaucer appears to understand that these are rare events in male-female communication. Usually, says Tannen, "evidence of . . . woman's superior knowledge sparked resentment, not respect," much less love, in men.[91] The happy outcome of the "Tale" shows the Wife's wish that men learn to appreciate women's values by listening to what they say. The knight must forsake hyper-male behavior and learn behavior conventionally considered feminine. He who has placed his own life in jeopardy by devaluing the worth of a woman has learned that, for women, "being listened to can become a metaphor for being understood and being valued."[92] All the controls imposed upon women throughout the stages of their lives, all the rules put forth in old books sacred and secular, have served to separate women from what they most desire: to be masters, *magistri,* authorities.

11

Authority and Experience, Books and Life

And as for me, though that my wit be lite,
On bokes for to rede I me delyte,
And in myn herte have hem in reverence,
And to hem yeve swich lust and swich credence
That there is wel unethe game non
That fro my bokes makes me to gon.

—*Legend*, G. Prol., 29–34

People say that life is the thing, but I prefer reading.

—Logan Pearsall Smith[1]

Addictive readers will identify with the narrator of *The Legend of Good Women*, a bookish man for whom very few attractions are strong enough to draw him from his study. Several of Chaucer's narrative personae are very like this one, besotted with books to the point of illness, "to curious / In studye, or melancolyous" (I., 29–30). The narrative voice at the beginning of *Troilus and Criseyde* is that of a writer transmitting an old tale to a reading audience. In *The Book of the Duchess*, the act of reading links the world of "reality" with the world of the dream. *The Parliament of Fowls* narrator reads for pleasure and enjoyment, "for lust" and "for lore" (15). When he finds an old book written in old script, he reads it all day long:

For out of olde feldes, as men seyth,
Cometh al this newe corn from yer to yere,
And out of olde bokes, in good feyth,
Cometh all this new science that men lere.

(22–25)

New learning comes from old books, he says. For all these narrators, reading is not only a central life experience, it is life itself. To the unbookish, this behavior seems bizarre. The *Legend* narrator knows this. He ponders the great question concerning those who spend their time being too curious of study, reading and writing books: what is the correct balance between books and life?

The *Legend* narrator believes that only certain kinds of truth can be found in books. To verify things unseen or unseeable, "olde thinges," one turns to "olde bokes" (F. Prol., 18, 25). No man dwelling in this country has seen heaven or hell, but because "he hath herd seyd or founde it writen" (F. Prol., 8), he believes. Believing in old words written in old books is the basis of Christianity. Yet, though the narrator reverences and gives credence to "olde appreved stories" (F. Prol., 21), his language shows a tension between things *read* and things "*assayed*" or *proven*. We must believe in such matters as heaven or hell by authority, because "by assay ther may no man it preve" (F. Prol., 9). We must "honouren and beleve / These bokes, there we han noon other preve" (F. Prol., 28). But the evidence of the written word does not necessarily constitute proof. The *House of Fame* narrator also distinguishes between that which "men may ofte in bokes rede" and that which men may "al day sen . . . in dede" (385–386). The rhyme reinforces the contrast: "rede" and "dede," what is written and what happens in life, authority and experience. But what is one to do, the *Legend* narrator ponders, when a matter is both discussed in books and also knowable through personal experience? The issue of books as instruments of authoritative discourse (things "writen") as set against life itself (things "assayed" or "preven") is a recurrent one in Chaucer's work, and important in the characterization of women.

The *Legend* narrator, reader, writer, and translator of books, must leave his "stodye" in the "joly tyme of May" (G. Prol., 39, 36) to have the experience that causes him to write. The events described in the poem send him back to his books again, to find in them and recast stories of good women. In his study, he must exercise his judgment as to which old approved stories represent goodness in women, then which elements of those stories must be suppressed to make the good women even better. Despite his "credence" and "reverence" for the "bokes olde," despite his "entent" to remain true to "the naked text in English" (G. Prol., 81–86), he alters his sources. On what basis shall he make all these literary choices? On the basis of the way life *is*, or the way it *should be*? Does literature *describe* or *prescribe* behavior? Chaucer depicts his *Legend* narrator as a poor candidate to make these choices. Stuck in his library, he knows little about life; he is a precursor of the stereotypical ivory-tower academic. The making and reading of books removes both writer and reader from life.

Then, the subject of women is essentially unknowable to medieval people through their books alone. No man, comments the *Legend* narrator, has been in heaven; but, similarly, no man has been a woman. When he gets his writing assignment, his assigned reading list includes "the epistel of Ovyde" and "Vincent in his Estoryal Myrour" (G. Prol., 305–307), works about women by men. When he turns to his sources, his "sixty bokes, olde and newe" (G. Prol., 273), he, a man, must select from the works of other men only those stories that reflect well on women. To offset his offense against women in retelling the old tale of Criseyde, he must unsay what he "mysseyde" (G. Prol., 430), by making an opposite kind of work. But to "make," say, Lucrece, is not to unmake Criseyde; rather, it is to stand the two made objects side by side and let the reader judge. Most modern readers feel that the virtuous *Legend* heroines are nowhere near as interesting as Criseyde. Readers always refer books to life, even if writers wish they would not; and no woman in any reader's lived experience acts like these women do. The god of Love has given the narrator a misbegotten assignment. Going back only to "olde auctours" (F. Prol., 575) is the wrong approach to learning about his subject. After all, Crisedye is in the old books too, just as much as are the clean maids, true wives, and steadfast widows. On what basis could such a bookish man, so removed from life, judge the accuracy of what he reads about women?

In order to depict a different kind of character, one more true to life, Chaucer must create a different kind of narrator. Take the narrator out of his study, place him in a situation where no books are available. Then the dramatic situation changes: the narrator does not read, but listens; and the mode of knowing can likewise change from the written word to the spoken voice. This narrative shift is the bold stroke that enables Chaucer to depict the Wife of Bath, a woman who is at once a compendium of everything negative ever written about women, and at the same time entirely new. The tension between books and life becomes Alisoun's famous dichotomy: authority versus experience.

On the subject of women, written words are flawed because, as the Wife says, men wrote the books. Women know themselves but cannot teach. Those with authority have no experience, and those with experience, no authority. Old books constitute authoritative discourse[2] by virtue of being old and being written. The speaking voice is feminine and identified with experience, but disadvantaged in being ephemeral. "Matere" in books seems truer than spoken words. Clerks, learned men, had been for centuries writing books telling women how to behave through all the stages of their lives. Theologians, preachers, law-givers, rule-givers of all sorts put words into books. But many women ignored these rules. What, then, constitutes truth: books or behavior? If behavior, then, in order to study women, a man must stop reading. The *Legend* narrator is hard pressed to leave his books; the result is a series of heroines the likes of which never lived. The *Legend* narrator's choice would have cost the hero his head in the "Wife of Bath's Tale." The ladies of King Arthur's court did not send him to the library to find out what women most desire. In fact, he must disregard what the books say and listen to women's talk.

The books-versus-life issue is, however, vastly complex to the medieval audience. The age's moral perception was that virtue consisted precisely in obedience to authoritative discourse. Chaucer was a man who could, in his "Retraction," reject as "worldly vanitees," chaff before God, any works of his "that sownen into synne"—works including those most favored by later readers—and affirm only his "othere bookes of legendes of seintes, and omilies, and moralitee, and devocioun." He could do this because he believed, with his age, that some books were conducive to what he calls "the salvacioun of my soule," some not (X.I., 1085–1090). Despite the fact that the rule books look to twentieth-century readers like mere instruments of patriarchal power, to the medievals they were aids to the salvation of souls. Unlike modern self-help books, their goal was not to make their readers more successful, healthier, or thinner, but to help them get to heaven by properly performing the duties of their estate. Behavior manuals, for example, customarily placed their *dicta* in a cosmic context by beginning with an exhortation to women to honor and serve God; only then did they work their way downward to the minutiae of domestic life. In this world view, the smallest detail of a woman's life—the size of her headdress, her location in her house—would ultimately take her toward or away from eternal salvation. Obedience to rules was a high-stakes enterprise for the medieval believer. So when Chaucer questions obedience to authority, when he shows characters disobeying the theological and social controls believed to contribute to their well-being not only in life but also in the hereafter, he is performing a much more radical act of intellectual rebellion than would a writer rejecting authority today. Chaucer was a man of his age in that the complex relationship of books to life was a vital issue because of a spiritual issue. *Sub specie aeternitatis,* under the aspect of eternity, it was crucial to know what kind of truth was found in books; which books were to be obeyed, which not; which books were conducive to "the salvacioun of [the] soule," which not. Chaucer was a Christian poet intellectually involved with theology.

At the same time, Chaucer was a man of the world and a humorist. A part-time poet, his life was spent largely away from his study. He was busy and active in public life, then hurried home to his study, probably feeling very like the *House of Fame* narrator, who

> goost hom to thy hous anoon,
> And, also domb as any stoon,
> Thou sittest at another book
> Tyl fully dawsed ys thy look.
>   (655–658)

In creating his bookish narrators, Chaucer mocks his bookish self, bleary-eyed with reading. He must have sensed in his personality a combination of those studious narrators with the pilgrim, a gregarious traveler with no intellectual pretensions. Chaucer understood the extent to which books, if taken seriously as he surely did take them, shaped lives. But, in the case of women, he questioned, on the basis of his lived experience, whether this should be so. As Chaucer's biographer Donald Howard commented, "*Chaucer liked women,*"[3] real women. His work showed that he listened to them and compared what he "assayed" to what was "writen."

The one bookish concept with which this book has been concerned—the purity of virgins, the fidelity of wives, the loyalty of widows—was believed in Chaucer's day to be a major shaping principle of women's lives. Chaucer, however, seriously questioned the validity of the rules emanating from it. The tension between reading and life is present throughout Chaucer's works, and it manifests itself clearly in the creation of his women characters. In *The Canterbury Tales,* no books are available. The spoken word is the only source of knowledge. Chaucer's master stroke is replacing the bookish narrator in his study with the sociable Geffrey on pilgrimage. This Geffrey does not automatically refer life to books; his job is to listen. Such a narrator allows a character like Alisoun to speak.

Notes

PREFACE

1. Quoted in Derek Brewer, ed., *Chaucer: The Critical Heritage*, 2 vols. (London: Routledge, 1978), Vol. 1, 86.

CHAPTER 1

1. *The Book of the Knight of the Tower*, trans. William Caxton, ed. M. Y. Offord (London: Oxford UP for EETS, 1971), 3.

2. *The Riverside Chaucer*, 3rd ed., ed. Larry D. Benson (Boston: Houghton, 1987). All references to Chaucer (given in parentheses in the text) are from this edition.

3. Colleen McDannell and Bernhard Lang, *Heaven: A History* (New York: Vintage, 1990), 77.

4. J. A. Burrow, *The Ages of Man: A Study in Medieval Writing and Thought* (Oxford: Clarendon P, 1986), 24, 34.

5. *Les Quatres Ages de l'Homme* (c. 1265), cited in Burrow, *The Ages of Man*, 25.

6. *Il Convivio* (1304–1307), cited in ibid., 33.

7. Ibid., 3.

8. Georges Duby, *The Three Orders: Feudal Society Imagined*, trans. Arthur Goldhammer (Chicago: U of Chicago P, 1980), 73.

9. Jill Mann, *Chaucer and Medieval Estates Satire* (Cambridge: Cambridge UP, 1973), 3, 8, 3.

10. Paul Strohm, *Social Chaucer* (Cambridge: Harvard UP, 1989), 2–4.

11. Ibid., 10.

12. Ibid., 23.

13. Elizabeth Sears, *The Ages of Man: Medieval Interpretations of the Life Cycle* (Princeton: Princeton UP, 1986), 139–140.

14. Duby, *Three Orders*, 57; see also 209.

15. Mann, *Medieval Estates Satire*, 5.

16. Barbara Tuchman, *A Distant Mirror: The Calamitous 14th Century* (New York: Ballantine, 1978), 57.

17. Quoted in Bonnie S. Anderson and Judith P. Zinsser, *A History of Their Own: Women in Europe from Prehistory to the Present*, 2 vols. (New York: Harper, 1988), Vol. 1, 12.

18. Ibid., xv.

19. Robert Hajdu, "The Position of Noblewomen in the Pays des Coutumes, 1100–1300," *Journal of Family History* 5 (Summer 1980): 125.

20. Eileen Power, *Medieval English Nunneries* (Cambridge: Cambridge UP, 1922).

21. See, for example, Graciela Daichman, *Wayward Nuns in Medieval Literature* (Syracuse: Syracuse UP, 1986).

CHAPTER 2

1. All citations from the Bible (given in parentheses in the text) are taken from the Revised Standard Version, Roman Catholic edition (Toronto: Nelson, 1965–1966).

2. Quoted in Katharine Rogers, *The Troublesome Helpmate: A History of Misogyny in Literature* (Seattle: U of Washington P, 1966), 37.

3. Elizabeth Clark, *Jerome, Chrysostom and Friends: Essays and Translations* (New York: Mallen, 1979), 1.

4. Ibid., 2.

5. Quoted in Duby, *Three Orders*, 267.

6. S. K. Heninger, Jr., "The Concept of Order in Chaucer's *Clerk's Tale*," *Journal of English and Germanic Philology* 56 (1957): 383, citing G. R. Owst, *Literature and Pulpit in Medieval England* (orig. 1933), (London: Blackwell, 1961), 551.

7. Natalie Zemon Davis, *Society and Culture in Early Modern France* (Stanford: Stanford UP, 1975), 127.

8. Ibid., 129.

9. Ibid., 129–131.

10. Doris Mary Stenton, *The English Woman in History* (New York: Schocken, 1977), 65.

11. Kenneth E. Kirk, *The Vision of God: The Christian Doctrine of the Highest Good* (Cambridge: James Clark, 1934), 4.

12. Kathleen Ashley, "Medieval Courtesy Literature and Dramatic Mirrors of Female Conduct," in *The Ideology of Conduct: Essays on Literature and the History of Sexuality*, ed. Nancy Armstrong and Leonard Tennenhouse (New York: Methuen, 1987), 25.

13. David Herlihy, "Women and the Sources of Medieval History: The Towns of Northern Italy," in *Medieval Women and the Sources of Medieval History*, ed. Joel T. Rosenthal (Athens: U of Georgia P, 1990), 136–146.

14. Clark, *Jerome, Chrysostom and Friends*, 4.

15. Ibid., 5.

16. Ibid.

17. Ibid., 10.

18. Ibid., 7.

19. Ibid., 11.

20. Kari Elizabeth Børreson, *Subordination and Equivalence: The Nature and Role of Women in Augustine and Thomas Aquinas* (Washington, D.C.: University Press of America, 1981), 93; cf. Brigitte Bedos-Rezak, "Medieval Women in French Sigillographic Sources," in Rosenthal, ed., *Medieval Women and the Sources of Medieval History*, 5.

21. For a survey of theology with reference to women, see Marie-Thérèse d'Alverny, "Comment les théologiens et les philosophes voient la femme," *Cahiers de Civilisation Médievale* 20 (1977): 105–129.

22. Elizabeth Clark and Herbert Richardson, *Women and Religion: A Feminist Sourcebook of Christian Thought* (New York: Harper, 1977), 53–54.

23. Marcia L. Colish, "Cosmetic Theology: The Transformation of a Stoic Theme," *Assays* 1 (1981): 11. On Jerome and women, see also Katharina M. Wilson and Elizabeth M. Makowski, *Wykked Wyves and the Woes of Marriage: Misogamous Literature from Juvenal to Chaucer* (Albany: SUNY P, 1990), 44–50.

24. Clark and Richardson, *Women and Religion*, 78–101; Børreson, *Subordination and Equivalence*, 93–133, 253–305.

25. Davis, *Society and Cultures*, 124–125.

26. Quoted in Julia O'Faolain and Lauro Martines, eds., *Not in God's Image: Women in History from the Greeks to the Victorians* (New York: Harper, 1973), 130.

27. John J. Clifford, "The Ethics of Conjugal Intimacy According to St. Albert the Great," *Theological Studies* 3 no. 1 (1942): 10.

28. Ibid., 16.

29. Quoted in Eric Fuchs, *Sexual Desire and Love: Origins and History of the Christian Ethic of Sexuality and Marriage*, trans. Marcia Daigle (New York: Seabury, 1983), 98; see his chapter 4, "Christianity and Sexuality," 84–134; and Derrick Sherwin Bailey, *Sexual Relation in Christian Thought* (New York: Harper, 1959), 103–166.

30. See Michael M. Sheehan, "The Formation and Stability of Marriage in Fourteenth-Century England: Evidence of an Ely Register," *Mediaeval Studies* 33 (1971): 228–263, and John T. Noonan, Jr., "Power to Choose," *Viator* 4 (1973): 419–434.

31. See Charles Donohue, Jr., "The Canon Law on the Formation of Marriage and Social Practice in the Later Middle Ages," *Journal of Family History* 8 (1983): 144–158, and Philippe Ariès, "The Indissoluble Marriage," in *Western Sexuality: Practice and Precept in Past and Present Times*, ed. Philippe Ariès and André Béjin, trans. Anthony Forster (Oxford: Blackwell, 1985), 140–157. The definitive work on the vastly complex subject of canon law and social custom concerning medieval marriage is James A. Brundage, *Law, Sex, and Christian Society in Medieval Europe* (Chicago: U of Chicago P, 1987).

32. Ariès, "Indissoluble Marriage," 149.

33. David E. Engdahl, " 'Full Faith and Credit' in Merrie Olde England: New Insight for Marriage Conflicts Law from the Thirteenth Century," *Valparaiso University Law Review* 5 (1970): 11. See also Michael M. Sheehan, "The Influence of Canon Law on the Property Rights of Married Women in England," *Mediaeval Studies* 25 (1963): 109–124.

34. George Eliot Howard, *A History of Matrimonial Institutions*, 3 vols. (New York: Humanities P, 1964), Vol. 1, 299–300.

35. Edwin Charles Dargan, *A History of Preaching*, 2 vols. (1905–1912; reprinted: New York: Burt Franklin, 1968), Vol. 1, 230, 308, 309.

36. Ibid., 271.

37. Ibid., 244–245.

38. Jean Delumeau, *Sin and Fear: The Emergence of a Western Guilt Culture 13th–18th Centuries*, trans. Eric Nicholson (New York: St. Martin's, 1990), 432.

39. See D. L. d'Avray and M. Tausche, "Marriage Sermons in *Ad Status* Collections of the Central Middle Ages," *Archives d'histoire doctrinale et littéraire du moyen age* 47 (1980): 71–119; see also Owst, *Literature and Pulpit*, especially 375–404, for further examples and analysis of what Owst calls the "harsh treatment of women usually meted out by the medieval pulpit" (20).

40. See, for example, d'Avray and Tausche, "Marriage, Sermons," 87–88, and Eugene F. Policelli, "Medieval Women: A Preacher's Point of View," *International Journal of Women's Studies* 1 no. 4 (1978): 285–286.

41. For these repeated themes, see, e.g., Thomas Frederick Crane, ed., *The Exempla or Illustrative Stories from the Sermones Vulgares of Jacques de Vitry* (New York: Burt Franklin, 1890; reprinted New York: Lenox Hill, 1971). See Crane's analysis of these *exempla*, especially numbers CCVI, CCXXI, CCXXII, CCXXVII, CCXXVIII, CCXXX, CCXXXI.

42. D'Avray and Tausche, "Marriage Sermons," 103.

43. Delumeau, *Sin and Fear*, 1.

44. Quoted in d'Avray and Tausche, "Marriage Sermons," 100.

45. Woodburn O. Ross, ed. *Middle English Sermons* (London: EETS, 1940), 235; never mind that Judith is used as an *exemplum* of virtuous womanhood when the need arises.

46. Ibid.

47. Siegfried Wenzel, ed. and trans., *Fasciculus Morum: A Fourteenth-Century Preacher's Handbook* (University Park: Pennsylvania State UP, 1989), 681.

48. Ibid., 663.

49. R. H. Hilton, *The English Peasantry in the Later Middle Ages* (Oxford: Clarendon P, 1975), 300.

50. See Donald Weinstein and Rudolph M. Bell, *Saints and Society: The Two Worlds of Western Christendom, 1100–1700* (Chicago: U of Chicago P, 1982), especially chapter 8, and Richard Kieckhefer, *Unquiet Souls: Fourteenth-Century Saints and Their Religious Milieu* (Chicago: U of Chicago P, 1984).

51. Lawrence Cunningham, *The Meaning of Saints* (San Francisco: Harper, 1980), 53.

52. See Brigitte Cazelles, *The Lady As Saint: A Collection of French Hagiographical Romances of the Thirteenth Century* (Philadelphia: U of Pennsylvania P, 1991).

53. Kieckhefer, *Unquiet Souls*, 14.

54. Ibid., 85.

55. Cazelles, *Lady As Saint*, 9.

56. Weinstein and Bell, *Saints and Society*, 237.

57. Kieckhefer, *Unquiet Souls*, 54.

58. Clarissa W. Atkinson, " 'Your Servant, My Mother': The Figure of Saint

Monica in the Ideology of Christian Motherhood," in *Immaculate and Powerful: The Female in Sacred Image and Social Reality,* ed. Clarissa W. Atkinson, Constance H. Buchanan, and Margaret R. Miles (Boston: Beacon, 1985), 152.

59. St. Augustine, *Confessions,* trans. Edward B. Pusey (London: Dent, 1907), Book IX, 192.

60. Kieckhefer, *Unquiet Souls,* 55.

61. Ross, *Middle English Sermons,* 319–320; cf. Theodor Erbe, ed., *Mirk's Festial: A Collection of Homilies by Johannes Mirkus* (London: Kegan Paul, 1905), 230.

62. Erbe, *Mirk's Festial,* 231.

63. #89 in Carleton Brown, ed., *English Lyrics of the XIIIth Century* (Oxford: Clarendon P, 1932), 155.

64. See, for example, Ross, *Middle English Sermons,* 248–249, 318–327.

65. Douglas Gray, ed., *The Oxford Book of Late Medieval Verse and Prose* (Oxford: Clarendon P, 1985), 102.

66. Ibid., 110–112.

67. See, e.g., "The Owl and the Nightingale," #79, in Brown, *Lyrics of the XIIIth Century,* 141–142; and #131 in Carleton Brown, ed., *English Lyrics of the XIVth Century* (Oxford: Clarendon P, 1924), 230–233.

68. See Joëlle Beaucamp, "Le vocabulaire de la faiblesse féminine dans les textes juridiques romains du IIIe au VIe siècle," *Revue historique de droit français et étranger* 54 (1976): 485–508.

69. See Stenton, *English Woman.* See also Florence Griswold Buckstaff, "Married Women's Property in Anglo-Saxon and Anglo-Norman Law," *Annals of the American Academy of Political and Social Science* 4 (1983): 233–264; Ruth Kittel, "Women under the Law in Medieval England, 1066–1485," in *The Women of England from Anglo-Saxon Times to the Present: Interpretive Bibliographical Essays,* ed. Barbara Kanner (Hamden, CT: Archon, 1979), 124–137; and Sheehan, "The Influence of Canon Law."

70. Stenton, *English Woman,* 32.

71. Judith M. Bennett, "Public Power and Authority in the Medieval English Countryside," in *Women and Power in the Middle Ages,* ed. Mary Erler and Mary Anne Kowalewski (Athens: U of Georgia P, 1988), 21; cf. Stenton, *English Woman,* 30, 32.

72. Stenton, *English Woman,* 30.

73. Judith Bennett, "Public Power and Authority," 22–23.

74. George Homans, *English Villagers of the Thirteenth Century* (New York: Russell, 1960), 112.

75. See Strohm, *Social Chaucer,* 1–23.

76. Homans, *English Villagers,* 137.

77. Stenton, *English Woman,* 29–30.

78. See Eleanor Searle, "Seigneurial Control of Women's Marriage: The Antecedents and Function of Merchet in England," *Past and Present* 82 (1979): 3–43, and Eleanor Searle, "*Merchet* and Women's Property Rights in Medieval England," in *Women and the Law: A Social Historical Perspective,* ed. D. Kelly Weisberg (Cambridge: Schenckman, 1982), 45–68.

79. See B. A. Windeatt, trans., *The Book of Margery Kempe* (Harmondsworth, UK: Penguin, 1985), especially chapter 11, 58–60.

80. Diane Bornstein, *The Lady in the Tower: Medieval Courtesy Literature for Women* (Hamden, CT: Archon, 1983), 13.

81. "Courtesy Literature," *Dictionary of the Middle Ages*, Vol. 3 (New York: Scribner's, 1983), 660–667.

82. Bornstein, *Lady in the Tower*, 11–12.

83. Arlyn Diamond, "Chaucer's Women and Women's Chaucer," in *The Authority of Experience: Essays in Feminist Criticism*, ed. Arlyn Diamond and Lee R. Edwards (Amherst: U of Massachusetts P, 1977), 62–63.

84. Ashley, "Medieval Courtesy Literature," 26.

85. Nancy Armstrong and Leonard Tennenhouse, introduction, in Armstrong and Tennenhouse, eds., *Ideology of Conduct*, 5.

86. "The Way of Christ's Love," #90 and "The Way of Woman's Love," #91, in Brown, *Lyrics of the XIIIth Century*, 161–163.

87. #394 and #395 in Richard Leighton Greene, ed., *The Early English Carols* (Oxford: Clarendon, 1935), 263–264; "In Praise of Woman," #34, in Rossell Hope Robbins, ed., *Secular Lyrics of the XIVth and XVth Centuries* (Oxford: Clarendon P, 1952), 31.

88. "Against Hasty Marriage, II," #41, and "A Henpecked Husband's Complaint, I and II," #43 and #44, in Robbins, *Secular Lyrics*, 37, 38–40; and #401 and #406–409 in Greene, *Early English Carols*, 267, 271–275.

89. "Contempt of the World," #8, in R. T. Davies, ed., *Medieval English Lyrics: A Critical Anthology* (Evanston: Northwestern U P, 1964), 56–57; and "On the Follies of Fashion," #74, in Brown, *Lyrics of the XIIIth Century*, 133–134.

90. "Scorn of Women," #211, and "Abuse of Women," #212, in Robbins, *Secular Lyrics*, 224–225.

91. Tauno Mustanoja, introduction in *The Good Wife Taught Her Daughter. The Good Wyfe wold a Pylgrimage. The Thewis of Gud Women*, ed. Tauno Mustanoja (Helsinki: Suomalaisen Kirjallisuuden Seuran, 1948), 80, 159–172.

92. Ibid., 159–172.

93. *The Goodman of Paris*, ed. Eileen Power (London: Routledge, 1928).

94. Eileen Power, *Medieval People* (New York: Harper, 1963), 97.

95. *Goodman of Paris*, 41–42.

96. Power, *Medieval People*, 98.

97. *Goodman of Paris*, 41–43.

98. Ibid., 3.

99. *Book of the Knight*, 11.

100. Ibid., 3.

101. Ibid., 25; cf. Rosemary Combridge, "Ladies, Queens, and Decorum," *Reading Medieval Studies* 1 (1975): 75, and Francesco de Barberino, in Alice A. Hentsch, *De la littérature didactique au moyen âge s'adressant spécialement aux femmes* (Geneva: Slatkine Reprints, 1975), 45, 75, 105.

102. Barberino, in Hentsch, *Littérature didactique*, 108.

103. Ibid.

104. *Book of the Knight*, 19–20, 37–38.

105. Jerome, in Hentsch, *Littérature didactique*, 27.

106. Barberino, in ibid., 113.

CHAPTER 3

1. *Goodman of Paris,* 94.

2. D. 1270; *Des quatre tens d'aage d'ome,* cited in Eileen Power, "The Position of Women," *The Legacy of the Middle Ages,* ed. C. G. Crump and E. F. Jacob (Oxford: Clarendon P, 1926), 404.

3. Christine de Pisan, *The Book of the City of Ladies,* trans. Earl Jeffrey Richards (New York: Persea, 1982), 225–227.

4. Ibid., 227.

5. Ibid., 230, 233.

6. Ibid., 228.

7. Ibid., 235, 236, 239.

8. Jane Tibbetts Schulenberg, "Saints' Lives As a Source for the History of Women, 500–1500," in Rosenthal, ed., *Medieval Women and the Sources of Medieval History,* 308.

9. Elaine Tuttle Hansen discusses this matter in her important article, "Irony and the Antifeminist Narrator in Chaucer's *Legend of Good Women," Journal of English and Germanic Philology* 82 no. 1 (1983): 11–31, to which the present discussion of characterization of the good women is indebted.

10. Ibid., 14.

11. Ann McMillan, introduction, in Geoffrey Chaucer, *The Legend of Good Women,* trans. Ann McMillan (Houston: Rice UP, 1987), 5.

12. Ibid., 3.

13. Ibid.; cf. John M. Fyler, *Chaucer and Ovid* (New Haven: Yale UP, 1979), 105, and Jill Mann, *Geoffrey Chaucer* (Atlantic Highlands, NJ: Humanities P, 1991), 5–7.

14. Compare *Ovid: Heroides and Amores,* trans. Grant Showerman (Cambridge: Harvard UP, 1921), XII, 142–159, to *Ovid's Metamorphoses,* trans. Rolfe Humphries (Bloomington: Indiana UP, 1955), VII, 153–167.

15. Lisa J. Kiser, *Telling Classical Tales: Chaucer and the Legend of Good Women* (Ithaca, Cornell U P, 1983), 100; see also Fyler, *Chaucer and Ovid,* 101–102.

16. Hansen, "Irony," 21.

17. McMillan, introduction to the *Legend,* 38.

18. Christine, *City of Ladies,* 237.

19. Ibid., 239.

20. Hansen, "Irony," 22.

21. Ibid.

22. Brundage, *Law, Sex, and Christian Society,* 264.

23. Donohue, "Canon Law," 146.

24. Brundage, *Law, Sex, and Christian Society,* 501.

25. See Frances Gies and Joseph Gies, *Marriage and Family in the Middle Ages* (New York: Harper, 1987), 244, citing R. H. Helmholz, *Marriage Litigation in Medieval England* (London: Cambridge UP, 1974), 29; also cf. Brundage, *Law, Sex, and Christian Society,* 501.

26. *Ovid: Heroides and Amores,* trans. Showerman, VII: 91; VIII: 97.

27. Virgil, *The Aeneid,* trans. Robert Fitzgerald (New York: Random, 1983), IV.

28. Gies and Gies, *Marriage and Family,* 244.

29. Hansen, "Irony," 22.

30. Mann, *Chaucer*, 44.

31. Robert Worth Frank, *Chaucer and the Legend of Good Women* (Cambridge: Harvard UP, 1972), 96.

32. *Ovid: Metamorphoses*, trans. Humphries, VI: l. 553.

33. Ibid., ll. 613–614.

34. Ibid., 11. 657–659.

35. John Marshall Carter, *Rape in Medieval England* (Lanham, NY: UP of America, 1985), 94.

36. Mann, *Chaucer*, 9.

37. Anderson and Zinsser, *History of Their Own*, Vol. 2, 30.

38. Hansen, "Irony," 14.

39. Mann, *Chaucer*, 44; see also Mann's chapter 1, "Women and Betrayal," for an explanation of the relationship between the *Legend* heroines and Criseyde.

40. Nicole Loraux, *Tragic Ways of Killing a Woman*, trans. Anthony Forster (Cambridge: Harvard UP, 1987), 9, 11–12.

41. Ruth M. Ames, "The Feminist Connections of Chaucer's *Legend of Good Women*," in *Chaucer in the Eighties*, ed. Julian N. Wasserman and Robert J. Blanch (Syracuse: Syracuse UP, 1986), 67.

42. Hansen, "Irony," 20.

43. Ames, "Feminist Connections," 67.

44. Frank, *Chaucer and the Legend*, 118.

45. Hansen, "Irony," 24.

46. McMillan, introduction to the *Legend*, 42.

47. Mann, *Chaucer*, 39.

48. See Elaine Tuttle Hansen's provocative discussion of male weakness in *The Legend of Good Women* in *Chaucer and the Fictions of Gender* (Berkeley: U of California P, 1992), 3–10. Hansen sees these tales in terms of the threat of "heterosexual union" to "stable masculine identity" (3); temporary weakness "signal[s] the heroes' feminization" (7), while the return of strength requires that they leave the "dangerous state" of subjection (5).

49. Frank, *Chaucer and the Legend*, 68, 75.

50. Ibid., 76–77.

51. Hansen, "Irony," 26.

52. Frank, *Chaucer and the Legend*, 119.

53. McMillan, introduction to the *Legend*, 8.

54. See G. L. Kittredge's important early work on this subject, "Chaucer's Discussion of Marriage," *Modern Philology* 9 no. 4 (1912): 1–33, especially 29–33.

55. Nevill Coghill, *The Poet Chaucer* (London: Oxford UP, 1967), 12.

56. Diamond, "Chaucer's Women," 80.

57. Velma Richmond, "Pacience in Adversitee: Chaucer's Presentation of Marriage," *Viator* 10 (1979): 350.

58. On the bachelor/lady situation, see Georges Duby, *Medieval Marriage: Two Modes from Twelfth-Century France*, trans. Elborg Forster (Baltimore: Johns Hopkins UP, 1978).

59. Hansen, *Chaucer and the Fictions of Gender*, 275.

60. Mann, *Chaucer*, 116.

61. Hansen, *Chaucer and the Fictions of Gender*, 280, 273, 269.

62. Ibid., 113.

63. Richmond, "Pacience in Adversitee," 331.

64. Bernard Huppé, *A Reading of the Canterbury Tales* (Albany: State U of New York P, 1964), 169.

CHAPTER 4

1. John of Salisbury, *Frivolities of Courtiers and Footprints of Philosophers: Being a Translation of the First, Second, and Third Books of the "Policraticus" of John of Salisbury [Bishop of Chartres] (1159)*, trans. Joseph B. Pike (Minneapolis: U of Minnesota P, 1938), 199.

2. Bartholomaeus Anglicus, *De Proprietatibus Rerum* (c. 1250), in *Chaucer: Sources and Backgrounds*, ed. Robert P. Miller (New York: Oxford UP, 1977), 387.

3. Eustace Deschamps (c. 1346–1406), *The Mirror of Marriage*, trans. Margaret Ehrhart, in ibid., 389.

4. John Boswell, *The Kindness of Strangers: The Abandonment of Children in Western Europe from Late Antiquity to the Renaissance* (New York: Pantheon, 1988), 226.

5. Georges Duby, *William Marshall: The Flower of Chivalry*, trans. Richard Howard (New York: Pantheon, 1985), 132.

6. Lynda E. Boose, "The Father's House and the Daughter in It: The Structures of Western Culture's Daughter-Father Relationship," in *Daughters and Fathers*, ed. Lynda E. Boose and Betty S. Flowers (Baltimore: Johns Hopkins UP, 1989), 33.

7. Thomas Pison, "Liminality in *The Canterbury Tales*," *Genre* 10 (1977): 158.

8. Homans, *English Villagers*, 195.

9. Georges Duby, *The Knight, the Lady and the Priest: The Making of Modern Marriage in Medieval France*, trans. Barbara Bray (New York: Pantheon, 1983), 47.

10. Ibid.

11. Duby, *Medieval Marriage*, 4–5.

12. Carolyn Dinshaw, *Chaucer's Sexual Poetics* (Madison: U of Wisconsin P, 1989), 57, citing Levi-Strauss.

13. Duby, *Medieval Marriage*, 11.

14. Dinshaw, *Chaucer's Sexual Poetics*, 96.

15. Derek Brewer, *Symbolic Stories: Traditional Narratives of the Family Drama in English Literature* (London: Longman, 1988), 9, 11.

16. Fuchs, *Sexual Desire and Love*, 93; cf. David Herlihy, "Family," *American Historical Review* 96 no. 1 (1991): 4–5.

17. Boose, "The Father's House," 63.

18. Ibid., 23.

19. Ibid., 63.

20. Ibid., 25, citing Levi-Strauss.

21. Ibid., 40.

22. Ibid., 67.

23. Anne Middleton, "The *Physician's Tale* and Love's Martyrs: 'Ensamples Mo Than Ten' As a Method in the *Canterbury Tales*," *Chaucer Review* 8 no. 1 (1973):

11. For Jean's version of the story, see *The Romance of the Rose*, trans. Harry W. Robbins (New York: Dutton, 1962), Chap. 27, 118–122.

24. See, for example, Karl Young, "The Maidenly Virtues of Chaucer's Virginia," *Speculum* 16 (1941): 340–349.

25. Weinstein and Bell, *Saints and Society*, 234.

26. Beryl Rowland, "The Physician's 'Historical Thyng Notable' and the Man of Law," *ELH* 40 no. 2 (1973): 166.

27. Quoted in Jane Tibbetts Schulenberg, "The Heroics of Virginity: Brides of Christ and Sacrificial Mutilation," in *Women in the Middle Ages and the Renaissance: Literary and Historical Perspectives*, ed. Mary Beth Rose (Syracuse: Syracuse UP, 1986), 32.

28. Middleton, *"Physician's Tale,"* 19.

29. Dinshaw, *Chaucer's Sexual Poetics*, 96–97.

30. Emerson Brown, "What Is Chaucer Doing with the Physician and His Tale?" *Philological Quarterly* 60 no. 2 (1981): 135, citing Middleton, *"Physician's Tale,"* 13.

31. Middleton, *"Physician's Tale,"* 15.

32. See Peter G. Beidler, "The Pairing of the *Franklin's Tale* and the *Physician's Tale*," *Chaucer Review* 3 no. 4 (1969): 277–278.

33. Emerson Brown, "What Is Chaucer Doing?," 136.

34. Schulenberg, "Heroics of Virginity," 34–36.

35. J. D. W. Crowther, "Chaucer's *Physician's Tale* and Its Saint," *English Studies in Canada* 8 no. 2 (1982): 135.

36. R. Howard Bloch, *Medieval Misogyny and the Invention of Western Romantic Love* (Chicago: U of Chicago P, 1991), 114.

37. Ibid., 105, 110.

38. Ibid., 100.

39. Ibid., 102.

40. Ibid., 114.

41. Brewer, *Symbolic Stories*, 97.

42. See James L. Boren, "Alysoun of Bath and the Vulgate 'Perfect Wife,' " *Neuphilologische Mitteilungen* 76 (1975): 247–256.

43. Herlihy, "Family," 8.

44. From the marriage ceremony in the Sarum Missal, trans. Frederick E. Warren (London: Alexander Moring, 1911), in R. Miller, *Chaucer: Sources*, 381.

45. Ibid., 386–387.

46. Donald R. Benson, "The Marriage 'Encomium' in the *Merchant's Tale*: A Chaucerian Crux," *Chaucer Review* 14 no. 1 (1979–1980): 48–51.

47. (London: Edward Marchant, 1616).

CHAPTER 5

1. Brian Stone, trans., *Medieval English Verse* (Harmondsworth: Penguin, 1964), 99.

2. *Goodman of Paris*, 136–137.

3. Homily 24 on Ephesians, cited in Gerard H. Ettlinger, "Church Fathers and Desert Mothers: Male and Female in the Early Church," *America* 164 no. 20 (1991): 561.

4. G. G. Coulton, *The Medieval Scene* (Cambridge: Cambridge UP, 1959), 35–36.

5. Bloch, *Medieval Misogyny*, 15, 21–23.

6. *Apostolic Constitutions*, Book 3, section 5, as quoted in Joann McNamara and Suzanne F. Wemple, "Sanctity and Power: The Dual Pursuit of Medieval Women," in *Becoming Visible: Women in European History*, ed. Renate Bridenthal and Claudia Koontz (Boston: Houghton, 1977), 94.

7. Duby, *Three Orders*, 28.

8. Duby, *William Marshall*, 38–39.

9. See Frederic Tubach, *Index Exemplorum: A Handbook of Medieval Religious Tales* (Helsinki: Suomalainen Tiedeakatemia Akademia Scientiarum Fennica, 1969), entries 1359, 5284–5285, 5289.

10. *Le Blasme de Fames*, in Gloria K. Fiero, Wendy Pfeffer, and Mathé Allain, *Three Medieval Views of Women: "La Contenance des Fames," "Le Bien des Fames," "Le Blasme des Fames"* (New Haven: Yale UP, 1989), ll. 147–148.

11. Owst, *Literature and Pulpit*, 387.

12. Ross, *Middle English Sermons*, 324.

13. Erbe, *Mirk's Festial*, 229–230; cf. Owst, *Literature and Pulpit*, 44.

14. Erbe, *Mirk's Festial*, 229.

15. G. G. Coulton, *Life in the Middle Ages*, 4 vols. (Cambridge: Cambridge UP, 1928–1930), Vol. 1, 222.

16. See, for example, Garin lo Brun in Hentsch, *Littérature didactique*, 45–48.

17. *Book of the Knight*, 24.

18. Cazelles, *Lady As Saint*, 59.

19. Ll. 146–151 in ibid., 115.

20. Ll. 221–224 in ibid., 116.

21. *The Romance of the Rose*, 385.

22. Garin lo Brun in Hentsch, *Littérature didactique*, 47.

23. Matfre Ermengau, in ibid., 92.

24. Bornstein, *Lady in the Tower*, 51, referring especially to the Knight of the Tower.

25. *Goodman of Paris*, 172.

26. *Book of the Knight*, 29, 35.

27. *Book of the Knight*, 124.

28. "*Good Wife Taught Her Daughter*," 161.

29. Elizabeth Salter, *Chaucer: The Knight's Tale and the Clerk's Tale* (Great Neck, NY: Barron's, 1962), 63.

30. Anne Middleton puts Chaucer's version of the Grisilde story in the context of other fourteenth-century versions in "The Clerk and His Tale: Some Literary Contexts," *Studies in the Ages of Chaucer* 2 (1980): 121–150.

31. For a survey of twentieth-century criticism of the *Clerk's Tale*, see Charlotte C. Morse, "Critical Approaches to the *Clerk's Tale*," in *Chaucer's Religious Tales*, ed. C. David Benson and Elizabeth Robertson (Cambridge: Brewer, 1990), 71–83.

32. Middleton, "Clerk and His Tale," 121.

33. Dolores Frese, "Chaucer's *Clerk's Tale:* The Monster and the Critics," *Chaucer Review* 8 (1973): 137.

34. Diana T. Childress, "Between Romance and Legend: 'Secular Hagiography' in Medieval English Literature," *Philological Quarterly* 57 no. 3 (1978): 318.

35. Cf. the situation of Marshall's wife in Duby, *William Marshall*, 136.

36. Owst, *Literature and Pulpit*, 389; Heninger, "Concept of Order," 383–384.

37. Deborah Tannen, *You Just Don't Understand: Women and Men in Conversation* (New York: Morrow, 1990), 24–25, 47.

38. *Book of the Knight*, 133.

39. As quoted in Sharon A. Farmer, "Persuasive Voices: Clerical Images of Medieval Wives," *Speculum* 61 no. 3 (1986): 517, 526, 535; see also Michael M. Sheehan, "Choice of Marriage Partner in the Middle Ages: Development and Mode of Application of a Theory of Marriage," *Studies in Medieval and Renaissance History* ns 1 (1978): 24.

40. Farmer, "Persuasive Voices," 526, 538.

41. Sharon A. Farmer, "Softening the Hearts of Men: Women, Embodiment, and Persuasion in the Thirteenth Century," in *Embodied Love: Sensuality and Relationship as Feminist Values*, ed. Paula McCooey, Sharon A. Farmer, and Mary Ellen Ross (San Francisco: Harper, 1987), 127.

42. Jane Cowgill, "Patterns of Feminine and Masculine Persuasion in the *Melibee* and the *Parson's Tale*," in Benson and Robertson, eds., *Chaucer's Religious Tales*, 173. Also see this essay for a discussion of feminine persuasion in the "Second Nun's Tale" and the "Wife of Bath's Tale."

43. Donald H. Reiman, "The Real 'Clerk's Tale'; or, Patient Griselda Exposed," *Texas Studies in Language and Literature* 5 (1963): 363.

44. Brundage, *Law, Sex, and Christian Society*, 183.

45. Jill Mann, "Satisfaction and Payment in Middle English Literature," *Studies in the Ages of Chaucer* 5 (1983): 31.

46. See, e.g., the Knight in Hentsch, *Littérature didactique*, 145.

47. Robert Stepsis, "*Potentia Absoluta* and the *Clerk's Tale*," *Chaucer Review* 10 (1975–1976): 142.

48. Homily 20 on Ephesians, cited in Ettlinger, "Church Fathers," 561.

49. In "Nominalism and the Dynamics of the *Clerk's Tale: Homo Viator* as Woman," in Benson and Robertson, eds., *Chaucer's Religious Tales*, 111–119, Elizabeth Kirk argues the contrary, that "Griselda's silence . . . is an affirmation of her autonomy, her selfhood, as an entity with the power of choice" and, further, that "Griselda defends the integrity of her will in a totally disempowering world" precisely by her voluntary silence (117); but Kirk does not discuss the function of the "Envoy" in articulating the opposing viewpoint.

50. See also illustration number 173 in Jonathan Alexander and Paul Binski, *Age of Chivalry: Art in Plantagenet England, 1200–1400* (London: Royal Academy of Arts, 1987).

51. Patricia Meyer Spacks, *Gossip* (Chicago: U of Chicago P, 1985), 44.

52. Mann, *Chaucer*, 64.

CHAPTER 6

1. Chap. 88, ll. 156–157.

2. #404 in Greene, *Early English Carols*, 271.

3. Georges Duby and Philippe Braunstein, "The Emergence of the Individual," in *Revelations of the Medieval World*, Vol. 2 of *A History of Private Life*, ed.

George Duby, trans. Arthur Goldhammer (Cambridge: Belknap P of Harvard UP, 1988), 509–511.

4. Alexander Rysman, "How the 'Gossip' Became a Woman," *Journal of Communications* 27 no. 1 (1977): 176; Spacks, *Gossip*, 25.

5. Owst, *Literature and Pulpit*, 44.

6. Spacks, *Gossip*, 25.

7. Tannen, *You Just Don't Understand*, 80.

8. Angela M. Lucas, *Women in the Middle Ages: Religion, Marriage, and Letters* (New York: St. Martin's, 1983), 123.

9. *The Good Wife Taught Her Daughter*, 161, 159.

10. #103 in Davis, *Medieval English Lyrics*, 198.

11. Bornstein, *Lady in the Tower*, 57.

12. *Goodman of Paris*, 179.

13. Ibid., 180–181.

14. Chap. 80, esp. ll. 9, 24, 167.

15. All quotations (line references in parentheses in the text) from the mystery cycle plays are from *English Mystery Plays: A Selection*, ed. Peter Happé (Harmondsworth: Penguin, 1975).

16. Spacks, *Gossip*, 5.

17. Ibid., 37.

18. Rysman, "How the 'Gossip' Became a Woman," 179–180.

19. Ray Oldenburg, *The Great Good Place* (New York: Paragon House, 1989), 232–233.

20. Tannen, *You Just Don't Understand*, 109–110.

21. Ibid., 98.

22. Rogers, *Troublesome Helpmate*, 93–94.

23. Quoted in Francis Gies and Joseph Gies, *Life in a Medieval Castle* (New York: Crowell, 1974), 81–82.

24. Katherine Asher Henderson and Barbara F. McManus, *Half Humankind: Contexts and Texts of the Controversy about Women in England, 1540–1640* (Urbana: U of Illinois P, 1985), 62.

25. "Abuse of Women," #212, in Robbins, *Secular Lyrics*, 225–226.

26. "Against Hasty Marriage II," #41, in ibid., 37–38.

27. Martin Stevens, *Four Middle English Mystery Cycles: Textual, Contextual, and Critical Interpretations* (Princeton: Princeton UP, 1987), 176.

28. Owst, *Literature and Pulpit*, 492.

29. Quoted in Coulton, *Life in Middle Ages*, 119.

30. Anderson and Zinsser, *History of Their Own*, Vol. 1, 439.

31. Herlihy, "Family," 5. See also court cases cited by Paul Hair in *Before the Bawdy Court: Selections from Church Court and Other Records Relating to the Correction of Moral Offenses in England, Scotland, and New England, 1300–1800* (London: Elek, 1972). This is a compilation of eccesiastical and civil cases in the British Isles from 1300 to 1800, showing men being punished for wife-beating. One Thomas Louchard pled guilty to the charge in 1300 and is recorded as being "whipped *in the usual way* around the market" (44; my italics). The implication is that this was a customary penalty.

32. Shulamith Shahar, *The Fourth Estate: A History of Women in the Middle Ages*, trans. Chaya Galai (London: Methuen, 1985), 89–90.

33. V. A. Kolve, *Chaucer and the Imagery of Narrative: The First Five Canterbury Tales* (Stanford: Stanford UP, 1984), 199.

34. Bornstein, *Lady in the Tower,* 63; Hentsch, *Littérature didactique,* 121.

CHAPTER 7

1. Early 14th century; in O'Faolain and Martines, *Not in God's Image,* 169.

2. A. D. Adams, C. H. Irwin, and S. A. Waters, eds., *Cruden's Complete Concordance to the Bible* (Grand Rapids: Zondervan, 1968), 242.

3. Lucas, *Women in the Middle Ages,* 121, citing Owst, *Literature and Pulpit,* 386.

4. Quoted in Mark Girouard, *Life in the English Country House: A Social and Architectural History* (New Haven: Yale UP, 1978), 46.

5. Ibid., 40, 45–46; Georges Duby, "The Aristocratic Households of Medieval France," in Duby, *Revelations of the Medieval World,* 60–61; Eric Mercer, *English Vernacular Houses* (London: Her Majesty's Stationer's Office, 1975), chapter 1; Margaret Wood, *The English Medieval House* (New York: Harper, 1965), chapters 4 and 5; Deborah S. Ellis, "Domestic Treachery in the *Clerk's Tale,*" in *Ambiguous Realities: Women in the Middle Ages and the Renaissance,* ed. Carol Levin and Jeanie Watson (Detroit: Wayne State UP, 1987), 105.

6. Duby, "Aristocratic Households," 62.

7. Sr. Mary Ernestina Whitmore, *Medieval English Domestic Life and Amusements in the Age of Chaucer* (New York: Cooper Square, 1972), 31; cf. Girouard, *Life in the English Country House,* 40.

8. Danielle Régnier-Bohler, "Imagining the Self," in Duby, *Revelations of the Medieval World,* 344.

9. P. A. Faulkner, "Domestic Planning from the Twelfth to the Fourteenth Century," *Archaeological Journal* 115 (1958): 180.

10. Girouard, *Life in the English Country House,* 53.

11. Régnier-Bohler, "Imagining the Self," in Duby, *Revelations of the Medieval World,* 332.

12. Charles de La Roncière, "Tuscan Nobles on the Eve of the Renaissance," in Duby, *Revelations of the Medieval World,* 189.

13. Ibid., 288.

14. Barberino, in Hentsch, *Littérature didactique,* 107–108.

15. *Rules of Marriage,* compiled c. 1450–1481, quoted in O'Faolain and Martines, *Not in God's Image,* 177.

16. La Roncière, "Tuscan Nobles," in Duby, *Revelations of the Medieval World,* 189.

17. Frank Crisp, *Medieval Gardens,* ed. Catherine Childs Paterson (New York: Hacker, 1966). The plate references in parentheses are to this text.

18. Régnier-Bohler, "Imagining the Self," in Duby, *Revelations of the Medieval World,* 322.

19. Whitmore, *Medieval English Domestic Life,* 63–64.

20. Jacques d'Amiens, *L'art d'amors,* in Hentsch, *Littérature didactique,* 71.

21. *Saint Hildegard of Bingen: Symphonia,* trans. Barbara Newman (Ithaca: Cornell UP, 1988), 135.

22. Quotes in this passage are as cited in Danielle Jacquart and Claude Thomas-

set, *Sexuality and Medicine in the Middle Ages,* trans. Matthew Anderson (Princeton: Princeton UP, 1988), 103–104.

23. Chap. 19: ll. 24–25, 26–27, 100.

24. McDannell and Lang, *Heaven: A History,* 76.

25. Quoted in Owst, *Literature and Pulpit,* 119.

26. See also, for example, plate 3, in Marina Warner, *Alone of All Her Sex: The Myth and the Cult of the Virgin Mary* (New York: Vintage, 1983), 111, and plates 164, 166, 457, 467, and 473, in George Zarnecki, *Art of the Medieval World* (Englewood Cliffs: Prentice, 1975).

27. Quoted in La Roncière, "Tuscan Nobles," in Duby, *Revelations of the Medieval World,* 285.

28. *La Contenance des Fames,* in Fiero et al., *Three Medieval Views,* 91.

29. Chap. 41: ll. 38–41.

30. Ibid., ll. 73–75.

31. Quoted in Owst, *Literature and Pulpit,* 119.

32. Ibid., 385–387.

33. As quoted in Rogers, *Troublesome Helpmate,* 69–70, and Owst, *Literature and Pulpit,* 395–396.

34. Quoted in Owst, *Literature and Pulpit,* 385–387.

35. *La Contenance des Fames,* in Fiero et al., *Three Medieval Views,* ll. 127–128.

36. *Book of the Knight,* 25.

37. Hentsch, *Littérature didactique,* 46, 76, 108.

38. Peter Brown, *The Body and Society: Men, Women, and Sexual Renunciation in Early Christianity* (New York: Columbia UP, 1988), 316.

39. Chap. 47: l. 35.

40. See Kenneth Kee, "Two Chaucerian Gardens," *Mediaeval Studies* 23 (1961): 154–162, on the gardens in the "Merchant's Tale" and the "Franklin's Tale."

41. Owst, *Literature and Pulpit,* 388.

42. Lucas, *Women in the Middle Ages,* 121.

43. Anderson and Zinsser, *History of Their Own,* Vol. 1, 192–193.

44. Christian K. Zacher, *Curiosity and Pilgrimage: The Literature of Discovery in Fourteenth-Century England* (Baltimore: Johns Hopkins UP, 1976), 108; Zacharias P. Thundy, "Matheolus, Chaucer, and the Wife of Bath," in *Chaucerian Problems and Perspectives,* ed. Edward Vasta and Zacharias Thundy (Notre Dame: Notre Dame UP, 1979), 48; Knight, in Hentsch, *Litérature didactique,* 129.

45. Joseph E. Grennen, "Chaucer's Man of Law and the Constancy of Justice," *JEGP* 84 no. 4 (1985): 505.

46. John Speirs, *Chaucer the Maker* (London: Faber, 1951), 135.

47. Paul Ruggiers, *The Art of the Canterbury Tales* (Madison: U of Wisconsin P, 1967), 172.

48. Huppé, *Reading of the Canterbury Tales,* 106.

49. Kolve, *Chaucer and Imagery,* 302. This is the image Edward Burne-Jones chooses to illustrate the tale in the Kelmscott edition of 1894. See *The Works of Geoffrey Chaucer: A Facsimile of the William Morris Kelmscott Chaucer with the Original 87 Illustrations by Edward Burne-Jones* (Cleveland: World, 1958), 43.

50. Kolve, *Chaucer and Imagery,* 302, 335.

51. Ibid., 326.

52. Ibid., 330.

53. Ibid., 339.

54. Ibid., 354.

55. Ibid., 356, citing II.B.¹356 and 347.

56. See Ellis, "Domestic Treachery," 104.

57. Ibid., 100–105.

58. See, among many others, Barberino, in Hentsch, *Littérature didactique*, 112.

59. Hansen, "Irony," 23.

60. Régnier-Bohler, "Imagining the Self," in Duby, *Revelations of the Medieval World*, 316.

61. Giovanni Boccaccio, *Concerning Famous Women*, trans. Guido A. Guarino (New Brunswick: Rutgers UP, 1963), 102.

62. Ibid.

63. Régnier-Bohler, "Imagining the Self," in Duby, *Revelations of the Medieval World*, 344.

64. J. B. Post, "Ravishment of Women and the Statutes of Westminster," in *Legal Records and the Historian*, ed. J. H. Baker (London: Royal Historical Society, 1978), 140–164.

65. Hansen, "Irony," 22.

66. Loraux, *Tragic Ways*, 7.

67. Ibid., 11.

68. Frank, *Chaucer and the Legend*, 95.

69. Erik Erikson, *Childhood and Society*, 2nd ed. (New York: Norton, 1963), 103–104.

CHAPTER 8

1. Owst, *Literature and Pulpit*, 404.

2. See Margaret Scott, *A Visual History of Costume: The Fourteenth and Fifteenth Centuries* (London: Batsford, 1986), 15; cf. James Laver, *Costume and Fashion: A Concise History* (New York, Thames: 1982), 71.

3. See Judith Shaw, "The Influence of Canonical and Episcopal Reform on Popular Books of Instruction," in *The Popular Literature of Medieval England*, ed. Thomas J. Heffernan, Tennessee Studies in Literature 28 (Knoxville: U of Tennessee P, 1985), 55.

4. Duby, *William Marshall*, 19.

5. Brown, *Lyrics of the XIIIth Century*, 133–134.

6. Scott, *Visual History of Costume*, 14; cf. Tuchman, *Distant Mirror*, 19.

7. McDannell and Lang, *Heaven*, 77–78.

8. Elizabeth Wilson, *Adorned in Dreams: Fashion and Modernity* (Berkeley: U of California P, 1985), 20.

9. Iris Brooke, *English Costume of the Later Middle Ages: The Fourteenth and Fifteenth Centuries* (New York, Barnes, 1935), 10.

10. Wilson, *Adorned in Dreams*, 20.

11. Frances Elizabeth Baldwin, *Sumptuary Legislation and Personal Regulation in England* (Baltimore: Johns Hopkins UP, 1926), 9. On the relationship of the sumptuary laws to the social class structure of Chaucer's England, see Strohm, *Social Chaucer*, 5–7.

12. Quoted in Baldwin, *Sumptuary Legislation*, 46–47.

13. Tuchman, *Distant Mirror*, 19.

14. Quoted in Baldwin, *Sumptuary Legislation*, 47.

15. Quoted in ibid., 48.

16. Ibid., 49.

17. Ibid., 51.

18. Ibid., 101.

19. Bloch, *Medieval Misogyny*, 99.

20. Scott, *Visual History of Costume*, 14.

21. Quoted in Owst, *Literature and Pulpit*, 314.

22. Scott, *Visual History of Costume*, 14.

23. Quoted in Owst, *Literature and Pulpit*, 96.

24. Wenzel, *Fasciculus Morum*, 659, 661.

25. Quoted in Owst, *Literature and Pulpit*, 392. For the visual arts' reinforcement of the preachers' condemnation "by personifying *luxuria* as a fashionable, richly-dressed woman," see also Ellen Kosner, "The 'noyous humoure of lecherie,' " *Art Bulletin* 55 (1975): 1.

26. Quoted in Owst, *Literature and Pulpit*, 395.

27. Ibid., 394; cf. *La Contenance des Fames*, in Fiero et al., *Three Medieval Views*, esp. ll. 76–77.

28. Quoted in Owst, *Literature and Pulpit*, 404–405.

29. Quoted in Fiero, Pfeffer, and Allain, "The Historical Context," in *Three Medieval Views*, 56. A mid-sixteenth-century penitential mandates three years of penance for a woman who "paints herself with ceruse or other pigment in order to please men"; cited in John T. McNeill and Helena M. Gomer, *Medieval Handbooks of Penance: A Translation of the Principle* Libri Penitentiales (New York: Columbia UP, 1938, 1990), 367. In addition to the obvious connection between cosmetics and lust, in their respective works Bloch (*Medieval Misogyny*, 9, 39–42) and Colish ("Cosmetic Theology") trace the early Christian theology on cosmetics to the distrust of Stoic philosophers for appearances and decoration.

30. D'Avray and Tausche, "Marriage Sermons," 102; cf. Owst, *Literature and Pulpit*, 520.

31. "Scorn of Women," #211, in Robbins, *Secular Lyrics*, 224–225; cf. "*La Contenance des Fames*," 111–121.

32. Jacquart and Thomasset, *Sexuality and Medicine*, 122.

33. See Anderson and Zinsser, *History of Their Own*, Vol. 1, 433–435.

34. D'Avray and Tausche, "Marriage Sermons," 103.

35. Lucas, *Women in the Middle Ages*, 127.

36. For a good short summary of fashion details in literature, see Fiero, Pfeffer, and Allain, "The Historical Context," in *Three Medieval Views*, esp. 44–47.

37. Anthony Weir and James Jerman, *Images of Lust: Sexual Carvings on Medieval Churches* (London: Batsford, 1986), 73.

38. Ibid.

39. Ibid., 58–79; cf. Christine Martineau-Genieys, "Modèles, maquillage et misogynie, a travers le littéraires français du moyen age," *Les Soins de Beauté*, Actes du IIIe Colloque International, Grasse, 1985 (Nice: Faculté des Lettres et Sciences Humaines, Université de Nice, 1987), 32.

40. Quoted in Weir and Jerman, *Images of Lust*, 61.

41. Laver, *Costume and Fashion*, 63.

42. Tubach, *Index Exemplorum*, 2489.

43. Wenzel, *Fasciculus Morum*, 705.

44. Quoted in Owst, *Literature and Pulpit*, 399.

45. Ibid., 398; cf. Wenzel, *Fasciculus Morum*, 705; Crane, *Exempla*, 235.

46. See, e.g., Jacques de Vitry, *exemplum* CCXLIII, in Crane, *Exempla*, 235.

47. "Costume," *Encyclopedia of World Art*, Vol. 4, 35.

48. Ibid.

49. Quoted in Owst, *Literature and Pulpit*, 369.

50. Mary G. Houston, *Medieval Costume in England and France: The 13th, 14th, and 15th Centuries* (London: Black, 1979), chapter 7.

51. Anne Hollander, *Seeing through Clothes* (New York: Avon, 1978), 2–3, 17, 47.

52. See Plate 7, Houston, *Medieval Costume*.

53. Umberto Eco, *Art and Beauty in the Middle Ages* (New Haven: Yale UP, 1986), 44–45; cf. "Costume," *Encyclopedia of World Art*, Vol. 4, 35.

54. Derek Brewer, *Chaucer in his Time* (London: Nelson, 1963), 104.

55. C. Willett Cunnington and Phillis Cunnington, *Handbook of English Medieval Costume* (Boston: Plays, 1969), 69.

56. Herbert Norris, *Costume and Fashion*, 3 vols. (London: Dent; New York: Dutton, 1950), Vol. 2, 398–399.

57. See, e.g., plate 65 in Joan Evans, *Dress in Medieval France* (Oxford: Clarendon P, 1952), and Herbert Druitt, *A Manual of Costume As Illustrated by Ornamental Brasses* (Baltimore: Genealogical Publishing, 1970), 264–267.

58. In Hentsch, *Littérature didactique*, 80–83.

59. *Knight of the Tower*, 72.

60. Ibid., 45, 72, 72.

61. *Goodman of Paris*, 50, 165, 165, 167.

62. William Langland, *The Vision of William Concerning Piers the Plowman*, ed. Walter W. Skeat (London: Oxford UP, 1886), A Prol., 17, 21–22, 23–24.

63. Ibid., A Passus I, 3.

64. Ibid., A Passus II, 8.

65. Note 15 in E. Talbot Donaldson, trans., *Piers Plowman: An Alliterative Verse Translation* (New York: Norton, 1990).

66. Langland, *Vision of William* (Skeat ed.), A Passus II, 9–10.

67. Ibid., A Passus II, 11–18.

68. Chap. 41, ll. 37–42.

69. Ibid., Chap. 42, ll. 70–147.

70. Ibid., Chap. 62, ll. 1–55.

71. Ibid., ll. 194–196.

72. Ibid., Chap. 62, l. 205.

73. Ibid., Chap. 62, l. 235.

74. Ibid., Chap. 97, ll. 87–152.

75. Giovanni Boccaccio, *Corbaccio*, trans. Anthony K. Cassell (Urbana, U of Illinois P, 1975), 24.

76. Ibid., 25.

77. Ibid., 39–41.

78. Ibid., 35.

79. Boccaccio uses clothing imagery in passing in connection with lust in his *Elegy of Lady Fiametta,* ed. and trans. Mariangela Causa-Steindler and Thomas Mauch (Chicago: U of Chicago P, 1990). The *Elegy* is another monologue, this time spoken by an unfaithful wife. On the day on which she fell in love with her paramour, she indicated her receptivity when she "dressed most carefully in robes resplendent with much gold and adorned every part of [herself] with a masterful hand" (6). This attire, it is suggested, drives her from the house to the public place in which she meets her lover (7). At the height of their love, in her anxiety to retain his affection, she "valued clothing, gold, pearls, and other precious things more than before," and her confidence in herself is diminished, causing her to "add art to [her] natural charms" (11–12). When her lover drops her, she signals her reluctant return to marital fidelity by going to visit her "women friends . . . dressed simply, in everyday clothes" (94).

80. See Muriel Bowden's detailed analysis, *A Commentary on the General Prologue to the Canterbury Tales,* 2nd ed. (New York: Macmillan, 1967).

81. William Matthews, "The Wife of Bath and All her Sect," *Viator* 5 (1974): 438; cf. Thundy, "Matheolus," 47.

82. Kristine Gilmartin, "Array in the *Clerk's Tale,*" *Chaucer Review* 13 no. 3 (1979): 235.

83. Ibid., 236.

84. Ibid., 237.

85. Bernard S. Levy, "The Meanings of the Clerk's Tale," in *Chaucer and the Craft of Fiction,* ed. Leigh A. Arrathoon (Rochester, MI: Solaris P, 1986), 390.

86. Ibid., 394.

87. Ibid., 396.

88. Gies and Gies, *Marriage and Family,* 55.

89. Duby, *William Marshall,* 19.

90. Gilmartin, "Array in the *Clerk's Tale,*" 243.

91. Quoted in Merry E. Wiesner, "Women's Defense of Their Public Role," in *Women of the Middle Ages and Renaissance: Literary and Historical Perspectives,* ed. Mary Beth Rose (Syracuse: Syracuse UP, 1986), 15.

CHAPTER 9

1. Diamond, "Chaucer's Women," 61; cf. Shahar, *Fourth Estate,* 95.

2. Eileen Power, *Medieval Women,* ed. M. M. Postan (London: Cambridge UP, 1975), 38; Power, "Position of Women," 417.

3. O'Faolain and Martines, *Not in God's Image,* 146.

4. Anderson and Zinsser, *History of Their Own,* Vol. 2, 29.

5. Shahar, *Fourth Estate,* 95.

6. Peter Brown, 147–148.

7. Duby, *Knight, Lady, and Priest,* 73; see also Zvi Razi's demographic study, *Life, Marriage and Death in a Medieval Parish: Economy, Society and Demography in Halesowen 1270–1400* (Cambridge: Cambridge UP, 1980), esp. 63.

8. Quoted in Clark and Richardson, *Women and Religion,* 59.

9. *Saint Hildegard: Symphonia,* 225.

10. See Newman's notes to Hildegard's poems, in ibid., 306.

11. Quoted in note 17, Anne Kernan, "The Archwife and the Eunuch," *ELH* 41 no. 1 (1974): 17.

12. See Robert W. Hanning, "From *Eva* to *Ave* to Eglentyne and Alisoun: Chaucer's Insight into the Roles Women Play," *Signs* 2 (1977): 580.

13. Summarized in Rogers, *Troublesome Helpmate*, 51–52.

14. Anderson and Zinsser, *History of Their Own*, Vol. 2, 29.

15. *Book of Vices and Virtues*, ed. W. Nelson Francis, EETS no. 207 (London, Oxford UP, 1942), 250. Cf. sermon in Owst, *Literature and Pulpit*, 119; Barberino in Hentsch, *Littérature didactique*, 113.

16. *Book of Vices*, 250–251.

17. Ibid., 251; cf. sermon in Owst, *Literature and Pulpit*, 119.

18. Philip of Novarre (d. 1270), *Des quatre tens d'aage d'ome*, in Hentsch, *Littérature didactique*, 86.

19. Anderson and Zinsser, *History of Their Own*, Vol. 2, 29.

20. J. D. Burnley, "The Morality of *The Merchant's Tale*," *Yearbook of English Studies* 6 (1976): 22.

21. *Book of the Knight*, 151.

22. In Hentsch, *Littérature didactique*, 113–114.

23. Jack Goody, "Inheritance, Property, and Women: Some Comparative Considerations," in *Family and Inheritance: Rural Society in Western Europe, 1200–1800*, ed. Jack Goody, Joan Thirsk, and E. P. Thompson (Cambridge: Cambridge UP, 1976), 25; Barbara A. Hanawalt, *The Ties That Bound: Peasant Families in Medieval England* (New York: Oxford UP, 1986), 220.

24. Hanawalt, *Ties That Bound*, 229; cf. Shahar, *Fourth Estate*, 129.

25. Razi, *Life, Marriage and Death*, 63.

26. Donald Howard, *Chaucer: His Life, His Works, His World* (New York: Dutton, 1987), 154. For a theoretical discussion of mourning in Chaucer, see Louise O. Fradenburg, " 'Voice Memorial': Loss and Reparation in Chaucer's Poetry," *Exemplaria* 2 no. 1 (1990): 169–202.

27. Hanawalt, *Ties That Bound*, 220, 225.

28. David Herlihy, *Medieval Households* (Cambridge: Cambridge UP, 1985), 110.

29. Martha C. Howell, *Women, Production, and Patriarchy in Late Medieval Cities* (Chicago: U of Chicago P, 1986), 13–14, 19.

30. "The Partnership Marriage," in Hanawalt, *Ties That Bound*, 205–219.

31. Hilton, *English Peasantry*, 99–102; Anderson and Zinsser, *History of Their Own*, Vol. 1, 324–331.

32. O'Faolain and Martines, *Not in God's Image*, 41.

33. See H. S. Bennett, *Life on the English Manor: A Study of Peasant Conditions* (Cambridge: Cambridge UP, 1937), 252–253; Anderson and Zinsser, *History of Their Own*, Vol. 1, 326; O'Faolain and Martines, *Not in God's Image*, 160–161.

34. Frances Gies and Joseph Gies, *Women in the Middle Ages* (New York, Barnes, 1980), 174, 178–179; Gies and Gies, *Marriage and Family*, 150–151.

35. See Gies and Gies, *Women*, 161–162; Hanawalt, *Ties That Bound*, 71; Goody, "Inheritance, Property, and Women," 10; Howell, *Women, Production, and Patriarchy*, 14.

36. Gies and Gies, *Marriage and Family*, 190; cf. Mark Amsler, "The Wife of Bath and Women's Power," *Assays* 4 (1987): 76.

37. Hanawalt, *Ties That Bound*, 121.

38. Katherine Usher Henderson and Barbara F. McManus, *Half Humankind: Contexts and Texts of the Controversy about Women in England, 1540–1640* (Urbana: U of Illinois P, 1985), 75.

39. See Sheila Delany, *Writing Woman: Women Writers and Women in Literature, Medieval to Modern* (New York: Schocken, 1983), 30–31; Power, "Position of Women," 417, 426–427; and Kathryn L. Reyerson, "Women in Business in Medieval Montpelier," in *Women and Work in Preindustrial Europe*, ed. Barbara Hanawalt (Bloomington: Indiana UP, 1986), 137.

40. Hanawalt, *Ties That Bound*, 220.

41. Hilton, *English Peasantry*, 101.

42. Gies and Gies, *Women*, 232.

43. Quoted in Rogers, *Troublesome Helpmate*, 51.

44. Quoted in Thundy, "Matheolus," 44.

45. Matthews, "Wife of Bath," 437.

46. *De miseria humanae conditionis*, cited in ibid., 418.

47. Ibid.

48. H. Marshall Leicester, Jr., "Of a Fire in the Dark: Public and Private Feminism in the *Wife of Bath's Tale*," *Women's Studies* 11 nos. 1–2 (1984): 172.

49. Gray, *Oxford Book of Verse and Prose*, 309–310.

50. Maureen Fries, " 'Slydynge of Corage': Chaucer's Criseyde as Feminist and Victim," in Arlyn Diamond and Lee R. Edwards, eds., *The Authority of Experience*, 48.

51. David Aers, "Criseyde: Woman in Medieval Society," *Chaucer Review* 13 no. 3 (1979): 181.

52. Ibid., 182.

53. Brewer, *Chaucer in his Time*, 101.

54. Notes to *The Riverside Chaucer*, 1032.

55. Houston, *Medieval Costume*, 117.

56. T. A. Kirby, *Chaucer's "Troilus": A Study in Courtly Love* (Gloucester, MA: Smith, 1958), 137.

57. Aers, "Criseyde," 185.

58. Ibid., 187.

59. Analyzed in detail by Kirby, *Chaucer's "Troilus,"* 200–201.

60. Mann, *Chaucer*, 101.

61. In R. Miller, *Chaucer: Sources*, 311.

62. E. Talbot Donaldson, *Speaking of Chaucer* (New York: Norton, 1970), 76.

63. Coghill, *The Poet Chaucer*, 60.

64. Mary Flowers Braswell, *The Medieval Sinner: Characterization and Confession in the Literature of the English Middle Ages* (East Brunswick, NJ: Associated University Presses, 1983), 13.

65. Ibid., 34.

66. Ibid., 16, 21.

67. Kirby, *Chaucer's "Troilus,"* 235.

68. Ibid.

69. *Ibid.*, his italics.

70. Peter G. Beidler, "Chaucer's *Merchant's Tale* and the *Decameron*," *Italica* 50 (1973): 271.

71. See George L. Haskins, "The Development of Common Law Dower," *Harvard Law Review* 62 (1948): 48–49, and Charles Donohue, Jr., "What Causes Fundamental Legal Ideas? Marital Property in England and France in the Thirteenth Century," *Michigan Law Review* 78 (1979): 65, 76.

72. Mann, *Chaucer*, 68.

73. Milton Miller, "The Heir in the *Merchant's Tale*," *Philological Quarterly* 29 (1950): 437–440.

74. Margaret Hallissy, "Poison Lore and Chaucer's Pardoner," *Massachusetts Studies in English* 9 no. 1 (1983): 54–63.

75. Burrow, *Ages of Man*, 156–161.

76. Delumeau, *Sin and Fear*, 216.

77. P. J. C. Field, "Chaucer's Merchant and the Sin Against Nature," *Notes and Queries* (1970): 84–86; Malcolm Andrew, "Januarie's Knife, Sexual Morality and Proverbial Wisdom in the Merchant's Tale," *English Language Notes* 16 no. 4 (1979): 273–277.

78. Quoted in Rogers, *Troublesome Helpmate*, 37.

79. Quoted in O'Faolain and Martines, *Not in God's Image*, 119.

80. Quoted in Vern Bullough, "Medieval Medical and Scientific Views of Women," *Viator* 4 (1973): 492.

81. John T. Noonan, Jr., *Contraception: A History of Its Treatment by the Catholic Theologians and Canonists* (Cambridge: Belknap P of Harvard UP, 1965), 337–338; cf. Bullough, "Medieval Medical Views," 495.

82. Quoted in Jacquart and Thomasset, *Sexuality and Medicine,* 130, cf. 61–64, 80–82; Brundage, *Law, Sex, and Christian Society,* 450; La Roncière, "Imagining the Self," in Duby, *Revelations of the Medieval World,* 214.

83. Quoted in Noonan, *Contraception,* 206.

84. Paul Delany, "Constantinus Africanus' *De Coitu:* A Translation," *Chaucer Review* 4 (1970): 61.

85. *The Art of Courtly Love,* trans. John Jay Parry (New York: Norton, 1969), 198–199.

86. Ibid., 32.

87. Brundage, *Law, Sex, and Christian Society,* 425; cf. 490–491.

88. Quoted in O'Faolain and Martines, *Not in God's Image,* 124.

89. Quoted in Burrow, *Ages of Man,* 68.

90. Paul Delany, *"De Coitu,"* 59.

91. Quoted in Noonan, *Contraception,* 202, 206; cf. Jacquart and Thomasset, *Sexuality and Medicine,* 93; La Roncière, "Imagining the Self," in Duby, *Revelations of the Medieval World,* 216.

92. Rowena E. Archer, "Rich Old Ladies: The Problem of Late Medieval Dowagers," in *Property and Politics: Essays in Later Medieval English History,* ed. Tony Pollard (New York: St. Martin's, 1984), 18.

CHAPTER 10

1. Thomas Jay Garbaty, "Chaucer's Weaving Wife," *Journal of American Folklore* 81 (1968): 342.

2. John A. Alford, "The Wife of Bath versus the Clerk of Oxford: What Their Rivalry Means," *Chaucer Review* 21 no. 2 (1986): 120.

3. Ann B. Murphy, "The Process of Personality in Chaucer's *Wife of Bath's Tale*," *Centennial Review* 28 no. 3 (1984): 205.

4. Amsler, "Wife of Bath," 74.

5. #43, in Robbins, *Secular Lyrics*, 38–39; my adaptation.

6. Quoted in Owst, *Literature and Pulpit*, 388.

7. Bornstein, *Lady in the Tower*, 63.

8. Tannen, *You Just Don't Understand*, 188.

9. Ibid., 125.

10. Ibid., 88.

11. Elaine Tuttle Hansen, "The Wife of Bath and the Mark of Adam," *Women's Studies* 15 no. 4 (1988): 399.

12. Quoted in Beryl Rowland, "Chaucer's Working Wyf: The Unraveling of a Yarn-Spinner," in Wasserman and Blanch, eds., *Chaucer in the Eighties*, 138, 141–142.

13. Ibid., 139, 141.

14. Mary Carruthers, "The Lady, the Swineherd, and Chaucer's Clerk," *Chaucer Review* 17 no. 3 (1983): 209–210.

15. Martha Howell, *Women, Production, and Patriarchy in Late Medieval Cities* (Chicago: U of Chicago P, 1986), 182.

16. Britton J. Harwood, "The Wife of Bath and the Dream of Innocence," *Modern Language Quarterly* 33 no. 3 (1972): 262; cf. Sheila Delany, "Sexual Economics, Chaucer's Wife of Bath, and *The Book of Margery Kempe*," *Minnesota Review* ns 5 (1975): 105.

17. Peggy A. Knapp, "Alisoun Weaves a Text," *Philological Quarterly* 65 no. 3 (1986): 395; see also 389.

18. Cecile Stoller Margulies, "The Marriages and the Wealth of the Wife of Bath," *Medieval Studies* [Toronto] 24 (1962): 210, 215.

19. Brundage, *Law, Sex, and Christian Society*, 199.

20. Quoted in ibid., 503.

21. Philippe Ariès, "Love in Married Life," in Ariès and Béjin, eds., *Western Sexuality*, 136; cf. James Finn Cotter, "The Wife of Bath and the Conjugal Debt," *English Language Notes* 6 (1969): 171.

22. Brundage, *Law, Sex, and Christian Society*, 242, citing Gratian.

23. Ibid., 93.

24. Amsler, "Wife of Bath," 76–77.

25. Rowland, "Working Wyf," 144–145.

26. Huppé, *Reading of the Tales*, 109.

27. Kernan, "Archwife and the Eunuch," 15.

28. Shahar, *Fourth Estate*, 142.

29. Daniel M. Murtaugh, "Women and Geoffrey Chaucer," *ELH* 38 no. 4 (1971): 473.

30. Margaret Deanesly, "Vernacular Books in England in the Fourteenth and Fifteenth Centuries," *Modern Language Review* 15 no. 4 (1920): 349–350.

31. Suzanne W. Hull, *Chaste, Silent, and Obedient: English Books for Women 1475–1640* (San Marino, CA: Huntington Library, 1982), 2.

32. James F. Murphy, *Rhetoric in the Middle Ages: A History of Rhetorical Theory from St. Augustine to the Renaissance* (Berkeley: U of California P, 1974), 102.

33. Hull, *Chaste, Silent, and Obedient,* 134.

34. Ibid., 135.

35. Policelli, "Medieval Women," 293.

36. See Murphy, *Rhetoric in the Middle Ages,* 102.

37. Hanning, "Eva/Ave," 597.

38. Quoted in Margaret L. King, "Book-Lined Cells: Women and Humanism in the Early Italian Renaissance," in *Beyond Their Sex: Learned Women of the European Past,* ed. Patricia A. Labalme (New York: New York UP, 1980), 73.

39. Bloch, *Medieval Misogyny,* 49.

40. Lee Patterson, " 'For the Wyves love of Bathe': Feminine Rhetoric and Poetic Resolution in the *Roman de la Rose* and the *Canterbury Tales,*" *Speculum* 58 no. 3 (1983): 686, 678.

41. Ibid., 678.

42. Hanning, "Eva/Ave," 597–599.

43. Robert W. Hanning, " 'I Shal Finde It in a Maner Glose': Versions of Textual Harassment in Medieval Literature," in *Medieval Texts and Contemporary Readers,* ed. Laurie A. Finke and Martin B. Schichtman (Ithaca: Cornell UP, 1987), 27. On the relationship of the Wife to the authority of patriarchal texts, see also Barbara Gottfried, "Conflict and Relationship, Sovereignty and Survival: Parables of Power in the *Wife of Bath's Prologue,*" *Chaucer Review* 19 no. 3 (1985): 206.

44. Hanning, " 'I Shal Finde It,' " 44, 47.

45. See John Mahoney, "Alice of Bath, her 'secte' and 'gentil text,' " *Criticism* 6 (1964): 144–155, discussing the Wife's association with heretical movements attracting women.

46. St. Augustine, *On Christian Doctrine,* II. 15. 22, as quoted in Peggy A. Knapp, "Wandrynge by the Weye: On Alisoun and Augustine," in Finke and Schichtman, eds., *Medieval Texts,* 148.

47. Quoted in Bloch, *Medieval Misogyny,* 74.

48. Amsler, "Wife of Bath," 73–74.

49. Quoted in ibid., 73.

50. Kittredge, "Chaucer's Discussion of Marriage," 440.

51. All quotations are from Barrie Ruth Straus, "The Subversive Discourse of the Wife of Bath: Phallocentric Discourse and the Imprisonment of Criticism," *ELH* 55 no. 3 (1988): 529–532.

52. Gottfried, "Conflict and Relationship," 207.

53. Robert A. Pratt, "Jankyn's Book of Wikked Wyves: Medieval Antimatrimonial Propaganda and the Universities," *Annuale Medievale* 3 (1962): 5–27.

54. Ibid., 6.

55. Ralph Hanna, "Jankyn's Book," *Pacific Coast Philology* 21 nos. 1–2 (1986): 31–32.

56. Hansen, "Wife of Bath," 404.

57. Martha Fleming, "Repetition and Design in the *Wife of Bath's Tale,*" in Wasserman and Blanch, eds., *Chaucer in the Eighties,* 156.

58. Mary Carruthers, "The Wife of Bath and the Painting of Lions," *PMLA* 94 (1979): 209.

59. T. L. Burton, "The Wife of Bath's Fourth and Fifth Husbands and Her Ideal Sixth: The Growth of a Marital Philosophy," *Chaucer Review* 30 no. 1 (1978): 43.

60. Carruthers, "Painting of Lions," 214, 216.

61. See "A Henpecked Husband's Complaint II," #44 in Robbins, *Secular Lyrics*, 39.

62. See Beryl Rowland, "The Horse and Rider Figure in Chaucer's Works," *University of Toronto Quarterly* 35 (1966): 246–259.

63. Quoted in Thundy, "Matheolus," 45.

64. Rowland, "Horse and Rider," 248. This device can be seen on exhibit at Warwick Castle.

65. Patterson, " 'For the Wyve's love,' " 682.

66. Burton, "Wife of Bath's Husbands," 40.

67. Quoted in Owst, *Literature and Pulpit*, 381.

68. See glossary in *The Riverside Chaucer*, ed. Benson.

69. Carter, 22; Barbara Hanawalt, *Crime and Conflict in English Communities, 1300–1348* (Cambridge, Cambridge UP, 1979), 104.

70. Robert J. Blanch, " 'Al was this land fulfild of fayerie': The Thematic Employment of Force, Willfulness, and Legal Conventions in Chaucer's *Wife of Bath's Tale*," *Studia Neophilologica* 57 (1985): 44, 47; see this article for a summary of fourteenth-century law on rape.

71. Ruth Kittel, "Rape in Thirteenth-Century England: A Study of the Common-Law Courts," in D. Kelly Weisberg, ed., *Women and the Law: A Social Historical Perspective* (Cambridge, MA: Schenckman, 1982), 101.

72. Ibid., 103.

73. Ibid., 106; cf. Carter, *Rape in Medieval England*, 156.

74. Kittel, "Rape," 103; Carter, *Rape in Medieval England*, 36; Hanawalt, *Crime and Conflict*, 105.

75. Kittel, "Rape," 110; cf. Carter, *Rape in Medieval England*, 38–39, 44–45, 124, 133–134.

76. Carter, *Rape in Medieval England*, 106–107.

77. Hanawalt, *Crime and Conflict*, 110.

78. Huppé, *Reading of the Tales*, 130–131; Richmond, "Pacience in Adversitee," 335.

79. Huppé, *Reading of the Tales*, 131.

80. Brundage, *Law, Sex, and Christian Society*, 313.

81. Ruggiers, *Art of the Canterbury Tales*, 207.

82. Brundage, *Law, Sex, and Christian Society*, 48–50.

83. Kathryn Gravdal, *Ravishing Maidens: Writing Rape in Medieval French Literature and Law*, (Philadelphia: U of Pennsylvania P, 1991), 8, 67.

84. Mann, *Chaucer*, 88.

85. H. Marshall Leicester, Jr., "Of a Fire in the Dark: Public and Private Feminism in the *Wife of Bath's Tale*," in *Women's Studies* 11 nos. 1–2 (1984): 160.

86. Brundage, *Law, Sex, and Christian Society*, 359–360.

87. Ibid., 36.

88. Peggy Knapp, "Alisoun of Bath and the Reappropriation of Tradition," *Chaucer Review* 24 no. 1 (1989): 49.

89. Mann, *Chaucer*, 86.

90. Tannen, *You Just Don't Understand*, 125.

91. Ibid., 128.

92. Ibid., 142.

CHAPTER 11

1. Logan Pearsall Smith, *All Trivia* (New York: Harcourt, 1935), 190.
2. See Straus, "Subversive Discourse."
3. Howard, *Chaucer*, 96; italics are Howard's.

Selected Bibliography

All sources are fully documented in the notes. The following bibliography high-lights main primary and secondary sources for the reader's convenience.

Aers, David. "Criseyde: Woman in Medieval Society." *Chaucer Review* 13 no. 3 (1979): 177–200.

Ames, Ruth M. "The Feminist Connections of Chaucer's *Legend of Good Women*." *Chaucer in the Eighties*. Ed. Julian N. Wasserman and Robert J. Blanch. Syracuse: Syracuse UP, 1986. 57–73.

Anderson, Bonnie S., and Judith P. Zinsser. *A History of Their Own: Women in Europe from Prehistory to the Present*. 2 vols. New York: Harper, 1988.

Ariès, Philippe, and André Béjin, eds. *Western Sexuality: Practice and Precept in Past and Present Times*. Trans. Anthony Forster. Oxford: Blackwell, 1985.

Baldwin, Frances Elizabeth. *Sumptuary Legislation and Personal Regulation in England*. Baltimore: Johns Hopkins UP, 1926.

Benson, C. David, and Elizabeth Robertson. *Chaucer's Religious Tales*. Cambridge: Brewer, 1990.

Benson, Larry D., ed. *The Riverside Chaucer*. 3rd ed. Boston: Houghton, 1987.

Bloch, R. Howard. *Medieval Misogyny and the Invention of Western Romantic Love*. Chicago: U of Chicago P, 1991.

Boose, Lynda E. "The Father's House and the Daughter in It: The Structures of Western Culture's Daughter-Father Relationship." In *Daughters and Fathers*. Ed. Lynda E. Boose and Betty S. Flowers. Baltimore: Johns Hopkins UP, 1989. 19–74.

Bornstein, Diane. *The Lady in the Tower: Medieval Courtesy Literature for Women*. Hamden, CT: Archon, 1983.

Brundage, James A. *Law, Sex, and Christian Society in Medieval Europe*. Chicago: U of Chicago P, 1987.

Bullough, Vern. "Medieval Medical and Scientific Views of Women." *Viator* 4 (1973): 485–501.

Burrow, J. A. *The Ages of Man: A Study in Medieval Writing and Thought*. Oxford: Clarendon, 1986.

Caxton, William, trans. *The Book of the Knight of the Tower*. Ed. M. Y. Oxford. London: Oxford UP for EETS, 1971.

Davis, Natalie Zemon. *Society and Culture in Early Modern France*. Stanford: Stanford UP, 1975.

Dinshaw, Carolyn. *Chaucer's Sexual Poetics*. Madison: U of Wisconsin P, 1989.

Donohue, Charles, Jr. "The Canon Law on the Formation of Marriage and Social Practice in the Later Middle Ages." *Journal of Family History* 8 (1983): 144–158.

———. "What Causes Fundamental Legal Ideas? Marital Property in England and France in the Thirteenth Century." *Michigan Law Review* 78 (1979): 59–88.

Duby, Georges. *The Knight, the Lady and the Priest: The Making of Modern Marriage in Medieval France*. Trans. Barbara Bray. New York: Pantheon, 1983.

———. *Medieval Marriage: Two Modes from Twelfth-Century France*. Trans. Elborg Forster. Baltimore: Johns Hopkins UP, 1978.

———, ed. *Revelations of the Medieval World*. Vol. 2 of *A History of Private Life*. 5 vols. 1987–1991. Trans. Arthur Goldhammer. Cambridge, MA: Belknap P of Harvard UP, 1988.

———. *The Three Orders: Feudal Society Imagined*. Trans. Arthur Goldhammer. Chicago: U of Chicago P, 1980.

———. *William Marshall: The Flower of Chivalry*. Trans. Richard Howard. New York: Pantheon, 1985.

Ellis, Deborah S. "Domestic Treachery in the *Clerk's Tale*." In *Ambiguous Realities: Women in the Middle Ages and Renaissance*. Ed. Carol Levin and Jeanie Watson. Detroit: Wayne State UP, 1987. 99–113.

Frank, Robert Worth. *Chaucer and the Legend of Good Women*. Cambridge: Harvard UP, 1972.

Gies, Frances, and Joseph Gies. *Marriage and Family in the Middle Ages*. New York: Harper, 1987.

———. *Women in the Middle Ages*. New York: Barnes, 1980.

Gilmartin, Kristine. "Array in the *Clerk's Tale*." *Chaucer Review* 13 no. 3 (1979): 234–246.

Hanawalt, Barbara A. *The Ties That Bound: Peasant Families in Medieval England*. New York: Oxford UP, 1986.

Hansen, Elaine Tuttle. *Chaucer and the Fictions of Gender*. Berkeley: U of California P, 1992.

———. "Irony and the Antifeminist Narrator in Chaucer's *Legend of Good Women*." *Journal of English and Germanic Philology* 82 no.1 (1983): 11–31.

Happé, Peter, ed. *English Mystery Plays: A Selection*. Harmondsworth: Penguin, 1975.

Hentsch, Alice A. *De la littérature didactique au moyen âge s'adressant spécialement aux femmes*. Geneva: Slatkine Reprints, 1975.

Herlihy, David. "Family." *American Historical Review* 96 no. 1 (1991): 1–16.

———. *Medieval Households*. Cambridge: Cambridge UP, 1985.

———. "Women and the Sources of Medieval History: The Towns of Northern

Italy." In *Medieval Women and the Sources of Medieval History*. Ed. Joel
     T. Rosenthal. Athens: U of Georgia P, 1966. 133–154.
Jacquart, Danielle, and Claude Thomasset. *Sexuality and Medicine in the Middle
     Ages*. Trans. Matthew Anderson. Princeton: Princeton UP, 1988.
Kiser, Lisa J. *Telling Classical Tales: Chaucer and the Legend of Good Women*.
     Ithaca: Cornell UP, 1983.
Kittredge, G. L. "Chaucer's Discussion of Marriage." *Modern Philology* 9 no. 4
     (1912): 1–33.
Kolve, V. A. *Chaucer and the Imagery of Narrative: The First Five Canterbury
     Tales*. Stanford, CA: Stanford UP, 1984.
Mann, Jill. *Chaucer and Medieval Estates Satire*. Cambridge: Cambridge UP, 1973.
———. *Geoffrey Chaucer*. Atlantic Highlands, NJ: Humanities P, 1991.
Miller, Robert, ed. *Chaucer: Sources and Backgrounds*. New York: Oxford UP,
     1977.
Murtaugh, Daniel M. "Women and Geoffrey Chaucer." *ELH* 38 no. 4 (1971):
     473–492.
Mustanoja, Tauno, ed. *The Good Wife Taught Her Daughter. The Good Wyfe
     wold a pylgrimage. The Thewis of Gud Women*. Helsinki: Suomalaisen Kir-
     jallisuuden Seuran, 1948.
O'Faolain, Julia, and Lauro Martines, eds. *Not in God's Image: Women in History
     from the Greeks to the Victorians*. New York: Harper, 1973.
Owst, G. R. *Literature and Pulpit in Medieval England* (1933). Rev. ed. London:
     Blackwell, 1961.
Power, Eileen. *Medieval People*. New York: Harper, 1963.
———. *Medieval Women*. Ed. M. M. Postan. London: Cambridge UP, 1975.
———. "The Position of Women." In *The Legacy of the Middle Ages*. Ed. C. G.
     Crump and E. F. Jacob. Oxford: Clarendon P, 1926. 401–433.
———, ed. *The Goodman of Paris*. London: Routledge, 1928.
Richmond, Velma. "Pacience in Adversitee: Chaucer's Presentation of Marriage."
     Viator 10 (1979): 323–354.
Robbins, Harry W., trans. *The Romance of the Rose*. By Guillaume de Lorris and
     Jean de Meun. New York: Dutton, 1962.
Rogers, Katharine. *The Troublesome Helpmate: A History of Misogyny in Litera-
     ture*. Seattle: U of Washington P, 1966.
Rosenthal, Joel T., ed. *Medieval Women and the Sources of Medieval History*.
     Athens: U of Georgia P, 1990.
Rowland, Beryl. "Chaucer's Working Wyf: The Unraveling of a Yarn-Spinner."
     In *Chaucer in the Eighties*. Ed. Julian N. Wasserman and Robert J. Blanch.
     Syracuse: Syracuse UP, 1986. 137–149.
———. "The Horse and Rider Figure in Chaucer's Works." *University of Toronto
     Quarterly* 35 (1966): 246–259.
———. "The Physician's 'Historical Thyng Notable' and the Man of Law." *ELH*
     40 no. 2 (1973): 165–178.
Schulenberg, Jane Tibbetts. "The Heroics of Virginity: Brides of Christ and Sac-
     rificial Mutilation." In *Women in the Middle Ages and the Renaissance: Lit-
     erary and Historical Perspectives*. Ed. Mary Beth Rose. Syracuse: Syracuse
     UP, 1986. 29–72.
———. "Saints' Lives as a Source for the History of Women, 500–1500." In *Me-*

dieval Women and the Sources of Medieval History. Ed. Joel T. Rosenthal. Athens: U of Georgia P, 1990. 285–320.

Shahar, Shulamith. *The Fourth Estate: A History of Women in the Middle Ages.* Trans. Chaya Galai. London: Methuen, 1985.

Sheehan, Michael M. "Choice of Marriage Partner in the Middle Ages: Development and Mode of Application of a Theory of Marriage." *Studies in Medieval and Renaissance History* ns 1 (1978): 3–33.

———. "The Formation and Stability of Marriage in Fourteenth-Century England: Evidence of an Ely Register." *Mediaeval Studies* 33 (1971): 228–263.

———. "The Influence of Canon Law on the Property Rights of Married Women in England." *Mediaeval Studies* 25 (1963): 109–124.

———. "Marriage Theory and Practice in the Conciliar Legislation and Diocesan Statutes of Medieval England." *Mediaeval Studies* 40 (1978): 408–460.

Spacks, Patricia Meyer. *Gossip.* Chicago: U of Chicago P, 1985.

Straus, Barrie Ruth. "The Subversive Discourse of the Wife of Bath: Phallocentric Discourse and the Imprisonment of Criticism." *ELH* 55 no. 3 (1988): 527–554.

Strohm, Paul. *Social Chaucer.* Cambridge: Harvard UP, 1989.

Tannen, Deborah. *You Just Don't Understand: Women and Men in Conversation.* New York: Morrow, 1990.

Index

About the Author

MARGARET HALLISSY is Professor of English at C. W. Post College, Long Island University, where her specialty is medieval literature, especially with regard to women. Her essays have appeared in such journals as *Christianity and Literature, Essays in Literature, Renascence, Studies in the Novel,* and *Studies in Short Fiction.* She is the author of *Venomous Woman: Fear of the Female in Literature* (Greenwood Press, 1987).